Protect Your Future

WIN YOUR INJURY CASE WITH HONESTY AND INTEGRITY

Matthew L. Bretz

SECOND EDITION

Protect Your Future
Win Your Injury Case with Honesty and Integrity
By Matthew L. Bretz

SECOND EDITION

Cover photograph from iStockPhoto
Photographs of Mr. Bretz by Landon Vonderschmidt

Published by Bretz Injury Law LLC
3 Compound Drive
Hutchinson, Kansas 67504-1782
620-662-3435
www.bretzinjurylaw.com

Bretz Injury Law, LLC
PO Box 1782
Hutchinson, KS 67504-1782
620-662-3435

ISBN 978-0-9906143-0-2

TABLE OF CONTENTS

INTRODUCTION v

PART ONE:
AUTO, TRUCK AND MOTORCYCLE WRECKS 1

I. Overview 1

II. Payment of Medical Bills From a Motor Vehicle Wreck 4

    A. Personal Injury Protection (PIP) or "No Fault" Insurance 5

    B. Bills After PIP Has Paid Its Limit (Or If You Don't Have PIP) 7

    C. Medical Bills When PIP Has Been Exhausted, Or When There
    is No PIP or Health Insurance 8

III. Special Issues with Mopeds, Bicycles and Pedestrians 10

    A. Mopeds 10

    B. Bicyclists and Pedestrians 11

IV. Motorcycles 12

V. Property Damage 15

VI. Liability Claims 17

    A. When Do You Pursue the Liability Claim? 18

    B. What is Included in a Liability Claim? 20

    C. Against Whom is the Liability Claim Pursued? 24

    D. No Pay, No Play Laws 28

VII. Commercial Truck Wrecks 28

VIII. Uninsured and Underinsured Motorist Claims—What if There
Isn't Liability Insurance or if There Isn't Enough Liability Insurance? 31

IX. Comparison of Fault—Contributory Negligence 32

X. Wrongful Death 34

XI. Liens 37

XII. Insurance Policies and Coverages 39

PART TWO:
PRODUCT LIABILITY / DEFECTIVE PRODUCTS 43

I. Overview 43

II. Types of Product Liability Claims 44

III. Theories of Liability 46

    A. Breach of Warranty 46

    B. Negligence 47

    C. Strict Liability 48

    D. Consumer Protection 49

IV. Damages 51

PART THREE:
NURSING HOME MALPRACTICE 53

I. Overview 53

II. Regulation of Nursing Homes 53

III. Claim Evaluation .55

IV. Pre-Suit Investigation and Retention of Experts 56

V. Jurisdiction and Venue 61

VI. The Petition or Complaint 62

VII. Conclusion 63

PART FOUR:
PREMISES LIABILITY 65

    I. Overview 65

    II. Duty of Care 67

        A. Types of Visitors 67

        B. Modern Standards 69

        C. Mode of Operation Rule—Conditions Created by Others 71

        D. Assaults 74

    III. Damages 75

PART FIVE:
WORKERS COMPENSATION 77

    I. Overview 77

    II. Coverage 78

    III. Benefits 78

    IV. Exclusions 81

PART SIX:
DO I NEED A LAWYER, AND HOW DO I PICK
A GOOD ONE? 83

APPENDICES. 91

    Appendix 1: Automobile/Truck Collision Complaint 91

    Appendix 2: Commercial Truck Interrogatories and
    Requests for Production 96

Appendix 3: Commercial Truck Demand/Mediation Letter 123

Appendix 4: Automobile/Truck Collision Petition 135

Appendix 5: Automobile Wreck Complaint 139

Appendix 6: Automobile Wreck Complaint 143

Appendix 7: Product Liability Petition 148

Appendix 8: Product Liability Interrogatories and Requests
for Production 159

Appendix 9: Ford Exploding Gas Tank Article 179

Appendix 10: Nursing Home Petition—Assault 199

Appendix 11: Nursing Home Petition—Neglect 207

Appendix 12: Medical Malpractice Complaint—Overdose 211

Appendix 13: Medical Malpractice Petition—Drug Addict
Surgeon 217

Appendix 14: Premesis Liability Petition 228

Appendix 15: Journal Entries of Judgment 233

ABOUT THE AUTHOR 238

INTRODUCTION

This book is designed to assist those who have been injured during what is often a difficult and frightening process. No one wants to get hurt, and unless you have been injured or have a close family member who has been seriously injured, it is impossible to understand how an injury can affect every aspect of your life.

In addition to the injuries, medical bills and lost wages, those who have been injured face a perception from the public that they are exaggerating or faking their injuries to get money. And attorneys who are perceived as "ambulance chasers" add to the credibility problem. To counter these perceptions and prejudices, it is imperative that both you and your attorney demonstrate absolute honesty and integrity in every aspect of pursuing your claim. Only by proving that you are different from the common perception can you recover what is fair for the medical bills, lost wages, and other damages that you and your family have suffered as the result of an injury.

We often explain to our clients that they don't want a million-dollar injury, because people who have million-dollar injuries do not have a quality of life which allows them to enjoy the financial recovery. Rather, people with million-dollar injuries have catastrophic injuries, severe physical or mental disabilities, enormous medical bills, a future of lost wages, and a future of uncertainty. Remember, the settlement which you obtain has to be used to pay for a lifetime of medical bills and lost income. You only get one chance, and you cannot risk your future or the future of your family by being anything less than brutally honest in every aspect of your case.

It is our goal to provide basic information in an easily understandable format to help you through the process even though many of the topics are highly technical and are governed by statutes, regulations and insurance policy language. We aim to provide practical information on issues which frequently arise in injury claims.

We also aim to provide guidance to and a resource for attorneys who do not have experience in these matters, or who have not litigated these cases through trial and appellate courts around the country.

And the disclaimer: While this book provides basic general information about a wide variety of topics, it is no substitute for legal advice from an authority in injury law concerning your specific claim. Often times there are differences in what laws apply given different insurance policy language, different ages of people involved, the location of the incident, the date that the incident occurred, and the like. If you have specific legal questions, call an experienced and honest lawyer who can guide you through the process.

PART ONE

AUTO, TRUCK AND MOTORCYCLE WRECKS

I.   OVERVIEW

Every year millions of people around the country are injured in motor vehicle wrecks. And while more and more safety devices are included in motor vehicles, many of the wrecks result in serious injuries.

Motor vehicle wrecks include many different sub-types of wrecks such as wrecks involving semis, trucks, cars and motorcycles. These claims can also include wrecks involving pedestrians, wrecks involving trains, wrecks involving vehicles striking cattle, and a variety of other wrecks involving a motor vehicle.

Motor vehicle wreck claims are generally decided using the law of "negligence." Negligence is doing something that a reasonably careful person would not do in the same or similar circumstances, or failing to do something that a reasonably careful person would have done in the same or similar circumstances. For example, if you are in a car stopped at a red light which is rear-ended by a drunk driver, the claim which is made against the drunk driver and his insurer is a negligence claim—the driver did something (drank alcohol and then drove a vehicle) which a reasonably careful person would not have done and, as a result, has caused injury to someone else.

> **Negligence** is doing something that a reasonably careful person would not do in the same or similar circumstances, or failing to do something that a reasonably careful person would have done in the same or similar circumstances.

Unfortunately many cases involve issues of negligence which are far more subtle than being rear-ended by a drunk driver. Some of the ways to prove negligence include:

- Disobeying traffic signs and lights
- Speeding or driving too slow
- Failing to yield the right of way
- Failing to pay full attention

- Failing to keep a proper lookout
- Installing illegal tint on windows, making it difficult to see pedestrians
- Driving under the influence of drugs or alcohol
- Driving while texting or using the cell phone
- Failing to take proper evasive maneuvers
- Failing to maintain the vehicle (brakes, tires, etc.)
- Commercial drivers driving beyond the allowed number of hours
- Driving too fast for conditions such as rain, snow or ice

This is, obviously, a non-exhaustive list, and it seems like there are always new ways for collisions to occur.

According to the United States Centers for Disease Control and Prevention (CDC), motor vehicle crashes are one of the leading causes of death in the U.S. Each year more than 2.3 million adult drivers and passengers are treated in emergency departments as the result of being injured in motor vehicle crashes. Statistics from the federal government show that the economic impact from motor vehicle collisions is significant. Lifetime costs of crash-related deaths and injuries among drivers and passengers in the United States are over $70 billion each year![1]

The greatest cause of motor vehicle wrecks is distracted driving. Distracted driving is driving while doing another activity that takes your attention away from driving. Distracted driving can increase the chance of a motor vehicle crash. Distracted driving generally includes three different types of distractions: (1) visual distractions (taking your eyes off the road); (2) manual distractions (taking your hands off the wheel); and (3) cognitive distractions (taking your mind off of driving).

Common distractions come from activities like using a cell phone, texting, using a navigation system, and eating. While all of these distractions can endanger the driver and others, texting while driving is thought to be especially dangerous because it combines all three types of distraction.[2]

---

1 Naumann R.B., et al. *Incidence and total lifetime costs of motor vehicle-related fatal and nonfatal injury by road user type, United States, 2005.* Traffic Injury Prevention, 11:353-60, 2010.

2 National Highway Traffic Safety Administration, September 2010. Publication Number DOT-HS-811-379. Available at www.distraction.gov/content/get-the-facts.

When driving a car, some speed and distance calculations are important. Consider the following:

20 miles per hour	=	29 feet per second
30 miles per hour	=	44 feet per second
55 miles per hour	=	80 feet per second
60 miles per hour	=	88 feet per second
75 miles per hour	=	110 feet per second
80 miles per hour	=	117 feet per second

It is fairly easy to calculate feet traveled per second at any given speed by using the following formula:

5280 x speed in miles per hour ÷ 60 ÷ 60 = feet traveled per second

When you consider the distance which is traveled each second that a person is driving while distracted, you can understand the risk to the driver, his passengers and the public at large. Taking one's mind or eyes off the road to adjust the radio or look at a text for just three seconds on the highway means that the person has traveled the length of a football field without watching!

Taking your eyes off the road for just three seconds at highway speed is equivalent to traveling the length of a football field without watching!

The problem of distracted driving seems to be getting worse as new technologies come to the market. For instance, in 2011, 3,331 people were killed in crashes involving a distracted driver, compared to 3,267 in 2010. In 2010, nearly one in five crashes (18%) in which someone was injured involved distracted driving. In June 2011, more than 196 billion text messages were sent or received in the US, up nearly 50% from June 2009.[3] Wrecks caused by motorists who are texting are expected to rise as texting becomes more prevalent.

A CDC study analyzed 2011 data on distracted driving, including talking on a cell phone or reading or sending texts or emails behind the wheel. The study found that 69% of drivers in the United States ages 18-64 reported that they had talked on their cell phone while driving within the 30 days before they were surveyed. A troubling 31% of U.S.

---

3 For additional statistics see the National Highway Traffic Safety Administration's official website for distracted driving, www.distraction.gov.

drivers ages 18-64 reported that they had read or sent text messages or email messages while driving at least once within the 30 days before they were surveyed.

To address this growing problem many states are enacting laws banning texting while driving. Other states have started issuing graduated driver licenses for teen drivers in an effort to raise awareness about the dangers of distracted driving and to keep it from occurring. In 2009, President Obama issued an executive order prohibiting federal employees from texting while driving on government business or with government equipment, and in 2010 the Federal Motor Carrier Safety Administration enacted a ban prohibiting commercial vehicle drivers from texting while driving.

II. PAYMENT OF MEDICAL BILLS FROM A MOTOR VEHICLE WRECK

When you have been injured in a motor vehicle wreck, one of the first claims which has to be pursued is related to payment of your medical bills. Payment of the bills is important for a number of reasons, some of which are more obvious and some of which are less obvious. Naturally, you will want your doctors to be paid, and you probably don't want to have to reach into your own pocket to get the bills paid when the need for medical treatment was caused by someone else's negligence. Also, you will want your doctor to be paid so that you can continue getting treatment, and you will want your medical bills to be paid so that you don't get turned over to collections.

The payment of medical bills following a motor vehicle wreck sometimes feels counterintuitive. For example, if you were rear-ended by a drunk driver you probably feel like the drunk driver and his insurer should pay the medical bills and you and your own auto insurance and health insurance should not have to pay. That type of sentiment is understandable, but that is not how it works under the law.

There are three reasons that it doesn't work that way. First, the person who caused the wreck may contest who was at fault and may even blame you for causing the wreck. As a result of playing "the blame game," the insurance company for the person who caused your injuries won't pay medical bills and lost wages as you are getting medical treatment. Second, the person who caused the wreck does not carry health insurance that covers you and likely does not have enough money sitting in his checking account to pay all of your bills as they are incurred. Third, the insurer for the person who caused the wreck and your injuries is a "liability insurer." Liability insurers pay a settlement only one time—they do not pay medical bills as they are incurred.

As a result of the controlling laws and the applicable insurance policies, it is very important that the proper steps are taken to make sure that all of your bills are paid and to make sure that you are able to obtain a full recovery.

A. PERSONAL INJURY PROTECTION (PIP) OR "NO-FAULT" INSURANCE

Many states around the country require automobile insurance policies to have a kind of coverage called "Personal Injury Protection" (PIP) or "No Fault." PIP insurance pays a portion of the initial medical bills, rehabilitation bills, lost wages and essential services arising from a motor vehicle wreck. Each state which requires PIP insurance sets certain minimums for this coverage. The minimum may be as low as $4,500.00 for initial medical bills and as low as $900.00 per month for initial lost wages. Other states have higher requirements. Many insurance policies offer higher amounts of coverage for an additional small premium.

PIP insurance also may provide payment for essential services, rehabilitation expenses, funeral and burial benefits, and other things. Insurance companies often do not tell the people they insure about these other coverages. "Essential services" coverage reimburses you for expenses which you incur in hiring someone else to do things for you while you are recovering from your injuries and are unable to do those things for yourself. This may include a variety of services such as mowing the lawn, shoveling snow, cleaning the house, driving to appointments, and other things which you normally would do but are unable to do as a result of your injuries.

> **Essential services** include services such as mowing the lawn, shoveling snow, cleaning the house, driving to appointments, and other things you would normally do but are unable to do as a result of injuries.

To present a claim for essential services you must keep track of a number of things: restrictions from your doctors, who you hired to do the work, the amount paid for the work, etc. Keep track of this information by getting a receipt book and asking the person who does the work for you to fill out what service was provided, when it was provided, and the amount of the charge or payment. The receipts or invoices for essential services then need to be presented to the PIP carrier for payment to the provider or reimbursement to you.

"Rehabilitation expenses" are generally separate from the medical expense coverage. Rehabilitation expenses are for physical or occupational therapy which is ordered so that you can get back to your job.

As the name suggests, "funeral and burial benefits" is for payment of a portion of funeral expenses resulting from the death of a person in a motor vehicle wreck. The amount of coverage available for this benefit is usually very limited, only covering a fraction of the total expense for a funeral and burial.

As mentioned, in states where PIP is required, PIP pays initial medical bills and other initial costs. PIP is sometimes also called "No Fault" insurance because these benefits are supposed to be paid automatically without having to prove who was at fault in causing a wreck and even if no one was at fault for causing a wreck. For example, in states where PIP or no fault insurance is required, PIP should pay regardless of whether you were rear-ended by a drunk driver while stopped at a red light, or whether you fell asleep at the wheel and drove into a bridge support.

One frequent question with PIP insurance is which insurance company is supposed to pay these benefits. The answer to this question depends on the state where the wreck occurred, the state where the insurance policy was issued, the language of each insurance policy, and vehicle ownership. In most states with PIP coverage, if you own a vehicle then your own PIP coverage is considered "primary." This means that your own PIP insurance should pay the PIP benefits regardless of whether you are in your own vehicle, in someone else's vehicle, or even if you are a pedestrian injured by a motor vehicle. If you do not own a motor vehicle, then PIP benefits are normally provided by the insurance company which insures the vehicle you were in at the time of the wreck or the vehicle which hit you if you were a pedestrian.

To get PIP benefits you will have to fill out a PIP application and sign a medical authorization form. You should not, however, have to sign any sort of a "release." Insurance companies frequently try to take advantage of those who are injured and try to get a release of claims form signed in exchange for providing PIP benefits. Don't be duped by their practices. You do not have to release any claims to get PIP benefits.

B. BILLS AFTER PIP HAS PAID IT'S LIMIT (OF IF YOU DON'T HAVE PIP)

PIP insurance has limits for what it will pay. If your bills go over the available PIP limit for medical bills and rehabilitation bills, you will need to get a "PIP exhaust" letter from your PIP carrier. The PIP exhaust letter will simply state that PIP has paid its limit and that remaining or future bills should be turned over to health insurance. After getting the PIP exhaust letter, provide a copy of the letter to each of your medical providers. The medical providers will, in turn, submit the rest of your bills to your health insurance company.

For those who do not have PIP coverage, or who have PIP coverage which has been exhausted, the medical bills should be submitted to your health insurance company. Health insurance should pay the balance of your bills. You will, however, have to pay the co-pay or deductible under your policy unless your health insurance policy has a provision waiving the co-pay or deductible in the event that the medical treatment was provided as a result of a wreck. For this and other reasons discussed elsewhere in this book, you should be absolutely clear with your doctor about the wreck causing the injuries and the need for treatment. This should be discussed with the scheduling person when you schedule the doctor's visit, should be written on the patient health history intake questionnaire, should be discussed with the nurse, and should be discussed with the doctor. **Be clear and consistent about the wreck and injuries. Absolutely do not exaggerate or minimize the injuries.**

Some health insurance companies have an exclusion in their policies or plan language and refuse to pay for medical treatment arising from a wreck where they believe that someone else was at fault in causing the injury. This type of exclusion is not found in most health insurance policies, but is frequently found in health "plans." Unlike traditional health insurance policies, these plans are self-funded by employers. If you have a health insurance policy or health plan which has this kind of exclusion, it may be possible to negotiate with them to obtain payment of medical bills while you are getting treatment in exchange for an agreement to reimburse them at the time that your case is eventually settled.

C. MEDICAL BILLS WHEN PIP HAS BEEN EXHAUSTED, OR WHEN THERE IS NO PIP OR HEALTH INSURANCE

As you would expect, if you do not have PIP insurance or health insurance you will have mounting medical bills and you may also have trouble getting medical treatment for your injuries. A federal law known as "EMTALA" may provide some help.

In 1986 Congress enacted the Emergency Medical Treatment & Labor Act (EMTALA) to ensure public access to emergency medical services regardless of the ability to pay. The law imposes specific obligations on hospitals which accept payment from Medicare and offer emergency services. Such hospitals are required to provide a medical screening examination when a request is made for examination or treatment for an emergency medical condition, regardless of an individual's ability to pay. Hospitals must also provide stabilizing treatment for patients with emergency medical conditions. If the hospital is not able to stabilize a patient within its capability, or if the patient requests it, an appropriate transfer should be implemented.

This federal law enables people to get emergency medical treatment at most hospitals, but does not require hospitals to provide ongoing care and treatment for injuries after the acute phase. This means that you may be able to get an emergency surgery right after a wreck but not get physical therapy or other treatment after discharge from the hospital. It may seem outrageous, but we repeatedly have seen a situation in which a person had emergency surgery after a wreck but later could not get the surgeon to see her to provide a follow-up examination or to even cut off the cast. We have also seen dozens, if not hundreds, of people who needed a surgery as a result of a wreck or other incident and could not go back to work until surgery was performed, but no surgeon would perform the surgery since there was no insurance.

Some medical providers may agree to provide medical care without payment up front. Other medical providers are less willing to provide treatment without payment. If your doctors are willing to provide treatment without payment up front, they can be paid when your injury case is eventually settled.

If your doctor is not willing to wait for payment there are a few, but limited, other options. One thing you can try is to find another doctor who is willing to provide treatment on credit with the promise of payment upon settlement of your injury claim.

Another option is to contact a medical treatment financing company which will pay for the treatment in exchange for a written agreement with you for reimbursement at the time of settlement of your injury claim. This option normally requires that you sign a "lien" against your injury claim. Medical financing companies sometimes have significant interest or fees for providing this service, so we typically try to exhaust all other avenues of obtaining medical treatment and getting medical bills paid prior to pursuing this option.

A third option for getting medical treatment when PIP has been exhausted, if you don't have PIP or if you don't have health insurance, is to get health insurance. Health insurance may be difficult to obtain but may still be available through your employer, your spouse's employer, your parents' employer, or on the private market. It may also be possible to obtain coverage through Medicare or Medicaid.

The Affordable Care Act (ACA), known affectionately as "Obamacare," may also provide an avenue for you to obtain health insurance. It is fairly easy to sign up and rates are based on the plan which is chosen, the number of people in your family that you want to include in your plan, and your income. If you are unable to work due to your injury and only choose to cover yourself, your premium will be exceptionally low. You can look into coverage under the ACA and can also sign up for coverage by going to www.healthcare.gov. If you do not have access to a computer, you can also call the federal Health Insurance Marketplace at 1-800-318-2596.

The option of obtaining health insurance through an employer, family member's employer, on the private market, or through the ACA can often be the most cost-effective and attractive option. If you are not working, it may be difficult to come up with the premium payment, but the premium payment is usually far less expensive than the medical treatment which is needed. Thus coming up with the premium payment through any avenue may be a small investment with a huge payoff.

Unfortunately, there are times when people just cannot afford to pay for health insurance and as a result cannot get the medical or surgical care which is needed to physically recover from the injuries and get back to work. This occurs most often in situations in which people have significant long-term medical needs following an injury. When this happens, and all other avenues for obtaining medical treatment have failed, your attorney may be able to negotiate a settlement which includes money for payment of future medical treatment. To include future medical costs in your claim you will need a report from your doctor about the need for additional medical treatment and the anticipated cost.

This is the least attractive way to get medical treatment because it means delaying treatment until the settlement is reached. This generally results in the doctor not being able to achieve as good of a result due to delayed treatment. This may also result in a lower amount of money paid for future medical expenses, as the insurance company will question whether future medical expenses will really be incurred. It also results in having to pay the full charge for the medical treatment rather than the discounted amount which would be paid by health insurance.

As previously stated, this is the worst way to get medical treatment so it is important to exhaust all other options before trying to rely on a settlement to get medical treatment.

III. SPECIAL ISSUES WITH MOPEDS, BICYCLES AND PEDESTRIANS

Every state has laws which deal with mopeds, bicycles, and pedestrians. These laws deal with both rules of the road and with insurance. For example, a pedestrian has different rules of the road which must be followed than a motorist but may have similar insurance issues. Likewise, the operator of a moped has to comply with the same rules of the road as does the driver of a car but has different requirements for insurance coverage than does the driver of a car.

A. MOPEDS

Those who are injured while operating mopeds have some different rules and regulations which apply. Moped operators have to follow the same traffic rules as do operators of cars, trucks and motorcycles. But from an insurance standpoint, they are treated in a much different manner.

Most states exclude mopeds from the definition of "motor vehicles." Typically two-wheeled vehicles with motors that have a displacement of less than 125cc, which are limited to 2HP, and which are limited to 30 miles per hour are not considered to be motor vehicles. Some states use different displacement sizes for the limit, such as 50ccs.

Using this definition of a motor vehicle, most states do not require mopeds to have liability insurance or PIP insurance. Thus the driver of the moped would get PIP benefits following a motor vehicle wreck from the insurer of the car, truck or motorcycle which was involved in the wreck with the moped.

Many states have started adopting "no pay no play" laws. These laws prevent a person who is driving an uninsured motor vehicle from pursuing a claim against the negligent driver who caused the wreck. There are many subtleties to these laws, including ownership of the uninsured vehicle, knowledge of its uninsured status, and coverage history, which are different from state to state. Insurance companies like to take advantage of these laws and misconstrue them to apply to claims made by moped drivers who do not have - and do not have to have - liability or PIP insurance. If your state does not require you to have insurance on your moped, then the no pay no play law should not apply to you.

"Uninsured motorist" (UM) and "underinsured motorist" (UIM) coverages and claims are discussed later in this book, but there are some special issues with UM and UIM claims when the driver on a moped is injured. After making a liability claim against the negligent driver who caused the wreck, the moped driver may think that she does not have a UM or UIM claim because she did not have insurance on the moped. However, if the moped driver also owns a car, truck or motorcycle, she may be able to pursue a UM or UIM claim against her insurer.

The rationale behind pursuing a UM or UIM claim is the same as the rationale behind pursuing PIP coverage for the moped driver. Essentially, the moped driver is not operating a "motor vehicle" and therefore her UM or UIM policy for any other vehicles which she owns applies. This is different than it would be if the moped driver was instead driving a car with no insurance. If driving an uninsured car, the driver would not be able to make a PIP claim or an UM or UIM claim against the insurance policy on other vehicles which she owned.

B. BICYCLISTS AND PEDESTRIANS

Bicyclists and pedestrians are also treated differently. Generally bicyclists have a hybrid mix of traffic laws which must be followed, some of which are the same as motorists and some of which are the same as pedestrians. For instance, in some communities bicycles are not allowed on sidewalks, and in other communities they are required to be on sidewalks if sidewalks are available.

From an insurance standpoint, bicyclists and pedestrians are treated the same. If you are involved in a motor vehicle wreck while riding a bicycle or while a pedestrian, your PIP coverage will come first from your own automobile insurance company if you own a vehicle. If you do not own a vehicle, then PIP coverage for a bicyclist or pedestrian involved in a motor vehicle wreck comes from the insurer for the vehicle involved in the wreck.

Many times people are walking or riding a bicycle because they own a car that does not run or because they do not have insurance on their car. Unfortunately, the effect of this is that in most states such a person does not get PIP coverage from anyone. The reason for this harsh outcome is because insurance is required if you own a vehicle regardless of whether it runs, and because the PIP insurer for the negligent driver excludes coverage for a person who does not have insurance when required to have insurance.

IV. MOTORCYCLES

Motorcycles can be fun to drive and might be more maneuverable in some instances than a car or truck. Most will agree however that motorcycles have the potential to be more dangerous than cars or trucks and that the risk of a severe or deadly injury is much higher for a motorcyclist than for others.

According to the most recent statistics from the CDC, between 2001 and 2008 more than 34,000 motorcyclists were killed and an estimated 1,222,000 persons were treated in a U.S. emergency department for a non-fatal motorcycle-related injury. Other statistics revealed:

- The highest death and injury rates were among 20-24 year-olds, followed by 25-29 year-olds.
- More than half of all nonfatal injuries treated in hospital emergency departments were to the leg/foot (30%) or head/neck (22%).
- Motorcyclist death rates increased 55% from 2001 to 2008 (1.12 per 100,000 persons in 2001 to 1.74 per 100,000 persons in 2008).
- The number of nonfatal motorcyclist injuries that were treated in hospital emergency departments also increased, from nearly 120,000 injuries in 2001 to about 175,000 in 2008.

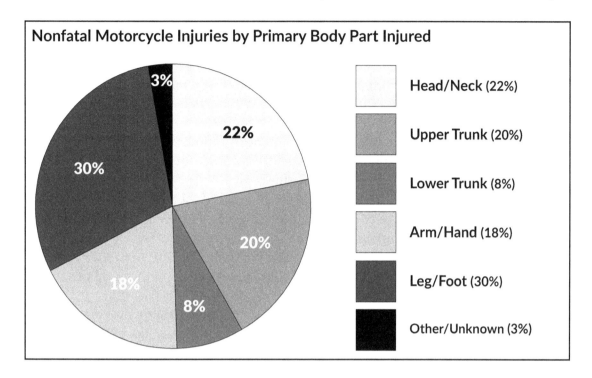

Nonfatal Motorcycle Injuries by Primary Body Part Injured

- Head/Neck (22%)
- Upper Trunk (20%)
- Lower Trunk (8%)
- Arm/Hand (18%)
- Leg/Foot (30%)
- Other/Unknown (3%)

With more people in the United States riding motorcycles today than ever before, motorcyclist deaths and injuries are an important public health concern. With these concerns in mind, the CDC recommends:

- Always wear a DOT-approved helmet.
- Never ride your motorcycle after drinking. Alcohol greatly impairs your ability to safely operate a motorcycle. If you have been drinking, get a ride home or call a taxi.
- Don't let friends ride impaired. Take their keys away.
- Wear protective clothing that provides some level of injury protection. Upper body clothing should also include bright colors or reflective materials so that other motorists can more easily see you.
- Avoid tailgating.
- Maintain a safe speed and exercise caution when traveling over slippery surfaces or gravel.

Even when motorcyclists follow all of the safety rules and are hyper-vigilant while driving, motorcycle wrecks still occur. Insurance companies recognize this increased risk for motorcyclists and have done a good job lobbying legislators to get laws passed which protect the insurers from a lot of claims arising from motorcycle wrecks. These laws make insurance companies more profitable but to the detriment of motorcyclists.

From an insurance standpoint, the primary difference for motorcyclists is that most states do not require insurance companies to provide PIP coverage for motorcycles. As a result of this law, the people who need PIP insurance the most usually do not have PIP insurance. With this law in mind, if you are a motorcyclist you should talk to your insurance agent or a lawyer about the coverage you have and the coverage you need. While many states do not require insurance companies to have PIP insurance on motorcycle policies, most insurance companies still offer PIP coverage as an option. This PIP insurance is a really good investment since it pays initial medical bills and lost wages in the event of a wreck.

People who own motorcycles often get low limits for their liability coverage, usually because their insurance agents suggest that motorcycles usually do not cause much damage to other vehicles in a wreck. This is a bad idea for the motorcyclist for a number of reasons. First, a passenger on your motorcycle may have a liability claim against you if you did something wrong to cause or contribute to a wreck, and the passenger has the same potential for a severe injury as does the driver. Second, uninsured (UM) and underinsured (UIM) motorist insurance limits are usually equal to your liability limits. If you are seriously injured by someone else who does not have sufficient insurance, then you will want high UM and UIM limits.

The cost of motorcycle insurance is typically much lower than the cost of insurance on a car or truck, so we always recommend to our clients that they use that savings to get higher liability, UM, UIM and PIP coverages on their motorcycles.

Passengers on motorcycles face different issues. First, if the passenger is not also the owner of the motorcycle, and if the passenger owns a vehicle with PIP coverage, then the passenger will have a PIP claim against her own insurer. Alternatively, if the passenger does not own a vehicle then she may have a PIP claim against the insurer for the motorcycle if the policy has PIP coverage.

V.   PROPERTY DAMAGE

Fortunately, there are some wrecks which result only in property damage and not in any injuries. If that is the case, hopefully you looked at the index and skipped straight to this section. On the other hand, if you were injured in the wreck you will likely get at least some initial medical treatment before you start worrying about the property damage caused by the wreck.

In most states, you can recover the cost of repairs for your vehicle unless the cost of repairs exceeds the fair market value of the vehicle. If the cost of repairs exceeds the fair market value of the vehicle, then you are limited to the fair market value.

In addition you can recover for rental car expenses while your vehicle is being repaired or replaced, and for damage to other property. Other property might include clothes which were cut off in the hospital following the wreck, computers, cell phones or other equipment damaged in a collision, or tools broken or lost in the collision.

You may have a couple of different avenues to pursue for property damage. When it appears that our client's car can be repaired, we normally start with the insurance company for the negligent driver and ask them to pay for the property damage. But sometimes the other driver's insurer will not pay for the repairs. This could be for a variety of reasons such as a dispute about liability, a dispute about insurance coverage, multiple property damage claims which might exceed the insurance policy's limit of coverage, a question regarding whether the driver was driving with permission, or any number of other reasons. In that instance you can look to your own insurer if you have "collision coverage" on your policy.

If, however, the cost of repairs exceeds the fair market value of the vehicle, then we normally contact both the negligent driver's insurance carrier and our client's insurance carrier and negotiate payment based on which insurance company provides the highest valuation of the vehicle. There are a number of resources which can be used to establish the value of a vehicle. These can include publications on vehicle values from NADA™ or Kelley Blue Book™, and can also include car dealerships, on-line automobile auctions, newspapers, and other publications.

Property damage claims can often be resolved fairly soon after a wreck and even before medical treatment is finished for your injuries. If an agreement cannot be reached on the property damage, then you may have to file suit to have a court determine the value of your property and the negligent party's liability for payment. This can create problems if you are still getting medical treatment for your injuries.

If the wreck only caused property damage, then some states allow recovery of attorney's fees for having to file a lawsuit for recovery of property damage arising from a motor vehicle wreck. This enables people to get an attorney to pursue a property damage claim without having to worry about losing a bunch of money to a lawyer.

A problem, which seems to be occurring more and more frequently, arises when a person owes more money on a vehicle than the vehicle is worth. Essentially, the person is "upside down" on the vehicle. This can happen when a person purchases a vehicle without much of a down-payment, or when a person trades in a vehicle with a loan for another vehicle and adds the first loan balance to the loan on the new vehicle. This can also happen when a person gets a very low interest rate loan on a long term, resulting in the vehicle depreciating faster than the loan is paid down.

As stated above, if repair costs for your vehicle exceed the vehicle's fair market value, then you can recover the fair market value of the vehicle. The amount a person owes on a vehicle does not have anything to do with the fair market value of the vehicle. So if you owe more on your car than what it's worth, then the property damage settlement likely will not pay off your loan balance. This tends to make people unhappy because they find themselves without a vehicle to drive, without a vehicle to trade in, and owing money to the lender without having money to pay off the balance.

There is not a great way to resolve this problem, but most people end up purchasing another vehicle and adding the loan payoff for the damaged vehicle into the loan on the new vehicle. Assuming you purchase a vehicle of the same value of the damaged vehicle, then mathematically you end up in the same position. Consider the following example: You own a vehicle with a $10,000.00 fair market value and a $12,000.00 loan balance, and the vehicle is destroyed in a wreck. The insurance company pays you $10,000.00 for the fair market value of your vehicle, leaving you with a $2,000.00 loan balance. If you go to a car dealer and purchase a $10,000.00 vehicle with a $10,000.00 loan and add the $2,000.00 balance from the old car, then you end up in the same position as you were before the wreck with a $10,000.00 vehicle and a $12,000.00 loan.

Replacing your damaged vehicle with a nicer vehicle can also create issues. Prospective clients frequently come in to our office to hire us because they are unhappy about what is going on with their property damage claim. Here is the situation: the prospective client owns a $10,000.00 vehicle that is paid off. The vehicle gets totaled in a wreck. The prospective client goes out and purchases a $25,000.00 vehicle with a $25,000.00 loan. Then the prospective client tries to resolve the property damage claim, gets a $10,000.00 offer since the fair market value of the damaged vehicle was $10,000.00, and is unhappy when he finds out that he now has a new car loan payment and a $15,000.00 balance. The person must remember, however, that he chose to purchase a $25,000.00 vehicle instead of another $10,000.00 vehicle like he had prior to the wreck.

The best way to avoid these potential problems is to talk to an experienced attorney before trying to settle the property damage claim and before purchasing a replacement vehicle.

VI. LIABILITY CLAIMS

A "liability claim" is the claim which is pursued against the driver and the insurance company for the driver, and possibly also against the owner or insurer of the vehicle. The idea behind a liability claim is that the claim is being pursued because someone else is "liable" for the injuries and damages which were suffered because of that person's conduct. Liability includes two concepts: negligence and causation. Essentially, and highly summarized, a driver and his insurer are liable for damages if the driver was negligent in driving and if that person's negligence caused or contributed to the injuries and damages.

You may have noticed that throughout this book we use the terms "incident" or "wreck," rather than the word "accident." This is intentional. The system of justice in the United States is based upon fault or negligence, i.e., that someone did something wrong or failed to do something that they should have done, causing an injury. The word "accident" suggests to many that the incident which caused injury was just an unfortunate occurrence with no one at fault. So referring to the incident which caused you injury as an "accident" helps the insurance company and the defense company destroy your own claim. Don't do it.

> Avoid referring to a wreck as an "accident." Doing so may suggest that the wreck is just an unfortunate occurence with no one at fault!

A. WHEN DO YOU PURSUE THE LIABILITY CLAIM?

The liability claim is usually pursued only after a person is finished with medical treatment. By waiting until a person is finished with medical treatment we can be sure to include all of that person's injuries and damages in the liability claim.

As you would expect, sometimes medical treatment takes longer than expected and surgeries are required which were not initially anticipated. For instance, something that might initially be diagnosed as a neck strain for which only muscle relaxers and therapy is expected, may eventually be diagnosed as a herniated disc which requires spine surgery for a discectomy or fusion. If the liability claim is settled early on before the doctors identify the herniated disc, then the person will not be able to include the medical bills for the surgery and the related losses for wages, loss of time, rehabilitation expenses, therapy, etc. By waiting until medical treatment is completed we can include all of the known damages for medical expenses, lost wages, lost time, pain and suffering, and all other damages suffered as a consequence of the negligence of the driver.

In some limited situations the liability claim can (or must) be pursued before the medical treatment is completed. The first situation in which this occurs is when your injuries are so severe that the value of your claim even before treatment is finished exceeds the available liability insurance limits. In this situation it may make sense to go ahead and pursue the liability claim before medical treatment is finished.

> The **statute of limitations** is state-specific and can be very tricky. Talk to a qualified lawyer about your specific situation to make sure you pursue your claim before the statute of limitations expires.

The second situation which frequently occurs is when your medical treatment continues until or past the "statute of limitations." In this situation you will have to pursue the liability claim before the statute of limitations expires. The statute of limitations is state-specific. The statute of limitations can be very tricky. And the statute of limitations is the most common error made by attorneys in handling injury cases.

Because the laws of each state are somewhat different when it comes to the statute of limitations, we use a generic definition for the statute of limitations in this book. It is important for you to speak to a lawyer about your specific situation to find out the statute of limitations which governs your case and to determine what must be done in order to comply with the statute of limitations.

Generically, the statute of limitations is defined as:

> The time frame set by legislation where affected parties need to take action to enforce rights or seek redress after injury or damage.[4]

If you fail to meet the requirements of the statute of limitations in pursuing your liability claim, then your liability claim will be forever lost and you will not be able to pursue it. Some states have statutes of limitations for some claims which are as short as 180 days. Other states have much longer statutes.

In addition to the controlling state law, the statute of limitations also depends on several other factors such as:

- The type of claim which is being pursued. (For example, the statute may be different for an auto wreck than for a medical malpractice claim, etc.)
- The type of damages which you are pursuing such as for bodily injury, property damage, etc.
- The party against whom you are pursuing the claim, such as an individual, a doctor, a governmental entity, a resident of your state, a foreigner, a person who has left or fled the country, etc.
- Whether it was a wreck caused by negligence, or whether it was an intentional act like battery, etc.
- Whether the injured person was an adult, a minor, or a disabled or incapacitated person, etc.
- Where the wreck occurred and where the injury occurred.
- Whether you were working at the time of the wreck and also have a workers compensation claim.
- Whether you have just a liability claim or whether you also have an uninsured, underinsured, or PIP claim.

Most states have special laws which deal with the statute of limitations for people who are minors, or who are incapacitated. Some of these statutes toll the statute of limitations while the person is a minor, or give a short time period after the person reaches the age of majority to file a claim. Some of these statutes extend the statute of limitations for a

---

4   "What is Statue of Limitations?" *The Law Dictionary*. Black's Law Dictionary Free, 2nd Edition and The Law Dictionary. www.thelawdictionary.org.

period of time, but the extended period of time might not be as long as it takes for the minor to reach the age of majority.

When a minor has been injured, some states have a different statute of limitations for pursuing a claim for recovery of medical bills than for pursuing a claim for bodily injuries. For instance, some states provide that a claim for recovery of medical bills for treatment of a minor is a claim which belongs to the minor's parents and is therefore governed by the parents' statute of limitations, and that only the bodily injury claim is governed by statute of limitations for minors.

Many states have a "statute of repose" which is different than a "statute of limitations." The statute of repose adds an outside time limit for pursuing a claim even if the statute of limitations might otherwise allow a longer time period.

Each state also has specific things which must be done to meet the statute of limitations. Some states only require that a petition or complaint be filed. Other states require filing the petition or complaint, and also require service of process on the person against whom the claim is being made. Still other states have certain requirements which must be met even before the petition or complaint is filed.

The subtle nuances surrounding the statute of limitations and the statute of repose have resulted in many cases being lost, and have also resulted in many lawyers getting sued for malpractice. Thus, it is vitally important that you discuss your case with a lawyer early on after a wreck and get specific advice which governs your specific wreck, injuries and claims. Don't take these requirements lightly, and don't wait until the eleventh hour to figure out what needs to be done or to hire a lawyer. Because there are so many legal requirements and potential pitfalls, many lawyers absolutely will not get involved in a case when it gets too close to the statute of limitations.

B. WHAT IS INCLUDED IN A LIABILITY CLAIM?

The liability claim includes all of the damages which have been suffered as a result of the wreck. These damages can include almost anything suffered as a result of the wreck, and most commonly include past and future medical bills, lost wages, pain, suffering and disability, other consequential damages, and loss of consortium.

Medical bills incurred prior to making the liability claim are fairly straight-forward. You get the medical records and bills and itemize the bills which are related to the wreck. What can be more difficult is establishing what injuries, medical treatment and bills were caused by the wreck. This can be especially difficult if you have had prior injuries, problems, or treatment to the body parts which were injured in the wreck. As attorneys, we frequently have to get reports from treating physicians or need to hire medical specialists to prove what injuries were caused by a wreck. By obtaining such reports and producing them as part of the initial liability claim we show the insurance adjuster that we know what evidence is needed to substantiate the claims and that we have the evidence to win at trial if they refuse to make a reasonable settlement offer.

Future medical bills are a bit less straight-forward. Most states only allow future medical bills to be recovered if you prove that it is probable that you will need medical treatment which was caused by the wreck in the future, and prove the value of the necessary future medical treatment. So, if it is possible but not probable that you will need medical treatment in the future then you don't get money for future medical treatment. And if you cannot prove the likely cost of necessary medical treatment then you don't get money for future medical treatment.

In order to make a claim for future medical bills it is important for your attorney to meet with your doctor or to hire a medical specialist to address likely future medical needs and costs. Frankly, it is easier for a lawyer to get the required information on future medical needs and costs than it is for a patient to get this information. While a doctor may tell you during the course of treatment that you may have more problems in the future, or may develop arthritis in the future, or that the problems may get worse over time eventually requiring a surgery, those statements do not meet the standard of proof which is required to get those opinions into evidence or to turn those statements into money for future medical treatment. An experienced lawyer who knows the standard of proof and who can explain the process to the doctor, will have much better success at getting a written opinion about future medical needs and costs.

> An experienced lawyer who knows the standard of proof and who can explain the process to the doctor, will have much better success at getting a written opinion about future medical needs and costs.

Making a claim for lost wages or future lost wages is similar to making a claim for past and future medical bills, but there are additional things which need to be done to make the wage loss claim. To make a wage loss claim you need proof of your job, a record of earnings, restrictions or an off-work slip from a doctor, and a statement from your employer verifying that you are off work due to injuries from the wreck. To make a claim for future lost wages you also need a statement from your doctor or from a medical expert which addresses the need to be off work in the future due to injuries from the wreck.

In cases involving serious or disabling injuries, we often retain vocational experts to address future lost wages. A vocational expert can review your medical records, medical restrictions, educational background and vocational history and address your anticipated future loss of income. We usually use a vocational expert who is a professor at a college or university in the state where our client lives, or in the state where trial will be held. This can help with credibility in front of a judge or jury, and can also help get a case settled without a trial.

A liability claim can also include money for pain, suffering and disability. There is no mathematical formula for calculating how much money should be given for pain, for suffering or for disability. Some insurance companies use a computer program to assist them in making this determination, and some lawyers say that money for pain and suffering should be a multiple of the medical bills. Both approaches are short-sighted as demonstrated by the following two examples.

First, consider the 45-year-old man who was rear-ended at a red light by a nun on her way home from Mass, went to ten different doctors who could not find anything wrong with him, and ended up with $20,000 in medical bills. A jury likely would not award much for pain and suffering.

Second, consider the 16-year-old girl who was rear-ended at a red light by a biker stoned on meth on the way home from a strip bar, went to the hospital and ended up having an arm amputation requiring $20,000 in medical bills. A jury likely would award a much larger amount for pain, suffering and disability.

Neither a lawyer who uses a multiple of the medical bills nor a computer program which crunches numbers based on medical bills will come up with good and accurate numbers for what a case is worth.

A good attorney will use his or her experience in handling cases like yours to make recommendations to you about the value of pain and suffering in your case.

Some states have limits (caps) on what you can recover for non-economic damages such as pain and suffering. Some states also cap what can be recovered for other damages, like medical bills and lost wages, as well. In states that have caps the person who was injured is not allowed to recover the full amount a jury awards for damages if the jury's verdict exceeds the cap, and instead suffers the loss but does not get full compensation. There are two obvious problems with caps on recovery for damages. The first is that caps result in some people not being fully compensated for their injuries. The second is that caps result in people being denied the Constitutional right to a trial by jury.

In states which have caps we have to look at other avenues for recovery. Sometimes we ask a jury to assess an economic value to losses. For example, when a person has been injured in a wreck and now has limitations on walking or pushing, we ask a jury to assign an economic value for this loss by assigning a value to having to hire someone to mow the lawn, shovel snow, or carry groceries. We may also ask for economic losses for loss of time which you spent in the hospital, going to doctor's appointments, or recovering from injuries. It is imperative that your lawyer know the law that applies and that your lawyer be creative to work around the limitations so that you are fully compensated for all of your injuries and damages.

It may also be possible to challenge the caps. Many state appellate courts have determined that caps are not Constitutional. And some appellate courts which previously have found caps to be Constitutional have since determined that caps are not Constitutional. In the right case it may be possible to mount another challenge in states where there are still caps.

Many states also allow claims for "loss of consortium." Loss of consortium deals with one spouse's losses as a result of injuries to the other spouse. These may include loss of economic contributions by the injured spouse to the household, care and affection, and even sex. These losses are normally divided into two categories including loss of services which normally would have been provided by the injured spouse, and emotional or romantic losses. Some states require the loss of consortium claim to be brought in the name of the injured spouse, and other states require the claim to be brought in the name of the non-injured spouse. Your lawyer should pay attention to the specific requirements in your state.

Most people who have been injured, and even many lawyers, fail to include loss of consortium as part of the liability claim. If your state allows a loss of consortium claim to be pursued it is something which should be investigated and considered. This is especially important given that a loss of consortium claim can be one way around statutory caps if it is properly pled and proven.

Finally, there may be other damages which you have suffered as a consequence of the wreck. These "consequential damages" can include almost any other losses which you have suffered or incurred, and like the other claims it must be proven that they were caused by the wreck.

C. AGAINST WHOM IS THE LIABILITY CLAIM PURSUED?

The idea behind a "liability claim" is that someone was negligent and caused your injury and is therefore "liable" to pay for the injury and your damages. With this concept in mind, the liability claim is usually pursued against the liable person, i.e., the person whose negligence caused the wreck. And while the liable person may have insurance which will step in and pay your damages, technically the liability claim is against the liable person.

In a motor vehicle liability claim there usually is insurance and, at least initially, the claim is pursued against the liability insurance company.

There may be more than one liability insurance policy. This can happen when the negligent driver owns a vehicle but was driving someone else's vehicle at the time of the wreck. In this instance both the policy covering the vehicle being driven by the negligent driver and the policy covering the driver may provide coverage. This can significantly increase the amount of available liability insurance.

> **Umbrella** and **excess insurance** policies offer broad coverage for damages which are in excess of other policies. These policies can potentially provide primary coverage for losses not covered by other insurance policies.

There may also be an "umbrella" or "excess insurance" policy. Umbrella and excess insurance policies cover damages which are in excess of other policies and potentially provide primary coverage for losses not covered by other policies. The term "umbrella" refers to the broad coverage provided by such a policy. Insurance companies usually do not volunteer any information about the existence of an umbrella or excess policy, and have been known to falsely claim that there is no such policy in existence. The careful attorney will investigate this and will require a statement in writing from the insurance company and negligent driver concerning the existence or non-existence of such a policy.

In addition to the liable person, there may be a number of people or entities against whom the liability claim may or must be pursued.

Some states also allow liability claims to be pursued against the owner of a vehicle even if someone else was driving and caused the wreck. In those states, both the negligent driver and the owner are named in a suit.

In states that do not make the owner automatically liable, the owner may be liable anyway if the owner was negligent in entrusting the vehicle to the person who was driving and who ultimately caused the wreck. This is also true if a person other than the owner of the vehicle negligently entrusted the vehicle to the driver. Negligent entrustment claims come up frequently because often a person will loan a car to a family member or friend who has lost his driver's license, has a history of drunk driving, or who has a history of being a reckless driver or habitual violator. These claims also come up when one intoxicated person gives the keys to another intoxicated person to drive home.

Sometimes the person who caused a wreck is working when the wreck occurred. If this is the case then the employer may also be included in the liability claim. The employer is "vicariously liable" under what is known as *respondeat superior*. *Respondeat superior* is a Latin term which means "let the master answer." In order for the employer to be liable you will have to prove that the person who caused the wreck was both in the course and in the scope of his employment when the wreck occurred. In cases of respondeat superior it is not necessary to prove that the employer was negligent.

> Sometimes an employer may be **vicariously liable** if the person who caused the wreck was both in the course and the scope of his employment when the wreck occurred.

There are also instances when the employer was negligent in addition to being vicariously liable for the employee's negligence. Consider the case where an employer makes an employee work 16-hour days driving a semi, and the semi driver falls asleep at the wheel, killing another motorist on the highway. In this instance the driver has been negligent, the employer is liable under respondeat superior, and the employer is also liable for its own negligence in making the driver work too many hours. If you can prove that the employer was also negligent, you likely can increase the dollars which a jury will award for the injuries and damages that you have suffered.

A few states allow you to name the insurance company as a defendant in a liability lawsuit. This is not allowed in most instances due to public policy considerations, but if you are allowed to name the insurance company then you should seriously consider doing so.

There may be other people or businesses against whom a liability claim can or should be included. For instance, some wrecks happen because a passenger in a vehicle does something to make the driver lose control. Some wrecks occur because of faulty maintenance of a vehicle's equipment or safety systems. Some wrecks occur because cows, horses or other livestock have not been properly fenced and get out on the highway at night.

Some wrecks occur because of negligent design or manufacture of a vehicle or other product. A problem which has persisted since the late 1960s has been seatbelts which release on impact. These seatbelts are known as "inertia release" or "open on impact" seatbelts. Strobe-light photography by Blick Engineering and Emtec Corporation has demonstrated that under certain conditions, especially rollover collisions and collisions involving multiple impacts, buckles can unlatch in crashes. This, obviously, negates the safety benefit provided by seatbelts.

Studies have demonstrated that unlatching may occur if more than two inches of slack is in the belt and belt tension is lower than 10 pounds. In the tests, buckles swinging against a human hip unlatched 40-50 times at impact speeds of 9 and 15 miles per hour.

The Federal Aviation Administration (FAA) has also found during airworthiness inspections that in some seat belt assemblies the buckle may open on impact. The buckles found to have this fault were similar to the type installed in many automobiles, including those manufactured by General Motors and Ford Motor Company. In 1996 the FAA recommended testing all such buckles and replacing them if the buckles failed to remain buckled during testing. At that time the FAA said it had searched without success for any automotive service bulletin, letter, or recall notice pertaining to such failures.

Also in 1996, the National Highway Traffic Safety Administration included Chevrolet and GMC pickup trucks in a recall, listing as the safety defect acceleration forces that had caused seat buckles to unlatch.

While this problem has persisted for over 40 years in the United States, European safety standards have been enacted requiring that a safety belt buckle "must withstand 5,000 opening and closing cycles.... Its self-release must be impossible, both with the belt slack and under the influence of inertia. The buckle, even when not under tension, shall remain closed whatever the position of the vehicle."[5]

---

5   For more information on "open on impact" seatbelts, please refer to the Kyle David Miller Foundation, www.homebizlifestyles.com/kyledavidmiller.

Police investigating a wreck routinely assume that if a belt buckle is disengaged after a crash, the occupant wasn't wearing the belt. Proving otherwise may make the difference between a full recovery and a wholly inadequate settlement. In a severe injury case, seatbelt failure is an important place to look when pursuing liability claims.

There are other types of negligent design or manufacturing problems which cause wrecks or which cause injury. These may be faulty seat-backs causing drivers to lose control, faulty brakes or accelerators, airbags which do not deploy when they should, etc.

Sometimes a person gets hurt in a wreck in which she might not otherwise have been hurt because of a faulty airbag, seatbelt, or other equipment. Depending on the facts of your incident there is an almost endless list of places to look for potential claims:

- City, county or state for traffic signals which aren't functioning properly, or weren't properly programmed.

- Adjacent landowner for creating a visual obstruction like trees, shrubs, equipment, etc.

- Passengers who divert a driver's attention, or whose actions cause a driver to lose control.

- People who create environmental issues like a farmer burning a field on a windy day and creating blowing smoke which covers the highway.

- Automotive manufacturer for poor design or for lack of safety equipment.

- Doctors who give medical clearance to truckers who have medical conditions (like high blood pressure, history of strokes or TIAs, sleep disturbances, narcolepsy, etc.) which make them a danger on the road.

> Some states allow **dram shop liability** claims against the person or business who served alcohol to a person who later causes a wreck while under the influence of alcohol.

Some wrecks happen because a bar, restaurant or social host kept serving alcohol to a person who was already drunk, resulting in the drunk person driving and causing a wreck. Some states allow claims against the person or business who served the alcohol. This is known as "dram shop liability." Other states do not allow such claims.

One common mistake that some injured people and their attorneys make is to settle the obvious or the easy claim first and then contact an experienced attorney to pursue the other claims. This is a BAD idea and may be fatal to your other avenues of recovery because by taking the money for one claim you will release all claims against all potentially liable parties and insurers. We have seen this mistake made literally hundreds of times by people without attorneys and even by attorneys.

Highly summarized, it is vitally important to fully investigate all of the potential causes for a wreck and your injuries. Only by an exhaustive investigation can you be assured of locating all of the potential avenues of recovery for your injuries and obtain full compensation. This is especially true in severe or catastrophic injury cases where at first blush there is only an auto insurance policy with low limits.

D. NO PAY, NO PLAY LAWS

In recent years some states have enacted what are known as "no pay, no play" laws. These laws take away an injured person's right to pursue a liability claim or to recover certain kinds of damages in the event that the injured person does not have insurance on his or her own vehicle.

These laws usually have many built-in conditions or exceptions which potentially keep the law from being applicable. For instance, some such laws only apply if you are driving your own uninsured vehicle, not if you are a passenger and not if you are driving someone else's vehicle. Some such laws only apply if you are driving an uninsured "automobile," so that the law doesn't apply if you are driving an uninsured truck or motorcycle. Some such laws only apply if you are driving a vehicle that is required to have PIP insurance but does not.

Most no pay, no play laws also have limitations so that they do not apply if the person does not realize she did not have the required insurance, or if the person has had uninterrupted insurance coverage for a certain length of time prior to a short lapse in coverage.

VII. COMMERCIAL TRUCK WRECKS

According to data released by the U.S. Department of Transportation (DOT), approximately 500,000 truck wrecks occur every year in the United States. About 5,000 of these wrecks result in fatalities. Statistics show that one out of every eight traffic deaths involve a commercial truck.

Commercial trucking revenues totaled $610 billion in 2012, and are expected to double by 2015.[6] While this is good for the trucking industry, it is bad for the people in cars, on motorcycles and in pickup trucks with whom truckers share the road.

Wrecks involving commercial motor carriers cannot be handled in the same way as a generic automobile case. There are complex federal regulations, multiple potential parties who may bear responsibility, product liability issues, and insurance questions which are specific to commercial motor carriers and wrecks with commercial trucks. This area of law is a minefield for the injured person and for the attorney who is inexperienced in commercial carrier litigation.

By way of example, consider the following list of potential parties who may be liable for a truck driver's negligence or who may be independently liable for their own negligence:

- Driver
- Tractor owner
- Tractor permanent and/or trip lessee
- Trailer owner
- Trailer lessees
- Employer for vicarious liability
- Employer for its own negligence
- Shipper or freight broker
- Manufacturer
- Maintenance company
- Physician who performed DOT physical
- Party or parties who loaded trailer

Common theories of liability impacting commercial truck wrecks include the following:

- Negligence
- Vicarious liability such as from *respondeat superior*
- Federal Motor Carrier Safety Regulation violations
- Joint venture

---

6   "Truck Accident Statistics" *Legal Info*. LegalInfo.com. www.legalinfo.com/content/truck-accidents/truck-accident-statistics.html.

- Negligent hiring, training, supervision or control
- Negligent entrustment
- Improper loading
- Failure to provide safe work place
- Agency
- Borrowed employee
- Conspiracy
- Product liability (brakes, tire failure, rim failures, etc.)
- Inadequate lighting
- Driver fatigue

In addition to damages to compensate a person who has been injured, or the family of a person who has been killed, commercial truck wrecks frequently warrant punitive damage claims. Punitive damages may be awarded in addition to compensatory damages when a person or company has behaved in a reckless, wilful, wanton, or grossly negligent manner. Punitive damages are designed to punish a wrongdoer for his conduct and to deter others from doing the same thing.

In trucking cases punitive damages may be appropriate when there is evidence of negligent hiring, retention, supervision, or entrustment; the intentional use of unsafe or broken equipment; allowing or requiring a driver to drive while fatigued; requiring a driver to falsify log books; not properly monitoring hours of service compliance; overloading a trailer; ignoring driver complaints about safety or maintenance issues; driving under the influence of drugs or alcohol; falsifying medical history information to get a DOT medical card; stopping the truck in a lane of travel; allowing the driver to use a radar detector; etc.

Wrecks involving commercial trucks should always be carefully investigated to determine the underlying cause of a collision, and only after a thorough investigation should there be any discussion about settlement. If there is evidence to support a punitive damage claim you owe it to yourself, your family, and the public at large to pursue the responsible parties and put an end to the reckless or wilful conduct.

For the legal practitioners who are reading this, the appendix contains a sample complaint as well as sample interrogatories and requests for production of documents for a commercial trucking case. These will help you identify potential parties who should be investigated and may have liability, and evidence to support your theories of liability.

VIII. UNINSURED AND UNDERINSURED MOTORIST CLAIMS— WHAT IF THERE ISN'T LIABILITY INSURANCE OR IF THERE ISN'T ENOUGH LIABILITY INSURANCE?

When there is not enough liability insurance to pay for all of your injuries and damages you may be able to pursue an uninsured or underinsured motorist insurance claim.

An "uninsured motorist," or "UM" claim comes into play when the negligent motorist does not have any insurance. In this instance you can pursue a UM claim against your own insurance policy if you have UM coverage. UM coverage may also be available in the event that the negligent motorist has insurance but his insurance company has denied coverage. An insurer may deny coverage for a number of reasons such as non-payment of premiums, lying on an insurance application, making incomplete disclosures when applying for auto insurance, intentionally causing a wreck, not listing a family member who is driving on the insurance policy, etc.

UM coverage may also apply if the negligent motorist flees the scene of the wreck and cannot be identified. We refer to this as a "phantom motorist" or "phantom vehicle." Your insurance policy will have written requirements for getting UM coverage to pay in the event that your damages were caused by a phantom motorist or vehicle.

An "underinsured motorist," or "UIM" claim is similar to a UM claim but comes into play when the negligent motorist has insurance but does not have enough insurance to pay all of your damages.

Many states make UM and UIM insurance mandatory, so that if you own a vehicle and have it insured then your insurance policy is required to have these coverages. Other states make UM and UIM coverages optional. Similarly, some states allow you to add together, or "stack," the UM or UIM limits for each of your insured vehicles, and other states prohibit stacking.

There may also be more than one UM or UIM policy which can be pursued. For example, if you own a vehicle but are a passenger in a friend's car at the time of the wreck, then you might be able to get UM or UIM coverage under both your friend's automobile insurance policy and your own automobile insurance policy.

> It is important to look at both the policy language of your UM or UIM policies and the statutory language governing such claims. Generally, the less restrictive language will govern.

To pursue UM or UIM claims it is of absolute importance to look at the policy language for each potential policy. And it is important to look at the statutory language which creates or governs UM and UIM claims. When you have the policy language and statutory language side-by-side you may note that there are differences. If your policy is more restrictive than your state statute, then the statute will govern. If your policy is more liberal than your state statute, then your policy will govern.

There are special laws which govern UM and UIM claims, and there is also specific insurance policy language which must be followed in order to pursue these claims. The claims are not automatic. There are lots of hoops you must jump through and numerous potential pitfalls for the unwary. There are specific procedural requirements which must be met as well. Don't finalize any liability settlement without first investigating the potential for a UM or UIM claim and what must be done to preserve and pursue such claims.

In the event that there isn't any or isn't enough liability insurance, or UM or UIM insurance, you may be forced to look at the negligent person's personal assets to pay for your damages. This is not particularly pleasant, and is usually difficult, time consuming and expensive to pursue. For the most part people who don't have insurance usually don't have a bunch of money either. So if the person who caused your injuries is uninsured and if you don't have UM or UIM coverage, your only avenue of recovery may be to file suit, go to trial, and try to collect your judgment against personal assets. This often results in the person filing bankruptcy to avoid having to pay for your damages.

IX. COMPARISON OF FAULT—CONTRIBUTORY NEGLIGENCE

There are some wrecks which occur where only one person was at fault, such as the driver who is drinking in the car and rear-ends someone else who is stopped five cars back from a red light. Most people would agree that the drunk driver was 100% at fault and that no one else shares any of the blame for the collision.

Other wrecks occur where perhaps more than one person was at fault, such as the left turn in front of oncoming traffic collision where the driver turning left failed to yield the right-of-way, but the driver of the oncoming vehicle was not keeping a careful lookout, was speeding, and failed to take evasive actions to try to avoid the collision.

The notion of "comparison of fault" takes into consideration that the fault of more than one person may have contributed to causing the collision, and allows a partial legal defense that reduces the amount of damages that an injured person (plaintiff) may recover in a negligence claim against another person (defendant). There are several different versions of comparison of fault.

> **Comparison of fault** takes into consideration that more than one person may have contributed to a collision.

Most states use one form or another of comparison of fault. In these states the amount which the injured person can recover is reduced by the percentage that her fault contributed to causing the wreck. So, for example, in the injured person was found to have been 25% at fault and the opposing driver was found to have been 75% at fault, then the injured person recovers only 75% of her damages.

In "pure comparative negligence" states, the injured person recovers whatever percentage of her damages that are found to be the fault of the other parties. In these states a plaintiff who was 95% at fault for causing a wreck can still recover 5% of her damages. Alaska, Arizona, California, Florida, Kentucky, Louisiana, Mississippi, Missouri, New Mexico, New York, Rhode Island and Washington all use pure comparative fault.

A second form of comparative negligence, "modified comparative fault," allows the injured person to recover only if her negligence is less than 50% of the total fault. So if fault is split 50/50 between the injured person and the other driver, then the injured person would recover nothing, but if fault is split 49/51 then the injured person could recover 51% of her damages. Arkansas, Colorado, Georgia, Idaho, Kansas, Maine, Nebraska, North Dakota, Tennessee, Utah and West Virginia, use modified comparative fault with the 50% standard. Twenty-two states use a slightly different form of modified comparative fault.

South Dakota stands alone using a slight/gross negligence form of comparative fault. Under South Dakota's version the parties' negligence is compared only if the injured person's negligence is "slight" and the defendant is "grossly negligent." Otherwise the injured person is barred from recovering anything.

Because of how the comparative fault laws work, it is even more important to bring all of the potentially liable parties to the claim or lawsuit. First, by including all of the potential parties you maximize the available insurance or assets from which your damages can be recovered. Second, by including all of the potential parties you likely reduce the amount of fault which may be attributed to the plaintiff, making it less likely that the plaintiff will be denied recovery.

Only four states, Alabama, Maryland, North Carolina, Virginia and the District of Columbia still have "contributory negligence" laws. In a contributory negligence state, if the injured person is found to be even 1% negligent in causing the wreck, then the injured person recovers nothing even though 99% of the fault was attributed to someone else. This is a harsh rule because even the slightest amount of negligence by the injured person bars all recovery regardless of how egregious or reckless the conduct of the defendant.

X.   WRONGFUL DEATH

The U.S. Department of Transportation National Highway Traffic Safety Administration (NHTSA) reports that approximately 35,000 Americans die each year in traffic wrecks. Traffic fatalities in 2011 were at the lowest level since 1949, but it is clear that much work needs to be done to further reduce the loss of life. Some key statistics from the NHTSA tell a chilling story:

- Most traffic fatalities involve motorcyclists and pedestrians.
- Most pedestrian fatalities occur in urban areas, not at intersections, and after sunset. Many involve alcohol.
- Ten times as many motorcycle riders die not wearing a helmet than die while wearing a helmet.
- Large truck occupant fatalities have increased in the last five consecutive years.
- In 2012 crashes involving drunk drivers claimed 10,322 lives. The majority of those crashes involved drivers with a BAC of .15 or higher.
- Almost two-thirds of the people that die in nighttime wrecks are not wearing seatbelts.

When a wreck has caused the death of a loved one, there may be two different legal claims which can be brought. The first kind of a claim is called a "survival claim," which refers to the claims which the injured person could have made had he not died. These losses may include medical bills incurred before death, lost wages incurred before death, conscious pain and suffering, funeral and burial expenses, and other potential compensatory damages. The survival action is pursued by the estate or personal representative of the deceased person, generally through the administrator or executor of the estate.

> When a wreck results in a death, there may be a **survival claim** for the claims the injured person might have made had he not died. There may also be a **wrongful death claim** for the losses sustained by those who lost a loved one.

The survival claim is investigated and proven the same way that claims are investigated and proven in cases where there was no death. We use medical records and bills to prove the injuries and medical expenses, tax returns and employment records to prove lost income, EMS or medical personnel or family members to prove conscious pain and suffering, the coroner to prove cause of death, and a family member or funeral director to prove burial expenses.

The second kind of claim is called a "wrongful death claim," which refers to the claim brought by the heirs of the person who died. In the wrongful death action the heirs bring a claim for their losses on account of the death of their loved one. These losses may include both economic and non-economic damages. "Economic damages" may include medical and funeral expenses caused by the death, loss of the loved one's future earnings and benefits, and the value of services that the loved one would have provided. Proving medical and funeral expenses is generally fairly easy. But proving loss of future earnings and benefits likely will require retention of a vocational expert or economist.

Proving the economic value of services that the loved one would have provided can be difficult. To convince a jury (or an insurance adjuster) that they should award money for the value of loss of services, you must explain how the things that a person does for her family have an economic or financial value.

Take for example the mother who in the morning gets her kids ready for school, works all day, prepares the family dinner, helps her kids with school work, cleans up around the house, and sleeps six hours a night. While the mother doesn't get paid for most of what she does, there is economic value in everything she does. If the mother was killed in a wreck, you would look at the cost of hiring a nanny to get the kids up and ready for school, the cost of a maid to shop for meal ingredients, prepare dinner and clean up around the house, and the cost of a tutor to help the kids with school work. And while the surviving father may try to make up these losses, the family still has suffered an economic loss because of the value of the services provided by the mother.

Convincing the insurance adjuster or the jury that what the decedent did for her family has an economic value—and the amount of value—is perhaps the hardest part of pursuing a wrongful death claim. Done well and with integrity, it can also be the biggest part of a wrongful death claim. Done poorly or overstated, it can also destroy a case since exaggerating claims and damages can result in a loss of credibility.

"Non-economic damages" may include damages for the survivors' mental anguish, loss of care, protection, guidance, advice training and nurturing, loss of love and companionship, and loss of consortium from a deceased spouse.

For the loss of a spouse or a parent the following, and other damages, are potentially recoverable:

Economic Damages
- Loss of marital (parental) care, attention, advice, counsel, or protection.
- Loss of educational, physical and moral training and guidance.
- Loss of earnings the deceased would have provided.
- Expenses for the care of the deceased caused by the injury.
- Funeral expenses.

Non-Economic Damages
- Mental anguish, suffering or bereavement.
- Loss of society, loss of comfort, or loss of companionship.

Recoverable damages for the wrongful death of a child are similar, but have some differences:

Economic Damages
- Loss of filial care, attention or protection.
- Loss of earnings the child would have contributed to the parent(s) during the remainder of the child's lifetime.
- Expenses for the care of the deceased caused by the injury.
- Funeral expenses.
- Loss of services, attention, care, advice, protection.
- Loss of educational, physical and moral training and guidance.

Non-Economic Damages

- Mental anguish, suffering or bereavement.
- Loss of society, loss of comfort, or loss of companionship.
- Loss of care and nurturing.
- Loss of aid and assistance.
- Loss of counsel and advice.
- Loss of continued family relationship.
- Loss of enjoyment and entertainment.

In states which have statutory caps, as discussed above, it is important for you and your attorney to map out a strategy to emphasize the damages which are recoverable and not capped. It may also be possible to couch some of the recoverable damages as economic rather than non-economic to avoid or minimize the impact of caps.

XI. LIENS

When evaluating your case and considering settlement offers which you may make or which you receive, you need to be aware of potential liens or claims against your settlement proceeds. This is also true when you are considering a verdict from a trial or collection of judgment proceeds.

A number of companies or individuals may want some of your money. Each must be considered. Some must be paid. A few may be negotiated.

The most obvious potential claim against your proceeds is outstanding medical bills. Your doctors, the hospital, radiologist, physical therapist, pharmacy, and anyone else who treated you or provided services to you to help you get better will want to be paid. Some states allow medical providers to obtain a lien against your claim, in which case you will have to pay the medical provider from your recovery. You may also be able to negotiate with the medical provider for a reduced payment amount in some instances. Other states only allow hospitals, and not doctors, to get liens.

> A PIP insurer's right to recovery is called **subrogation**, and is dependent on many different factors.

The PIP insurer may also have a right to be repaid out of your settlement or judgment proceeds. The PIP insurer's right to recovery, known as "subrogation," depends on the controlling state law, the insurance policy language, the extent of your injuries, and the available liability insurance limits.

Medicare and Medicaid both have reimbursement rights. Medicare's claim and reimbursement rights are handled by MSPRC out of Oklahoma. Medicare requires an initial report about the injury and claim and then a follow-up when the case is resolved. Medicare reduces its claim for reimbursement by a proportionate share of litigation expenses and attorney's fees and for other liens such as PIP.[7]

Some states allow health insurance companies to get reimbursement from a settlement or judgment if they have paid bills related to treatment for your injuries. By statute or by regulation most states do not allow such reimbursement provisions in health insurance policies based on the fact that the health insurance company charges a premium for providing the health insurance and therefore should have to fulfill its contractual obligation and pay the bills. These states reason that the injured person paid the premium for the health insurance so should get the benefit of the health insurance, regardless of whether there is a settlement or judgment from an injury claim.

Health plans organized under the federal ERISA laws are not technically health insurance and are instead "group-funded plans." ERISA plans may have enforceable reimbursement claims, but only if the plan language contains such a reimbursement right and only if the plan is truly group funded and not insurance.

If you are dealing with a health plan or policy which claims to have reimbursement rights, be sure to investigate. Request copies of the plan documents, and be sure to get copies of the 5500 and 5310 forms. These forms contain information such as company contact information, plan renewal dates, plan financial data, information about service providers and carriers, and other information. The plan financial data, specifically the information about whether there is insurance, will help establish whether it has enforceable reimbursement rights.[8]

---

7   Contact Medicare at: MSPRC, P.O. Box 138832, Oklahoma City, OK 73113. Fax: (405) 869-3309.

8   If you cannot get the plan documents from the plan or employer, you may be able to get the information which you need from BenefitsPro at freeerisa.benefitspro.com.

XII. INSURANCE POLICIES AND COVERAGES

Auto, motorcycle and pickup truck insurance policies typically have a number of different kinds of coverage as well as definitions and exclusions that affect the coverage available.

State Farm ®
Your Policies and Accounts
State Farm Agent - CRIS COREY

Associated Customers:	PRIMARY NAMED INSURED	Inception Date: 11/9/09
	ADDITIONAL NAMED INSURED	BRETZ, MATTHEW L
		BRETZ, AMY K

Term Start: 5/9/14
Term End: 11/9/14

DISCOUNT - ACCIDENT FREE
DISCOUNT - MULTICAR
DISCOUNT - MULTILINE
DISCOUNT - VEHICLE SAFETY

PACKAGE: SINGLE LIMIT LIABILITY	2000000 (LIMIT PER OCCURRENCE)
BODILY INJURY	2000000 (LIMIT PER OCCURRENCE)
COMPREHENSIVE	1000 (OVERALL DEDUCTIBLE)
COLLISION	1000 (OVERALL DEDUCTIBLE)
NO FAULT	0 (LIMIT PER OCCURRENCE)
MEDICAL EXPENSES	50000 (LIMIT PER OCCURRENCE)
REHABILITATION EXPENSES	4500 (LIMIT PER OCCURRENCE)
SURVIVOR LOSS	25 (LIMIT PER OCCURRENCE)
SUBSTITUTE SERVICES EXPENSES	25 (LIMIT PER OCCURRENCE)
FUNERAL EXPENSES	2500 (LIMIT PER OCCURRENCE)
UNINSURED/UNDERINSURED MOTOR VEHICLE	2000000 (LIMIT PER PERSON) /2000000 (LIMIT PER OCCURRENCE)
PROPERTY DAMAGE	2000000 (LIMIT PER OCCURRENCE)

A sample declarations page from a State Farm policy.

"Comprehensive coverage" pays for your car to be repaired in the event that it is damaged by something other than a collision. This may include any number of things such as theft, vandalism, natural disasters, tornados, hail, falling objects, fire, flooding, or animals. Comprehensive coverage is required by most lenders if you have a loan against your vehicle, so that the lender's security interest in the car is protected in the event of loss or damage. Comprehensive coverage pays for the cost of repairs, but only up to the fair market value of the vehicle, subject to a deductible.

Comprehensive coverage is not as comprehensive as the name suggests, as there are exclusions from this coverage. Typical exclusions include intentional damage done to your vehicle by you or a family member, theft of personal belongings stored inside the vehicle, normal wear and tear items such as worn tires, and damage resulting from improper vehicle maintenance.

"Collision coverage" pays for your car to be repaired in the event that it is damaged in a collision. If you have collision coverage then it does not matter who was at fault for causing a collision, because you are covered for damage to your car regardless of whether the collision was your fault, someone else's fault, or no one's fault. Collision coverage is also required by most lenders if you have a loan against the vehicle. Again, collision coverage pays for repairs to your vehicle, up to the value of your vehicle, subject to a deductible.

Collision coverage has exclusions as well. Most policies exclude coverage for damages or loss to a vehicle while being used to carry persons or property for a fee, for damage resulting from intentional acts or racing, for damage to custom parts or equipment, and damage to CDs and other media.

For collector cars and antiques many insurance companies offer "agreed value coverage." With agreed value coverage, as the name suggests, you and the insurance company agree on the value of your vehicle at the time that the insurance policy is obtained. This means that you should not have to argue with the insurance company about the fair market value of your vehicle if it is damaged or destroyed. If you want agreed value coverage the insurance company will likely require proof of purchase price and value at the time the policy is issued, and will also likely require a reduced number of driven miles per year.

"Personal injury protection" (PIP) or "no-fault" insurance is explained earlier in this book in much more detail. PIP essentially acts as health insurance to pay medical bills, rehabilitation expenses, lost wages, and essential services in the event that you are injured in a motor vehicle wreck. It may appear on the policy as "medical expenses," "rehabilitation expenses," or "substitution services." In the event of a fatal wreck, PIP coverage also pays funeral and burial expenses.

Uninsured and underinsured motorist coverage are explained in detail earlier in this book. In short, "uninsured motorist coverage" pays the insured person who is injured by the negligence of a motorist who does not have liability insurance or whose liability insurer has denied coverage. "Underinsured motorist coverage" pays the insured person in the event that the negligent driver has insurance but doesn't have enough insurance to pay all of the injuries and damages.

"Liability coverage" pays other people, not you, in the event that you are negligent in driving a motor vehicle and cause an injury to someone else. Stated another way, liability coverage pays when an insured person is legally liable for bodily injury or death caused by your vehicle or your operation of most non-owned vehicles. Liability coverage may be listed on the policy as "bodily injury" coverage.

Your liability insurance normally follows you even if you are driving someone else's car, a loaner car, or a rental car and negligently cause injury to someone else. And your liability insurance normally covers someone else who is driving your car with your permission if that permitted user negligently causes injury to someone else.

Common exclusions from liability insurance coverage include: (1) when you are using your vehicle to carry people or property for a fee (such as use as a taxi or to deliver newspapers); (2) bodily injury or death to an employee; (3) bodily injury or death caused by an intentional act; (4) damage to property owned by the insured; (5) bodily injury or death to you or a resident relative; or (6) bodily injury or death resulting from your operation of a motor vehicle which you own but which is not covered under the policy.

Clients and people in the community often ask how much liability insurance they should get. Liability insurance has limits expressed by three numbers in a policy. For example: 25/50/10. The first number is the limit on coverage for bodily injury suffered by one person hurt in a wreck; the second number is the total payment limit for everyone who was injured; and the third number represents the total amount of property damage coverage available per wreck. The numbers are stated in thousands. So, a 25/50/10 policy will pay one person up to $25,000, but no more than $50,000 for all of the people injured, and just $10,000 for property damage.

Most states require only a bare minimum for liability coverage, like 15/30/10, but that is not enough liability insurance for anyone who might actually be in a collision. Think about it for a moment. Other than high mileage old vehicles, $10,000 isn't enough insurance for property damage you, your spouse or your children might cause. And an ER bill with x-rays, a CT scan and an MRI may cost more than $15,000. Add in a surgery and rehabilitation expenses for someone you have hurt and any minimum-limits policy will run far short – exposing you to a lawsuit and personal liability in excess of your insurance policy and potentially leading to your financial ruin.

While liability insurance pays someone else that you might hurt, it also protects you from having to come up with money out of your own pocket and from losing your assets to the injured person. So, consider your assets, your house, vehicles, wages, business, checking and savings accounts, retirement accounts, and ask yourself how many of these things do you want to put at risk in the event that you, your spouse, or your children seriously injure someone. Also ask yourself the moral question: if you, your spouse, or your children injure someone, do you want to make sure that that person is treated fairly and can get medical treatment and lost wages paid?

Keep in mind that high liability insurance limits don't cost significantly more than low limits. Let us explain. There are many more $25K claims than there are $50K claims, there are many more $50K claims than there are $100K claims, there are many more $100K claims than $500K claims, and there are many more $500K claims than there are $1M claims. So, the first $25K in liability insurance coverage is more expensive than the next $25K in coverage, and so on. For this reason a $1,000,000 policy does not cost much more than a $100,000 policy even though it provides ten times more coverage.

After giving a long explanation, we always answer the question about how much insurance to get with the following—get the highest limits that the insurance company will write for you, and make up for the slightly higher premium by increasing your deductible for comprehensive and collision coverage to the amount of one or two weeks of your wages.

PART TWO
PRODUCT LIABILITY / DEFECTIVE PRODUCTS

I.   OVERVIEW

"**P**roduct liability" refers to the legal liability of product manufacturers and sellers to compensate those who are injured by their products for damages or injuries suffered because of defects in the product or because of the dangerous nature of some products.

According to statistics from Santa Clara University, every year over 34 million people in the United States are injured or killed as a result of dangerous products. Product related injuries are the leading cause of death in people from age 1 to 36, accounting for more deaths in this age group than cancer and heart disease. Injuries and deaths from products have a $12 billion annual cost.[9]

Consider these statistics regarding various products sold in the United States:

- More than 200,000 infants are hospitalized each year for injuries from toys, or nursery or recreational equipment.

- Almost 1.8 million people each year require emergency treatment because of injuries involving home furnishings, and more than 1,200 of these are fatal.

- More than 1.7 million people per year require treatment for injuries involving home construction materials, and 1,300 of these people die.

- Around 443,000 people in the United States die per year due to smoking or second-hand smoking, with another 8.6 million living with a serious smoking related illness, resulting in $75 billion in direct medical costs and $82 billion in lost productivity.

- More than 107,000 people die each year from asbestos-related lung cancer, mesothelioma, or asbestosis resulting from occupational exposure.

---

9   Andre, Claire and Manuel Vclasquez. "Who Should Pay? The Product Liability Debate." *The Markkula Center for Applied Ethics*, Santa Clara University. www.scu.edu/ethics/publications/iie/v4n1/pay. html.

- Toyota has been in the news during the last few years for selling cars which have acceleration and braking defects.

- Ford has been haunted for years by deaths resulting from exploding gas tanks.[10]

II. TYPES OF PRODUCT LIABILITY CLAIMS

Product liability claims may be divided into three main categories including design defects, manufacturing defects, and a failure to warn. These are not generally considered to be legal claims in and of themselves, but are included as part of the theories of liability which are discussed below.

A "design defect" occurs where the design of a product is dangerous or useless regardless of how carefully manufactured. One may look at whether the product fails to meet normal consumer expectations or whether the risks created by the product outweigh its benefits.

> A **design defect** occurs when a product is poorly designed, while a **manufacturing defect** occurs as a result of poor materials or workmanship. **Failure to warn** occurs when a product lacks proper warnings for inherent and non-obvious dangers.

A "manufacturing defect" is a defect which occurs during the manufacturing process, making the product dangerous not because of its design but, rather, because of poor quality materials or poor workmanship.

A defect in "failure to warn" occurs when a product is designed and manufactured properly, but still has inherent dangers which are not obvious and which could be avoided with proper warnings.

To explain the differences between these three types of product liability claims, consider the real-life example of a wheel which was installed on the back of a cruiser motorcycle which is normally used for long distance highway travel carrying a passenger, loaded saddle bags, and possibly a small pull-behind trailer. While returning from Sturgis the driver of such a motorcycle, for an unknown reason, lost control of the motorcycle, crashed, and the passenger suffered severe injuries.

Most attorneys would pursue a liability claim for the passenger against the driver of the

---

10 See the Appendix for an in-depth history and analysis of the Ford cases.

The wheel rim which broke while the motorcycle was traveling at highway speed, causing loss of control of the motorcycle, a single-vehicle crash, and our client's catastrophic injuries.

motorcycle in such a case. But when we handled this case, we first investigated to see whether there was an underlying cause for the driver to lose control. Was the wheel damaged in the wreck, or did damage to the wheel cause the wreck? Was the wheel properly designed, with the proper type of metal thick enough to handle the increased load associated with a heavy cruiser motorcycle, passenger, packed saddle bags, and trailer? Was the wheel manufactured to specifications, or was an improper cheaper metal with impurities used, making the wheel weak and susceptible to failure? If the wheel was designed and manufactured properly, was there a failure to warn about overloading the motorcycle? Through investigation and discovery, we were able to determine that in this case, the crosss section of the metal in the rim was too thin for the load carried on this type of motorcycle.

Also consider the example of several exploding gas tank cases where people were burned to death after their vehicles were rear-ended at a fairly low speed. Many of these claims were pursued only against the drivers of the vehicles which rear-ended the other vehicles, without the attorneys even considering why the gas tanks exploded.

While we did not handle these cases, in one such case a careful and experienced attorney also looked into the underlying cause of the gas tank rupture and explosion. This attorney found that the fuel tanks were positioned behind the rear axle and in front of the rear bumper, that the fuel filler neck would tear away from the sheet metal tank and spill fuel beneath the car upon impact, and that the tank was also easily punctured by bolts protruding from the rear differential and nearby mounting brackets. In short the vehicles were manufactured properly, but had several inherent design defects which rendered them unsafe. For an excellent book on this see Ralph Nader's *Unsafe at Any Speed*.

III. THEORIES OF LIABILITY

A. BREACH OF WARRANTY

Warranties are representations by a product manufacturer or seller concerning a product. Liability for breach of warranty usually focuses on breach of an express warranty, breach of an implied warranty of merchantability, or breach of an implied warranty of fitness for a particular purpose.

"Express warranties" are usually in writing, since the Magnuson-Moss Warranty Act provides that a company must provide a written express warranty if a product is sold for more than $15.00. A warranty that "guarantees all furniture against defects in construction for one year" is an express warranty. If the furniture breaks within that year due to a defect in construction, the express warranty has been breached. Most express warranties are provided by the product manufacturer, are included in the seller's contract, are stated on the product's packaging materials or owner's manual, or can be contained in an advertisement or sign in a store.

> An **express warranty** is usually in writing, while **implied warranties** deal with reasonable expectations of products that are not expressly written.

An "implied warranty of merchantability" deals with expectations common to all products. An implied warranty of merchantability means that the product seller impliedly warrants that the product will be fit for the ordinary purpose for which such products are intended. For example, there is an implied warranty that a screw driver will be fit for the purpose of installing screws. If the screwdriver breaks while being used for this purpose, and shards of metal lodge in your eye and blind you, the implied warranty of merchantability has been breached. However, if the screw driver is being used as a pry-bar and breaks causing the same injury, the implied warranty of merchantability may not have been breached.

The "implied warranty of fitness for a particular purpose" deals with a situation where the purchaser tells the seller about a particular purpose he has and then relies on the seller's skill and expertise to select a specific item to fulfill that purpose. Consider the motorcycle example above. If the buyer went to the dealer and told the dealer that he was newly into motorcycles and wanted a motorcycle which he could use to take his girlfriend, with loaded saddle bags and loaded trailer cross country, and the seller picked out a motorcycle and said that it would meet those requirements, but it was later found that the motor was not strong enough, that the tires were not highway rated, or that the wheels could not handle those loads, then the implied warranty of fitness for a particular purpose would be breached by the dealer.

One should note that the implied warranty of fitness for a particular purpose can be very broad and may be breached without the implied warranty of merchantability or the express warranty being breached. Again using the motorcycle example, if there was an express one-year manufacturing defect warranty but the wheel did not break for three years, the express warranty wasn't broken. And if such motorcycles don't normally have saddlebags or trailers, and it was the added load from the saddlebags and trailer which caused the wheel to fail, then the implied warranty of merchantability might not have been broken. But if the buyer consulted the dealer for the buyer's specific needs and relied on the dealer to select a motorcycle to meet those needs, then the dealer breached the implied warranty of fitness for a particular purpose.

B. NEGLIGENCE

Negligence in a products liability case is similar to negligence in a car wreck case. In a products liability case, "negligence" is the failure to do what a reasonable product designer (manufacturer, distributor, seller) would do in the same or similar circumstances, or doing something that a reasonable product designer (manufacturer, distributor, seller) would not have done in the same or similar circumstances.

A basic negligence claim requires proof of four things: (1) a duty which is owed; (2) breach of that duty; (3) that the breach of the duty was the cause of the plaintiff's damages; and (4) that the plaintiff suffered actual damages.

In a products liability case, one can pursue negligence claims arising from the negligent design of the product, arising from the negligent manufacture of the product, and/or from negligently failing to warn of risks or dangers associated with the product. For example, consider a commercial slicer and conveyer belt used in a pizza manufacturing plant. The slicer has belts and gears which pose a risk to workers when they clean the machine, and the product designer fails to include a safety switch which turns off the machine when the safety guard is removed for cleaning. There could be a negligent design claim due to the lack of a safety switch. There may also be a negligence claim for lack of warnings if the machine did not have any warnings about the risk of injury from the moving belts and gears or warnings to shut off and disconnect the power when cleaning the machine.

C. STRICT LIABILITY

Perhaps the greatest development in injury law in the last 50 years was the adoption of "strict liability" for defective products. Instead of looking at the actions of the manufacturer as is done in a negligence claim, strict liability looks at the product itself. Under strict liability the manufacturer of a product which is defective is liable, even if the manufacturer was not negligent in making the product defective.

The adoption of strict liability in most states centers on the disparity of knowledge about a product between the product's seller and the consumer who is injured by the product. The rational behind strict liability was explained in a 1944 case, *Escola v. Coca Cola Bottling Co.*, in which a waitress was injured when a defective Coke bottle exploded:

> Even if there is no negligence, however, public policy demands that responsibility be fixed wherever it will most effectively reduce the hazards to life and health inherent in defective products that reach the market. It is evident that the manufacturer can anticipate some hazards and guard against the recurrence of others, as the public cannot. Those who suffer injury from defective products are unprepared to meet its consequences. The cost of an injury and the loss of time or health may be an overwhelming misfortune to the person injured, and a needless one,

for the risk of injury can be insured by the manufacturer and distributed among the public as a cost of doing business. It is to the public interest to discourage the marketing of products having defects that are a menace to the public. If such products nevertheless find their way into the market it is to the public interest to place the responsibility for whatever injury they may cause upon the manufacturer, who, even if he is not negligent in the manufacture of the product, is responsible for its reaching the market. However intermittently such injuries may occur and however haphazardly they may strike, the risk of their occurrence is a constant risk and a general one. Against such a risk there should be general and constant protection and the manufacturer is best situated to afford such protection.[11]

In the years since the *Escola* case was decided in California, nearly every state has adopted strict liability for product manufacturers, distributors and retailers of defective products. Many states now follow *Escola*, or a modified version of strict liability found in Section 402A of the Restatement of Torts which provides, in pertinent part:

One who sells any product in a defective condition unreasonably dangerous to the user or consumer or to his property, is subject to liability for physical harm thereby caused to the ultimate user or consumer, or to his property, if (a) the seller is engaged in the business of selling such a product, and (b) it is expected to and does reach the user or consumer without substantial change in the condition in which it is sold.

The difference between true strict liability and Section 402A is that Section 402A adds a requirement that the defective condition be "unreasonably dangerous." True strict liability does not have such a requirement.

D. CONSUMER PROTECTION

Many states have enacted consumer protection statutes in addition to the existing common law theories of liability dealing with warranty, negligence and strict liability. Consumer protection statutes generally codify the common law claims of breach of

---

11   *Escola v. Coca Cola Bottling Co.*, 24 Cal. 2d 453, 462, 150 P.2d 436, 440-41 (1944) (Traynor, J., concurring).

warranty, negligence and strict liability, and also add remedies for defective products.

These statutes often provide remedies for defects which render a product unusable, but don't cause injury to other property or people. "Lemon laws" are a common example of consumer protection laws. Consumers are protected from products which don't work, like a new car which repeatedly is in the shop due to continual mechanical or electrical problems.

Consumer protection laws also frequently provide remedies for a consumer aggrieved by unconscionable or deceptive acts or practices by product sellers, and may allow recovery of attorney's fees in certain cases.

Typically, "deceptive acts and practices" are things like the following:

- Representing that property or services have approval, characteristics, or qualities that they don't have.

- Representing that the property is original or new when it isn't or when it has deteriorated.

- Representing that property is of a particular quality, if it is not and differs materially from the representation.

- Representing that the consumer will receive a rebate or discount in return for giving the supplier the names of prospective consumers, if receipt of the rebate or discount is contingent on an event occurring after the consumer enters into the transaction.

- Willful use of exaggeration, falsehood or ambiguity as to a material fact.

- Willful failure to state a material fact.

- Disparaging the property, services or business of another by making knowingly false or misleading representations of material facts.

- Offering property or services without intent to sell them; also known as "bait and switch."

- Offering property or services without intent to supply enough for the expected public demand, unless the offer discloses the limitation. For example: "Only 5 available at this price."

- Sending or delivering a solicitation for goods or services which looks like a bill without required disclosures.

"Unconscionable acts and practices" include a variety of things which a seller might do before, during or after the transaction. Typically state consumer protection laws consider:

- Whether the supplier took advantage of the consumer's physical infirmity, ignorance, illiteracy, language barrier, etc.

- Whether the price grossly exceeded the price at which similar property was readily obtainable.

- Whether the consumer was unable to receive a material benefit from the subject of the transaction.

- Whether there was no reasonable probability of the consumer being able to pay at the time the transaction was made.

- Whether the transaction was excessively one-sided in favor of the seller.

- Whether the supplier made misleading statements of opinion on which the consumer was likely to rely to the consumer's detriment.

- Whether the seller improperly attempted to exclude, modify or limit the implied warranties of merchantability and fitness for a particular purpose.

When considering an injury which was caused in whole or in part by a product, think about all of the different parties which are involved in the design, manufacturing, testing, distribution and sale. Consider the components of the product, and the designer and manufacturer of the component parts. Also consider all of the different possible types of product liability claims and all of the different potential theories of liability.

The thought that "one size fits all" doesn't work in product liability cases. Each case has different parties and a different combination of claims.

IV.   DAMAGES

The damages which are recoverable in a product liability case are the same damages as are recoverable in an automobile liability claim. (Look back at Section VI. B. for a refresher.) Similarly, if the product causes death then a wrongful death claim with its included recoverable damages is also pursued.

In addition, many states have other damages which are recoverable for violation of their consumer protection laws. These damages typically include actual damages, additional damages in instances of deceptive or unconscionable acts and practices, and attorney's fees.

Given the potential to recover attorney's fees, many attorneys attempt to include consumer protection act claims so that the product seller ends up paying the fees for the injured person's attorney rather than the injured person having to pay the fees out of her settlement or judgment.

PART THREE
NURSING HOME MALPRACTICE

I.   OVERVIEW

Elder abuse and neglect must not be tolerated. Our parents and grandparents should be treated with respect and compassion, and should not be forgotten. When neglect, abuse and injuries are found, the responsible persons should be pursued in the same manner in which we would pursue someone who neglected or abused our children and grandchildren.

This area of law is growing as our population grows. Pursuing these cases against nursing homes which abuse and neglect our elders is difficult but necessary.

II.   REGULATION OF NURSING HOMES

In order to handle an elder abuse or neglect case, it is necessary to be thoroughly familiar with the rules and regulations which govern nursing homes. Lack of understanding of the technical rules and regulations will result in failure to identify all of the potential causes of action, statutory and regulatory violations, and potential defendants. On the other hand, thorough familiarity with the rules and regulations will arm you with the tools which are necessary to advance a persuasive case on your loved one's behalf.

All nursing homes are required to be licensed. State licensure requires the home to follow state administrative regulations. The regulations govern virtually every aspect of nursing home care including administration and management standards, administrative standards for resident care policies and procedures, health and nursing services standards, physician and pharmacy services standards, medical records standards, dietary standards, social and activities standards, and environmental and safety standards which include standards for infection control, housekeeping, maintenance, and laundry.

In addition to the requirement that the nursing home comply with state administrative regulations, if the facility receives any Medicare or Medicaid money, the home must also comply with the Omnibus Budget Reconciliation Act of 1987 (OBRA). OBRA

The **Omnibus Budget Reconciliation Act of 1987 (OBRA)** sets regulations for licensed nursing homes that have residents who are Medicare or Medicaid beneficiaries.

regulations apply to "certified" nursing homes, that is, licensed nursing homes that have residents who are Medicare or Medicaid beneficiaries. In exchange for the ability to be directly reimbursed by the government at the governmental fee schedule, certified nursing homes must contractually promise the Federal government, the state where the nursing home is licensed, and all of the nursing home's residents that the home will comply with the federal regulatory standards.

The OBRA regulations thus apply to all residents in the certified nursing home, regardless of whether the particular resident is a Medicare or Medicaid beneficiary or is a private pay resident.

The OBRA regulations, found at 42 CFR Ch. IV, Part 483 et seq, are more broad and detailed than their state administrative regulations counterparts. The OBRA regulations, at the outset, define their scope as follows:

> The provisions of this part contain the requirements that an institution must meet in order to qualify to participate as a [skilled nursing facility] in the Medicare program, and as a nursing facility in the Medicaid program. They serve as the basis for survey activities for the purpose of determining whether a facility meets the requirements for participation in Medicare and Medicaid.[12]

The OBRA regulations establish basic resident rights. Upon a review of the regulations, you will find more than five pages of specifically enumerated rights. By way of example, OBRA requires notice of the resident's rights, production to the resident of "all records pertaining to himself or herself ... within 24 hours," notification of physician and family members regarding any accident or significant change of condition, protection of resident property, and production of survey results. OBRA also regulates admission and discharge rights, use of physical and chemical restraints, abuse, and resident assessment.

One of the major provisions of OBRA is the requirement that nursing homes provide their residents with a quality of life. 42 CFR Ch. IV, 483.15 provides:

---

12   42 CFR Ch. IV, 483.1(b).

A facility must care for its residents in a manner and in an environment that promotes maintenance or enhancement of each resident's quality of life.

This quality of life requirement is further defined to include dignity, self-determination, activities, social services, and environment. Quality of life issues must be considered in all cases. Rarely is there an instance that the nursing home provided care in such a manner as to cause injury to your family member without also being negligent by providing a substandard quality of life.

Quality of care is also required by OBRA. Much like quality of life, the quality of care requirement relates to all aspects of physical, mental and psycho-social well-being. Common quality of care violations include injury or death from bedsores, over-medication, malnourishment and dehydration, misuse of bed side rails, medication errors, or using physical restraints or chemical restraints for staff convenience rather than for patient needs.

III. CLAIM EVALUATION

In a typical personal injury case such as an automobile wreck, or even in a medical negligence case, you must look at the type of damages which may be recovered. These damages typically include medical expenses, provable lost wages, and something for disability, suffering and pain. You then set out attempting to demonstrate the losses.

Elder abuse and neglect cases are different. You probably don't have any lost wages, medical expenses may be minimal or may well have been paid by Medicare or Medicaid leaving a hefty lien, and future losses are quite uncertain due to the age and frailty of the patient. Your loved one may already have a disability, or may even already be totally disabled and adjudicated incompetent. Historically, attorneys and others have thought that since the elderly have a relatively short life expectancy, the value of future pain, suffering, and disability was relatively small. Many a defense lawyer has argued that any verdict that a jury returns will not benefit the resident, but rather will be a gift to family members who are behind the lawsuit. Other defense lawyers have argued that the resident would have suffered the skin tears, decubitus ulcers, hip fractures, and more, regardless of the care provided.

In recent years, an increasing number of civil lawsuits over elder abuse and neglect have demonstrated a growing public consciousness, and are leading to long-overdue changes in the industry. Juries have been demonstrating great empathy for victims of abuse, and now consider quality of life an important factor, often more so than life expectancy.

Thus, in evaluating an allegation of elder abuse or neglect, you must look primarily at the liability issue. You cannot neglect proving damages, but you can trust that the jury will want to protect the victims of abuse and neglect and will try to make them whole. Once the jury has concluded that the nursing home abused or neglected a disabled person in their charge, and was paid for doing so, they will probably not believe the nursing home's excuse as to causation or the nature and extent of your loved one's damages.

Juries recognize the frailty of human life, and understand that they, themselves, someday will be faced with the decision of whether to put mom or dad in the home. They recognize that they, themselves, may face going to a nursing home. Perhaps this is the reason that juries have awarded substantial sums for skin tears and bruises as well as for more significant injuries like fractured hips and deaths.

For lawyers who are reading this book, consider yourself to be the voice of the unheard. Your evaluation of the case must be based, in large part, on your moral conviction. If you believe – really believe – that your client was neglected or abused, and that there was no excuse for the way in which your client was treated, then the case is worth pursuing.

IV.   PRE-SUIT INVESTIGATION AND RETENTION OF EXPERTS

Once you have decided to pursue a nursing home, you must be prepared to vigorously pursue it. These claims are usually very record intensive and a thorough investigation is absolutely necessary.

First, get a copy of the records from the nursing home. OBRA regulations, 42 CFR Ch. IV, 483.10(b) requires, in pertinent part:

> (2) The resident or his or her legal representative has the right--(I) Upon an oral or written request, to access all records pertaining to himself or herself including current clinical records within 24 hours (excluding weekends and holidays); and (ii) After receipt of his or her records for inspection, to purchase at a cost not to exceed the community standard

photocopies of the records or any portions of them upon request and 2 working days advance notice to the facility.

Obtaining the nursing home records at the outset is crucial. The time limits imposed by OBRA may keep the nursing home from making "late entries" in the chart. Additionally, anything which was not produced at the outset will be suspect and potentially subject to objection if later produced and represented to be part of the chart.

Note that the quoted regulation requires access to "all records" pertaining to the resident. This, of course, includes the medical and nursing chart. This provision also provides ammunition to obtain copies of incident reports and quality assessment or assurance committee meeting minutes. Nursing homes and their attorneys often try to play a game of "hide and seek" in which they hide any records which relate to an incident or an injury, or try to prevent disclosure of the records after their existence has been discovered.

We have had many cases where the first record of an injury in the documents which are voluntarily produced is from an emergency room visit, but have found later on that the patient was dropped in the shower, taken to bed, and then left there for hours before obtaining treatment. And we have had one case where testimony revealed that the nursing home's director of nursing ordered the staff to re-write the nursing notes and delete reference to an injury to the resident.

State licensing agencies conduct surveys (inspections) of licensed and certified nursing homes. These surveys are conducted annually and are supposed to be conducted whenever the state receives a complaint about resident abuse or neglect. The results of the surveys, as well as the nursing home's required "plan of correction" should be available as a public record. Get these for all of the years of your loved one's residence at the home, as well as the few years before admission and the year after dismissal. Carefully review the reported deficiencies. See whether your family member's chart was reviewed, or whether the injuries to your loved one were reported and investigated. See whether the home has had previous similar problems.

There may well be a pattern that you can define. In one elder abuse case we recently handled, a review of the state licensing agency's surveys showed that the home had been given a deficiency related to other patients in each of the preceding three years for the exact same condition that was suffered by the client whose case was being investigated.

A frequent problem in nursing homes relates to medication errors. Given that nursing homes try to have as many residents as possible and staff the facility with as few workers as possible, there frequently are errors in dosages, times, patients, route, and in medications. The facility should keep a record of medication errors which have been reported, but probably won't want to share it. If your loved one suffered a medication error, get the records.

Obtain copies of any newspaper articles about the nursing home. Collect copies of any advertisements or newsletters which the home has distributed. The promises made in the newsletters of some homes provide evidence as to what the standard of care should be at the facility in a case concerning resident abuse and neglect.

Collect everything that the home has provided, such as the admissions agreement, the "resident bill of rights," and copies of billing. It is amazing how frequently nursing homes continue to bill for services even after the resident has been discharged. We have even seen times where a nursing home charted a resident's vitals after the client was taken out of the nursing home! Collect and analyze everything.

PHARMACY & THERAPEUTICS COMMITTEE
MEDICATION ERROR SUMMARY - 2002

	Time – Late	Time – Early	Time – Comission / On Hold & Given	Time – Omission	Transcription – Order to Medex	Transcription – Medex to Medex	Wrong Route	Wrong Patient	Wrong Medication	Wrong IV	Wrong Dose	Wrong Rate	Wrong Drug from Pharmacy	Wrong Dose from Pharmacy	Pyxis – Discrepancy	Wrong Med In Drawer /-Box	Pyxis – Waste Not Recorded	Other
JANUARY	4	3	2	2	10	3	1		1	3	8		1		6			4
FEBRUARY	4	1	1	5	6		2	1	3		3				5	1	1	7
MARCH	4	2	3	2	9	2			4	1	5	3			3	1		4
APRIL	4	2	2	1	10				6	2	3		2	1	5			4
MAY	3	1	1	5	8	1	1		1	2	2	1		1	3	1		6
JUNE	4	4	2	2	17			1	1	3	2							5
JULY	3	2	3	3	9			2	1		3	1			2		1	7
AUGUST	5	3	5	2	12		1	1		1	1	1			2	4	2	8
SEPTEMBER																		

(Data Source – Variance Reports processed through Risk Management)

This medication error chart was used as an exhibit in a case to demonstrate the frequency of medication errors.

Consider the evidence that you need to prove how the injuries have affected your loved one. A day-in-the-life video, a summary of medical bills, a calendar of medical treatments, and photographs of the family together will make the case more personal. This is especially necessary if your loved one died at the hands of the nursing home, or if it is likely that she will die before the case gets to trial. Lawyers who are reading this should consider perpetuating the client's testimony in the event that it is unlikely that she will survive until trial. Also, consider video depositions of other residents who observed the abuse or were abused in the same way before your client was abused.

Collect all of the medical records. Resist the temptation to limit the request to only related medical or recent medical. The defense, without a doubt, will collect all of the prior medical records and you should be prepared to address any issues which may be raised.

Interview witnesses. You or your attorney can interview other residents who your client or her family can identify. You may be able to interview some of the employees. Try to reach them at their homes in order to avoid the facility's administrator standing over their shoulders when you ask questions. Consider doing this before notifying the nursing home that you are investigating and pursuing a claim, because otherwise they will retain an attorney and the attorney will try to hinder your ability to talk to employees.

Once you have done the initial investigation you will need to retain experts. Nursing home cases are expert intensive. In all likelihood, you will need at least two, if not more, experts. When the suit revolves around deficient nursing care, you will need, at a minimum, a nursing expert to testify as to standard of care and breach, and a physician to testify as to causation. When skin injuries are an issue, you may need nurse, nutritional and medical experts. When medication or chemical restraints are an issue, you may need nurse, pharmacologist and medical experts. When policies and procedures are in dispute, an expert administrator, in addition to the other experts, should be considered.

The expert witnesses should be able to identify the proper persons who should be named as defendants. You may need to name the individual nurse, the director of nursing, the administrator, the medical director, or even the treating physician as defendants.

After the expert has reviewed the records, discuss standards of conduct such as "negligence," "willfulness," "wantonness," and "recklessness." Discuss in detail and pin the expert down on issues of standard of care and causation as defined in the your

LAWRENCE • STATE — Thursday, August 26, 2010 | **5A**

HUTCHINSON

Lawsuit over death at retirement home settled

By Darcy Gray
The Hutchinson News

HUTCHINSON — A Reno County civil lawsuit filed last year by the family of an 85-year-old woman who was sexually assaulted and killed while living in a Buhler retirement community has been settled.

The lawsuit against Sunshine Villa Inc., Buhler Sunshine Home Inc. and its administrator, Keith Pankratz, was filed in January 2009 by the estate of Pearl Arthaud, the 85-year-old woman who was strangled to death in her bed May 18, 2008, by Marvin J. Gifford Jr.

Gifford, 46, housed in the El Dorado Correctional Facility, is serving a life sentence without possibility of parole for Arthaud's death and attacks on two other elderly women in Reno County.

A hearing in the civil case scheduled for Wednesday in Reno County District Court was canceled, as the two sides have reached an agreement, District Judge Tim Chambers confirmed. Terms of the settlement are confidential, however.

The lawsuit, filed on behalf of Arthaud's heirs, sought $510,000 in damages, including $250,000 for wrongful death, $250,000 for pain and suffering and $10,000 for funeral expenses.

The lawsuit claimed officials at the retirement community failed to take appropriate precautions to protect Arthaud after she'd reported a man entered her apartment and attempted to have sex with her. Arthaud had reported to Buhler Sunshine Home staff she awoke to find a man in her bed in March 2008, and he left after she refused his advances and asked him to leave.

Retirement-home officials were accused of being negligent by failing to investigate the attack, failing to warn other residents and staff of the attack, and failing to provide additional security in the retirement community. In a response to the lawsuit, Sunshine officials denied the allegations, arguing they had no control over Gifford's actions or the events that led to Arthaud's death.

A motion in the civil case filed July 29 also sought punitive damages for Arthaud's heirs.

Matthew Bretz, the local attorney representing Arthaud's estate, obtained sworn testimony from Gifford, who admitted attacking and sexually assaulting elderly women in 2008 in the Hutchinson area. According to the motion, Gifford also admitted to being in Arthaud's Buhler Sunshine apartment twice before killing her in May 2008: once pretending to be a friend of her son, and a second time when he attempted to sexually assault her after she found him in her bed.

Gregory S. Young, a Wichita lawyer representing Buhler Sunshine Home, said Gifford's statements to Bretz contained many inaccuracies that contrasted with his confessions to law enforcement, including his claim Arthaud's door was locked and that if there were security at the retirement home he would have gone elsewhere.

"Ultimately the parties resolved it as everyone agreed that Mr. Gifford's crimes were horrible and it was unfortunate for everyone involved," Young said in an e-mail to The News.

Aviation's economic impact in state set at $10.4B

CONTINUED FROM PAGE 3A — Community airports — Kansas was one of the last

Media coverage of a settlement obtained in favor of a client in a nursing home case.

state. If you have an out-of-state expert, provide the expert with a copy of the applicable administrative regulations so that the expert can identify any which have been violated.

Given the volume of records which are generated by nursing homes, the volumes of policy and procedure manuals which will be in issue, and the number of depositions which are necessary, expect that the cost of experts will be significant.

Residents in nursing homes are frequently the victims of assaults. Some of these results are perpetrated by other residents, some by facility employees, and some are by outsiders. Assaults in nursing homes, on people unable to protect themselves, require extra attention. For an assault by another resident, look at the resident's history of abuse and acting out, and also at what (if anything) the facility did to protect your family member and others from the danger.

For an assault by an employee, investigate the employee's work history, prior complaints and write-ups, criminal history, and reports of abuse or neglect. Get the employee's personnel records from prior employers and find out about disciplinary issues.

For assaults by an outsider, investigate the perpetrator's history, how the perpetrator gained entry to the facility, prior times that the perpetrator had been to the facility, other similar crimes in the community, what knowledge the business had about criminal activity in the area and at it's own facility, what information was disclosed to the residents and families of residents, and what the facility did to prevent assaults by outsiders.

V.   JURISDICTION AND VENUE

This section is mostly for lawyers, as it addresses legal issues and considerations for filing suit. Most nursing home cases have to be filed in state court since, usually, the nursing home will be a local facility and will be incorporated in the same state where the facility is located and where the resident is a citizen.

Some cases, however, can be filed in federal court. This is possible when the case is between citizens of different states and where the amount in controversy is greater than $75,000.00. This is called "diversity of citizenship" jurisdiction for federal court cases.

There are times when you will want to pursue a claim in state court in the same or a nearby community. For instance, if the nursing home has a particularly bad reputation in the community, you may prefer to file the lawsuit in the same community. There are other times when you may prefer to file the case so that if it goes to trial you won't have jurors who are familiar with the parties. For instance, you may prefer to file the lawsuit in a different venue if the nursing home has a particularly good reputation in the community.

You may be able to get your case into federal court based on the citizenship of the person pursuing the claim. This may mean taking the victim of abuse out of the facility and moving across the state border so that you can go to trial in federal court instead of state court. In a wrongful death case, consider naming an out-of-state heir as the plaintiff to create diversity.

Thoughts about the choice of places to litigate an elder abuse case seem to be almost directly opposite the thoughts about the choice of places to try a medical negligence case. If you have a medical negligence claim against a local doctor in a small town or county, most trial lawyers would have long thoughts about the client moving out of state and litigating in federal court. However, in an elder abuse claim, a jury of people who themselves may have to go to the same nursing home when they are older may well be the best cross-section of the community that you can find.

Consider the issue of venue. If you have not tried cases in the county where the nursing home is located, talk to trial lawyers who have. Talk to trial lawyers who have handled elder abuse cases. Ask whether your client and future nursing home residents would be better off locally or in a different city where the federal court is located.

VI.   THE PETITION OR COMPLAINT

Again, this section is mostly for lawyers since it deals with legal requirements which must be met when filing a nursing home suit. The importance of a detailed petition or complaint cannot be over-emphasized. When you represent the victim of elder abuse, you must educate everyone else who is involved in the case. In addition to educating your client, you must educate the defendant, the defense attorney, and the insurance carrier. Often you have to educate the trial judge who, probably, has never had an elder abuse case go to trial. For your reference, the appendix includes sample petitions for nursing home wrongful death cases arising from an assault and arising from neglect.

In order to properly educate the other people involved in the suit, you will need to explain the facts of the case, the various injuries sustained by your client, the various statutes and regulations which have been violated, and how the violations and injuries affected your client.

Bland notice pleading will set the stage for the defense to limit your case to the one primary injury, when, in fact, your client has numerous injuries and a quality of life claim. In another case we litigated, the client had sustained a number of minor skin tears and had one significant decubitus ulcer which progressed and required extensive medical treatment. The defense tried to limit the discovery and presentation of evidence to the decubitus ulcer alone. However, since the complaint was detailed, with exhibits attached, and explained the facts, injuries, regulatory violations, and quality of life issues, the trial judge gave a long leash on the presentation of evidence.

Fact intensive pleading also may be used to expand the inquiry into patterns of abuse by the target nursing home when you allege—and support with exhibits—a history of the nursing home's deficiencies and a history of other residents with similar injuries and complaints. Such allegations with evidentiary support in the form of state surveys may enable you to discover evidence of injuries suffered by other residents and claims information. When the nursing home is owned by a national chain instead of being locally owned, this kind of evidence can be particularly damning.

There are a number of specific legal claims which should be considered. Consider breach of contract for breach of the admissions agreement, negligence, state administrative regulation and OBRA violations, negligence *per se*, loss of chance, wrongful death, and potential violations of the False Claims Act. Be mindful of the procedural requirements for pursuing each of these claims, especially for the False Claims Act violations.

VII. CONCLUSION

Nursing home residents have the right to be free from abuse and neglect, and nursing homes should not have to be told to be nice to their residents. The implementation of the OBRA regulations have helped in improving conditions in nursing homes in recent years, but nursing homes have become good at covering up abuse and making documentation look good.

People who are injured and pursue claims sometimes suffer attacks from many segments of society—legislators, manufacturers, physicians, defense lobbyists, and the insurance industry, to name a few. But when you are advocating for a loved one who was injured or killed by a nursing home, you and your lawyer have the unique opportunity to protect the infirm, to be the voice of the unheard, and to change the course of how our parents, grandparents, and eventually ourselves, are treated during what are supposed to be the "golden years."

PART FOUR
PREMISES LIABILITY

I.   OVERVIEW

"Premises liability" refers to the liability of the owner or occupier of land for injuries which occur on his property. Most premises liability claims arise from "slip and fall" or "trip and fall" incidents but can include a variety of other kinds of incidents arising from the physical condition of the property such as falling into open holes, stumbling over uneven pavement, slipping in water collected in a pothole in a parking lot, falling due to snow which has not been carefully cleared from a sidewalk, or falling on old safety mats which have become bubbled.

In addition to claims arising from the physical condition of the property, premises liability claims may also include injuries suffered as a result of physical assault such as during a robbery or a rape when the landowner has not provided sufficient security or lighting and the assault occurs in an area known for high crime or prior assaults.

Premises liability claims may also be appropriate as part of another claim such as when a business owner does not provide a protected place for shoppers to walk from the parking lot into the business and as a result gets hit by a car. There may be both a claim against the driver and a claim against the business owner.

There are also some accidents which occur because a motorist drives into a store. The obvious claim is against the motorist for not stopping in the parking lot, but there may also be a claim against the business owner for not having parking stops, for not having tall enough curbs to reduce the risk of such an accident, or for not having some sort of barrier to prevent this from occurring. In a recent case we litigated there was also a claim against the contractor who built the premises because the contractor failed to follow the architect's plans which called for a 6-inch curb and instead only constructed a 2-inch curb, thus reducing the safety protection that a 6-inch curb would have provided.

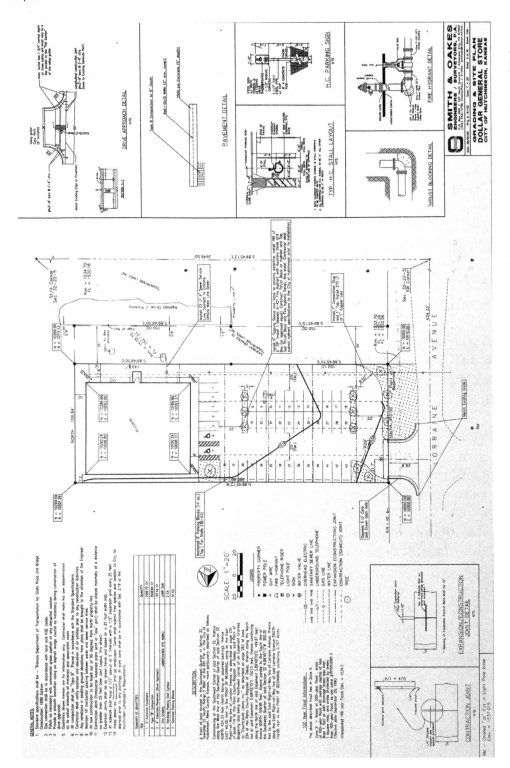

This schematic was used in a recent case against Dollar General, who constructed a 2-inch curb despite plans which called for a 6-inch curb. The failure to adhere to the plans reduced the safety protection provided by the curb.

These claims are usually based upon a claim of negligence where you prove that the owner or occupier of land was negligent and that as a result of that negligence you or your loved one suffered injuries.

Premises liability claims can be pursued against both the landowner or the occupier of the land, since frequently the land is owned by one person or entity but a business is operated on the land by a different person or entity. Similarly, some houses are owned by the people who live inside, but some are owned by landlords and tenants live inside. Although premises liability claims can be pursued against both (or either) the owner or occupier, we will refer to these claims as claims against the owner throughout this section to make reading less cumbersome.

II.   DUTY OF CARE

A. TYPES OF VISITORS

Historically a landowner's duty to people on his property depended on whether the person was considered an invitee, a licensee, or a trespasser.

An "invitee" is a person who comes on the property for the benefit of the landowner or for the benefit of both the landowner and the visitor. This might be a person invited to come on the property as a member of the public. This might be a business invitee, a person invited to enter or remain on the property for purposes of doing business with the landowner, such as when you go to a store to shop. And this might also be a social invitee going to a friend's home.

> In premises liability, an **invitee** is a person who comes on the property for the benefit of the landowner or for the benefit of both the landowner and visitor.

The landowner is liable for an injury suffered by an invitee if he has failed to inspect the premises and make it reasonably safe, or if he has failed to give a proper warning about defects on the property about which he knows or should know. The injured person must prove that the landowner had actual notice of the dangerous condition or that the dangerous condition had existed so long that the owner should have known of the dangerous condition, and that the landowner failed to take reasonable steps to make the premises safe or to warn of the dangerous condition.

The landowner is not liable for "latent defects"—hazards about which the landowner did not know and could not have been reasonably discovered or anticipated.

> A **licensee** is a person allowed on the owner's property whether by invitation or permission.

A "licensee" is a person who is allowed to enter or remain on land because the owner allows it either by invitation or permission. This might be a hunter who asks permission to hunt on the landowner's property, or a neighbor who asks to swim in your swimming pool. The landowner owes the licensee a duty to warn of dangerous hidden hazards about which he actually knows, to watch out for licensees if the owner is engaged in a dangerous activity, to exercise due caution, and to not intentionally harm the licensee.

The landowner is also subject to liability to the licensee for injuries caused by a natural or artificial condition of the land if he knows of the condition, recognizes that it involves an unreasonable risk, should realize that the licensee will not discover the risk, and permits the licensee to enter onto or remain on the premises without taking reasonable steps to make the condition reasonably safe or to warn of the risk. For example, if the owner knows that there is an abandoned mine shaft on the property and that the entrance is obscured by brush, the owner will need to take precautions to close the entrance or warn the licensee of the presence of the open shaft.

As you can see from comparing the duty owed to an invitee versus the duty owed to a licensee, the landowner has a higher duty of care to the person invited onto the property for the benefit of the owner than is owed for a person who is merely allowed to enter the land because he asked permission.

The lowest duty of care is owed to a trespasser. A "trespasser" is a person who enters or remains on property without the owner's or occupier's express or implied consent

> A **trespasser** is a person who enters and remains on property without the owner's express or implied consent and without right or authority.

and without any right or lawful authority. This might be a person who stays in the restroom of a business until after closing hours so he can rob the business, a person who breaks in, or a person who enters land to hunt without permission.

The duty of care owed by an owner to a trespasser is pretty low. The owner merely owes a duty to refrain from willfully, wantonly or recklessly injuring the trespasser. So the owner has no duty to the trespasser who falls in an old abandoned mineshaft while hunting without permission, but the owner is not allowed to shoot the trespasser simply because he is on the property.

In states which still use different standards for invitees, licensees and trespassers, children who trespass are given a little deference. This is because children may not recognize they are trespassing or may not recognize the risks associated with what they are doing. Most of these states have adopted the Restatement (Second) of Torts which provides that a landowner is liable for harm to trespassing children caused by an artificial condition if five requirements are met: (1) the owner knows or should know that children are likely to trespass, (2) the owner knows or should know that the condition poses an unreasonable risk of injury to children, (3) that the child because of his youth did not discover the condition or risk, (4) the cost or effort required to make the condition safe is minimal compared to the risk involved, and (5) the owner fails to use reasonable care.

The easiest example of such a risk to trespassing children is the backyard swimming pool. Kids like swimming pools. And young kids don't realize the risk associated with water, and may not realize that they cannot go to a neighbor's house and go for a swim. So most pool owners put a fence with child-proof gates and locks around their pools in order to prevent injury to children.

B. MODERN STANDARDS

More modern laws do not distinguish between whether the injured person was an invitee or a licensee, instead utilizing the same duty of care to both. These laws typically require the owner to have some knowledge of the dangerous condition and then establish a duty to remedy the problem and to warn.

Under these more modern standards, owners have a duty to others of reasonable care under all the circumstances. In order to determine whether the owner breached that duty a number of factors are to be considered:

- The foreseeability of harm to the injured person.
- The magnitude of risk of injury to others by maintaining the land in its condition.
- The individual and social benefit of maintaining the land in such a condition.

- The cost and inconvenience of providing adequate protection whether incurred by the owner or the community.

- Other factors as may be appropriate under the facts of your case.

Modern laws also provide a duty for the owner to warn of any dangerous condition in a location which is open to the public of which the owner knows or should know. This duty to warn usually applies only to parts of the property which are designed to be open to the public or to which the public may reasonably be expected to go. So, for example, a department store owner probably would not be found negligent for failure to warn customers about the risk of burns from the boiler in the mechanical room in the basement.

The duty of care and the duty to warn of a dangerous condition are normally limited to instances where the owner has actual knowledge of the condition, or where the condition has existed for such a length of time that the owner should have known of the condition if the owner had exercised reasonable care. However, if the owner created or maintained the dangerous condition, then knowledge of the condition is assumed. So, for example, if it was raining and a roof leak just started the owner might not be liable for a customer

A4 Saturday, August 27, 2011   The Hutchinson News

WIDE WEST

Lawsuit over man's fall names Hutch, Reno

He later died, and state of pavement outside the courthouse is a key issue.

By Mary Clarkin
The Hutchinson News
mclarkin@hutchnews.com

A widower scheduled to attend an Aug. 11, 2009, court hearing for the estate settlement of his late wife fell outside the Reno County Courthouse, suffering head injuries and dying about six weeks later.

The estate of Leo Stygles and Stygles' daughter, Lynne, is suing Reno County and the city of Hutchinson, alleging the pavement leading to the courthouse's handicap-accessible entrance was "uneven, deteriorated, pock marked with holes, and was rough," making it "unreasonably dangerous for a handicapped person."

The alley belongs to the city, the plaintiffs assert.

The county doesn't maintain the alley, said County Maintenance Director Harlen Depew. It's the city's responsibility, said County Counselor Joe O'Sullivan.

The county is named in the suit, though, because the alley lies between the courthouse's handicapped parking spaces and the handicap-accessible entrance on the rear, or north side, of the courthouse.

"Mechanically, the only way to get to the handicapped entrance is to walk up to it," said Hutchinson attorney Matthew Bretz, representing the plaintiffs.

Bretz said the case was referred to him after attempts by another attorney to reach a settlement failed.

"They both claimed they didn't have responsibility. They offered us nothing, not

Lindsey Bauman/The Hutchinson News
Uneven and broken pavement in an alleyway leads to an entrance on the north side of the Reno County Courthouse.

even medical bills," Bretz said.

He said the city's insurance provider, Travelers, sent a brief letter stating there was no finding of any liability.

After the courthouse fall, Stygles, 80, experienced a loss of equilibrium and had a number of additional falls in the ensuing days, the suit states. He was treated at Promise Regional Medical Center, Hutchinson, and at a hospital in Wichita, dying there Sept. 26, 2009. A 93-page billing from Via Christi

Health is included in estate court filings, and Bretz said medical costs overall exceeded a half-million dollars.

Stygles was using an aluminum cane with a rubber footing at the time of the fall, Bretz said.

The death certificate, signed by Reno County's coroner, Dr. Jaime Oeberst, described the cause of death as "complications of left subdural hemorrhage" and the manner of death as "accident."

The death certificate said the place of injury was "multiple locations" and that Stygles had a "reported history of numerous falls." It listed other conditions contributing to the cause of death, including post polio syndrome.

The lawsuit says the Reno County coroner "has determined that the location of the fall which caused the

subdural hemorrhage" causing Stygles' death was the "alley behind Reno County Courthouse."

A check Friday by The News found cracks and crumbled pavement in the alley.

Hutchinson City Manager John Deardoff said he couldn't see the alley when he drove by recently because of a parked UPS truck.

The city has many alleys downtown, and typically, Deardoff said, the central user – in this case, the county – contacts the city when repairs are needed.

"We don't drive every alley in town and fix cracks," he said, but rather, he said, they respond to calls.

The county's closest handicapped parking space lacks the proper painted handicap symbol on the pavement. Depew said painting was on the list of things to do.

Media coverage about a case in which our client's father was injured and eventually died as the result of a decayed walkway leading to the handicapped entrance to the courthouse.

who slips on water on the floor. But if the owner or its employees were stocking shelves and dropped a case of water, creating the dangerous condition, then it is not necessary that you prove notice.

Crumbling sidewalks, raised sidewalk slabs, parking lots, and potholes in driveways and parking lots frequently cause trip and fall injuries. These hazards typically develop over long periods of time so there usually is not any difficulty in proving that the owner had knowledge of the condition or that the owner should have known of the condition. Owners may also be forced to admit that they knew that people could be seriously hurt or even killed as a result of not making proper repairs. This can open the door to a punitive damages claim when you are pursuing a claim against most property owners.

C. MODE OF OPERATION RULE—CONDITIONS CREATED BY OTHERS

Back before most of us were born, stores were full service. When you went to the gas station a crew of workers would fuel your car, clean your windshield, check your oil and air your tires. Or a customer would go to the store with a list of items to purchase, would hand the list to a clerk, the clerk would pick the items off the shelves behind the counter, and would then ring up the purchases on a mechanical register. Does anyone remember Laura and Mary Ingalls going to Olesen's Mercantile on *Little House on the Prairie*? With this type of full service there was little risk that a customer would drop something on the floor and another customer would end up falling on it.

Those days are gone. Now most businesses are operated in such a way that customers regularly create dangerous conditions. Think about modern grocery stores or convenience stores. Customers walk through the store, perhaps sip a Starbucks coffee while shopping, pick items off the shelves, put the items in their carts, continue walking through the store, eventually check out, and then push the cart or carry the bags out of the store. Customers spill and drop things all the time. Sometimes customers report the spills, sometimes they do not. Sometimes spills are promptly cleaned up, sometimes they are not.

Most states have a **mode of operation rule** in which the owner or operator of a business may be held liable for injuries that result from dangerous conditions on the property created by another customer.

Due to the way that most stores are now run, many states have adopted what is known as the "mode of operation rule." Under the mode of operation rule the owner or operator of a business is liable for an injury that results from a dangerous condition on the property if two conditions are met: (1) the business adopted a mode of operation in which the dangerous condition could regularly occur, and (2) the owner or operator failed to use reasonable measures to discover the dangerous condition and remove it.

When considering liability against a business owner it is important to look at what the dangerous condition was, how it was created, who created it, and what the business owner did to get rid of it. If the dangerous condition was created by the owner, then you don't have to worry about the mode of operation rule. But if the dangerous condition was created by another customer, then you need to investigate these additional factors.

For instance, if you fall on spilled milk in a grocery store, look at the floor. Is there just one puddle or do the drops of spilled milk go up and down the aisles of the store. Look at where the drops are located. Are they in low traffic aisles or in one of the main aisles where employees should have seen them? When did employees last inspect the area where the spill was located? What level of customer traffic was present at the time? How much milk was sold in the store per hour?

Business owners will want to argue that they have a policy of periodic inspection, and may even have a sweep or inspection log that employees sign every hour representing that they have inspected and cleaned the area. You may see these inspection logs on the back of restroom doors. With a filled-out inspection log the store will argue that they inspected the area every hour and thus were not liable for your injury. The counter to this argument is that the store sells X gallons of milk per hour, that some of those containers leak, that customers carry the leaking milk cartons through the store, that spilled milk is immediately slick, that checking the floors every hour is not frequent enough given the volume of milk sales, and that inspecting only every hour creates a situation where dangerous conditions exist for up to 59 minutes of every hour.

In mode of operation cases it is important to get a number of things from the defense to help prove your case. Consider getting copies of the following:

- Surveillance video of the area of the fall.
- Surveillance video of the employee or customer who created the condition.
- Sweep/inspection logs for each area of the store where the spill was located.
- Sales record for the product which was sold. (Be generic. Ask for "all dairy products," rather than "2% Hiland Dairy Milk," so that the frequency of sales is higher, allowing you to argue for a higher level of risk.)

- Sales records for all products which have the potential for spilling and which can create dangerous conditions.

- Total sales figures and employee wages, so you can argue about the minimal cost required to make the store safe for customers.

- Written policies and procedures concerning floor safety.

- Policies and procedures concerning product placement.

The last item on the above list—policies and procedures concerning product placement —is included because businesses often argue that the customer who was injured was negligent for not keeping a proper lookout and that it was therefore the customer's own fault that she fell. To counter this, you have to show where you were looking and why you didn't see the dangerous condition.

Businesses know that customers want what customers see, so businesses place high profit items on shelves that are at eye-level, and lower profit items on lower shelves. Businesses hang sale banners from the ceiling. Essentially many things that businesses do to increase sales and profits draw the eyes of customers up from the floor. So, to be prepared to counter the defense argument that the person who was injured was negligent, you must use the store's own actions as one of the reasons for not seeing and avoiding the condition.

The sweep logs seem to have a tendency to be carefully and completely filled out by the time a lawsuit has been filed and discovery exchanged. When you compare sweep logs produced during discovery to sweep logs that you may see when visiting the store you may see some significant differences. It makes one wonder whether the sweep logs for the day and time of the accident may be fraudulent. With this in mind it may be appropriate to go to the facility before filing suit and take photos of the sweep logs which can be found in the restrooms and other locations, and then compare those to what is produced after suit is filed.

The mode of operation rule does not apply when the dangerous condition was created by the business owner or one of its employees. So if an employee stocking shelves spilled the product on which you fell, or if a store employee ran a cart into you and knocked you down, you don't have to worry about mode of operation.

D. ASSAULTS

Business owners may be liable for injuries suffered by their customers as a result of assaults, robberies, or other criminal actions. These can be separated into two categories: assaults by employees or assaults by third persons.

Normally a business owner is not liable for the criminal conduct of its employees since criminal conduct would not ordinarily be within the scope of the employment. But there are times when the criminal conduct does occur within the course and scope of employment. Consider the bar patron who is removed from a bar and beat up by the bouncer. The key to proving employer liability for actions of its employees is to prove that the employee's actions or inactions occurred both within the course of employment and within the scope of employment.

There may also be a claim against the business owner for negligent hiring, retention, or supervision of the employee. If the bouncer had a criminal history or a history of fighting, the owner may be held negligent for hiring the person to work as a bouncer. By employing the person the employer is creating the dangerous condition.

If the assault is by a third person, i.e. someone not employed by the business owner, then there may still be a claim against the business owner if the business owner has not taken reasonable steps to provide a safe place for its customers. Shopping malls are well known as targets for criminal activity. There are people with money, people whose hands are occupied holding packages, huge parking lots, and lots of noise and activity. Consider:

People with money	=	Attractive targets
Hands occupied	=	Hard for customers to fight back, and easy for criminals to snatch packages and purses
Huge parking lots	=	Hard to patrol by businesses, and easy escape for criminals
Noise and activity	=	Distraction for customers, and easy cover for criminals

Shopping malls are not the only places which are attractive to criminals. Convenience stores, jewelry stores, pawn shops, payday loan shops, and grocery stores are also frequent venues for criminal activity.

Because of these risks business owners have a duty to take reasonable precautions to make their business property reasonably safe. Laws in most states require the owner of a business to provide security for customers on the premises when circumstances exist from which the owner could reasonably foresee that there is a risk of criminal conduct beyond the ordinary level of risk and that appropriate security measures should be taken. The legal test used by the courts is whether under the totality of the circumstances a reasonable landowner could foresee that patrons have a risk of being victims of criminal acts which is higher than is ordinarily expected.

In investigating and pursuing such a claim you should look at the following, and other, factors:

- Whether the location is in a known high-crime area.
- The time of day that the crime was committed.
- The amount of lighting.
- Prior incidents involving crimes upon patrons.
- The economic feasibility of a reasonable level of security.
- What other businesses do in the same or similar circumstances.

We also see instances where a person who is required to have dealings with a business is assaulted, attacked or raped by an employee of the business. These include the child who has been taken out of the home and placed in foster care who is subsequently beaten up or raped by a foster care worker. These types of situations also seem to frequently occur to a person who is in jail and is raped by a guard.

Among the most egregious kinds of claims to pursue are those cases where a person in a position of trust, such as a foster care worker, takes advantage of that position and victimizes a person in his care. As with the other cases in this section it is vitally important to prove the employer's negligence in hiring, retention, supervision, and control.

III. DAMAGES

The damages which are recoverable in a premises liability case are the same damages as are recoverable in an automobilc liability claim, so please look back at Section VI. B. Similarly, if the incident causes death then a wrongful death claim may also be pursued.

In addition to actual damages, punitive damages may be recovered in some instances where you can prove that the landowner had knowledge of the dangerous condition but chose to ignore the probable consequences of his actions and inactions.

PART FIVE
WORKERS COMPENSATION

I.   OVERVIEW

Workers compensation is a form of insurance which provides certain benefits in exchange for giving up other rights when a person is injured while on the job.

Historically, before states adopted workers compensation laws, people who were injured on the job did not have any right to get medical treatment or to get wages paid while they were off work recovering from an injury. The employer did not have to provide a doctor for treatment, did not have to pay lost wages while the worker was off work getting medical treatment, and the employee was not entitled to money for permanent impairment or future loss of income or earning ability.

If the employer's negligence caused the injury, the worker could file a lawsuit and get damages similar to those available for a motor vehicle negligence case. But if the employee's own negligence caused the injury, there were no benefits. If no one was negligent in causing the injury, there were no benefits. And if the employer did not have money sitting in a bank account, the worker could not collect damages even if he won at trial. As a result, a sheriff's deputy who was shot by a robber got no benefits. A cowboy thrown off a horse got no benefits. And a railroad brakeman crushed between two rail cars got no benefits.

People died due to lack of medical treatment. Families lost their homes due to lost wages. Employers profited by using up their employees and then sending them out onto the street when they were no longer physically able to work due to injuries.

In the early 1900s many states started to recognize the inequalities and other problems created by this system. Workers compensation was the result. Under workers compensation laws, workers receive the right to what are supposed to be automatic benefits for work-related injuries in exchange for giving up the right to pursue a civil lawsuit for injuries caused by the employer's negligence.

II.   COVERAGE

The first thing to look at if you have been injured while on the job is whether your employment is covered by workers compensation in your state. Most states have a minimum payroll for an employer before requiring the employer to carry workers compensation insurance. If your employer is not required to have workers compensation insurance then you may not be able to get workers compensation benefits.

Some states also exclude certain types of employment from workers compensation. Interestingly, while farming was a major source of employment in the early 1900s when many workers compensation laws were enacted, farmers were frequently excluded from having to provide workers compensation insurance. Realtors frequently don't have to provide workers compensation insurance, and businesses which only employ relatives may not have to provide workers compensation insurance.

There are also some injuries which are not covered by workers compensation. For instance, many states do not provide benefits for employees who suffer heart attacks or strokes on the job unless certain very restrictive conditions are met. The heart attack and stroke exclusions from coverage are particularly damning for people in manual labor jobs and for people who have continued working past the point where workers traditionally retire.

Sometimes employers who are required by law to have workers compensation insurance do not get the required coverage. If that is the case for your employer, then you may have a remedy against a state insurance fund.

III.   BENEFITS

Under most modern workers compensation laws employees have rights to certain benefits. The available benefits vary widely from state to state, so if you were injured on the job then you should talk to an attorney who is familiar with the workers compensation laws in your state. In this book we will address some of the benefits which are common in most states so that you will have a reference as you are going through the process.

The first benefit for the injured worker is authorization of medical treatment and payment of medical bills. This benefit is designed to get the injured worker the treatment which is needed to cure or relieve the effects of the injury. Some states allow the worker to choose the physician who will provide treatment. Other states allow the employer or insurer to choose the authorized physician.

As you would expect, if the employer and insurer get to choose the authorized physician and the employee does not get any say in the decision, a significant amount of distrust may develop between the worker and the doctor chosen by the insurance company. Insurance companies generally choose a physician who they know will limit the medical treatment which is provided and who will return the employee to work as soon as possible, even if returning the employee to work may have long term negative effects on the employee's injury and condition.

In these states, the employee who is not getting adequate medical treatment from the physician chosen by the insurance company may or may not have the ability to get a change of physician from a workers compensation judge. Obtaining a change of physician in this instance can be very expensive and time consuming.

The second benefit for the injured worker is payment of lost wages while the worker is off work getting medical treatment. The lost wage benefit is usually a percentage of the worker's pre-injury wage and may also be subject to a weekly cap.

The widespread public perception is that lots of people fake injuries so that they can get paid for not working. Nothing could be further from the truth. The reduced compensation while a person is off work for a work-related injury acts as a penalty for those who are injured and is designed to get the employee back to work as soon as possible. This penalty of reduced wages frequently results in situations where the injured worker faces repossession of vehicles, foreclosure of a house, loss of a rental house, and collection lawsuits from other creditors. We have seen people unable to pay electric and gas bills because they have been injured on the job, resulting in no heat in the winter, and even resulting in young children being taken out of the home since the lack of heat endangers the child.

As with other kinds of injuries and claims, to pursue and win a workers compensation claim requires both the injured worker and his attorney to be absolutely honest in every aspect of the claim. When you have been injured on the job you will be faced with increased scrutiny from your employer. Your employer may have your co-workers report on your activities. The insurance company may hire an investigator to follow you, talk to your neighbors, and videotape you. And the insurance adjuster or defense lawyer will talk to your doctor and ask if you are faking the injury. If you lack honesty or integrity at any stage of the process then you lose all credibility with the court and will lose your claim.

Consider the worker who suffers an un-witnessed injury, has real injuries but exaggerates his physical limitations to the doctor, and then is caught on surveillance video doing something that he told his doctor he couldn't do. The insurance company will claim that there was no accident or injury and the worker will have no credibility with the workers compensation judge. So even a real injury ends up with no treatment because of the exaggeration.

On the other hand, if you are absolutely honest in all of your dealings with your employer, with your co-workers, with the insurance company, with the doctor, and with the judge, then you probably will win your case because you will show everyone that your are different than the stereotype—that you have integrity, that you really were hurt, and that you really need medical treatment and the other benefits available under the law.

The third benefit for an injured worker is based on permanent impairment. It may also be based on a combination of permanent impairment, loss of actual earnings, loss of earning potential, or loss of ability to perform job duties. Proof of these losses generally comes from physicians who are hired by the insurance company or your lawyer, or from vocational experts who address wage loss, loss of earning potential or loss of ability to perform job duties.

Most states have a formula for calculating the amount which is owed for these losses, though some states give the judge more discretion and latitude when making the decision.

The fourth commonly available benefit for the injured worker is future medical treatment. Some states make future medical treatment available for all injured workers, while other states significantly limit the availability of future medical treatment.

Insurance companies are frequently willing to offer a little extra money, or to pay all of the amount which is owed for permanent impairment in one lump sum rather than over time, in exchange for a worker giving up the right to future medical treatment. This may be reasonable for some injuries where future medical treatment is not likely to be needed but may be the worst decision you could make for other more severe injuries which are likely to require ongoing or future medical treatment.

Attorneys usually charge their workers compensation clients a percentage of the settlement. So the higher the settlement the higher the fee. Many attorneys looking out for themselves more than for their clients recommend closing future medical in exchange for a small payment of additional money. For the client who has been seriously injured, that kind of lawyer cannot be trusted. The ethical lawyer will recommend to her seriously injured client that he keep open future medical—even though that may mean a somewhat lower settlement and corresponding lower fee.

IV. EXCLUSIONS

As one might expect, most workers compensation laws exclude or severely limit benefits for those who are injured on the job when the injured person is under the influence of drugs or alcohol. The "drug and alcohol exclusion" generally has rather onerous standards before a drug or alcohol test can be admitted into evidence and considered by the court, but can result in a complete loss of benefits even in the most horrendous injury or death case.

> Most workers compensation laws exclude or limit benefits for those under the influence of drugs or alcohol, though the exclusion has rather onerous standards that must be met.

We certainly are not advocating use of drugs or alcohol while working but recognize that sometimes a person can have a positive test result even though it may have been a day since alcohol was used or weeks since drugs were used. And we recognize that sometimes a person takes a leftover old pain pill from the medicine cabinet after an injury and then tests positive for opiates. If you are injured and a positive drug or alcohol test is possible, talk to an experienced lawyer without delay (perhaps while you are on the way to take the drug test).

Another exclusion in some states is for injuries suffered by people with pre-existing conditions. In some states people with pre-existing conditions do not get any workers compensation benefits unless the work accident was the "predominant factor" in causing the injury, need for treatment, and impairment. Other states use a "caused or contributed" standard, providing workers compensation benefits to those who had an accident which caused or contributed to the injury, need for treatment or impairment.

To understand the difference between these two standards, consider the firefighter with 25 years on the force who has had back strains several times from carrying people out of fires, from training exercises, from pulling hose, and from other strenuous work activities, but each time gets better and can keep working. The firefighter then suffers another back strain while extricating a person trapped in a car, but this time the pain doesn't go away and instead gets worse to the point that he needs surgery. In states with the caused or contributed standard the firefighter gets medical treatment, payment of medical bills and payment of lost wages while off work. But in states with the predominate factor exclusion he does not get any benefits whatsoever since he had pre-existing back issues and the most recent activity was not the predominate factor in causing the problems in his back.

Since workers compensation laws are created by the legislatures of each state, workers compensation laws are frequently changed. At times the laws will become more conservative in response to publicity about perceived abuses by injured workers, and at other times the laws will become more liberal in response to publicity about perceived abuses by employers and insurance companies. As a result, familiarity with the current state of the law is paramount in order to identify the potential claims, legal procedures, and statutory standards.

PART SIX

DO I NEED A LAWYER, AND HOW DO I PICK A GOOD ONE?

There is one good reason not to hire a lawyer to help you with your injury claim: fees. If you have a very minor injury it may make sense to try to handle it on your own without a lawyer. That way you can keep all of your settlement—after payment of any medical bills or liens—for yourself.

On the other hand, if you have a significant injury or have lost a loved one, you are far better off with an experienced and ethical lawyer than without a lawyer. There are a number of reasons to hire a lawyer.

First, insurance companies pay you more to settle your case when you have a lawyer and pay much more when you have a good lawyer. Varying statistics show that when a lawyer is involved, the average amount paid for medical treatment and the average amount paid for a settlement is between four and seventeen times higher than when no lawyer is involved. That means a person with a lawyer is able to get more medical treatment so that she can make a better physical recovery from an injury and also is able to get a higher settlement to compensate for all of her losses.

> Statistics show that when a lawyer is involved, the average amount paid for medical treatment and for a settlement is between four and seventeen times higher than when no lawyer is involved.

Insurance companies know that from a practical standpoint a person without a lawyer cannot do anything about a lowball settlement offer. Insurance companies know that a person without a lawyer is forced to take their settlement offer and cannot do anything about it not being fair. Insurance companies know the traps that the unrepresented person faces, such as:

- Not knowing about the availability of PIP or no-fault coverage.
- Not knowing about essential services reimbursement.
- Not knowing about the deadline for filing suit to avoid losing your claim to the PIP carrier's subrogation claim.
- Not knowing about the statute of limitations, how to calculate it, or how to meet it's requirements.

- Not being able to identify all of the potentially responsible parties and their insurers.

- Not being able to accomplish service of process on the defendant(s).

- Not knowing which insurance policies provide primary or excess coverage.

- Not being able to meet the statutory or contractual requirements to pursue an uninsured or underinsured motorist claim.

- Signing something that releases all claims, avoiding further liability for your injuries and damages.

- Not meeting the statutory and procedural requirements for stating a claim.

- Not knowing the regulatory requirements for product liability or nursing home claims.

This is obviously not an exhaustive list of the traps faced by those who are unrepresented. These are just a small handful of the traps at the very beginning of the case. Insurance companies also know that the unrepresented person cannot conduct discovery, take depositions to establish a claim, subpoena and question witnesses at trial, and so on.

This book will help you identify many of these issues and provides information about how we resolve them, but is not a substitute for 30 years of experience pursuing these claims in state and federal courts around the country.

Second, insurance companies know the difference between good lawyers and bad lawyers, and make different evaluations of your claim based on the lawyer you choose. They know which lawyers are ethical, vigorously advocate for their clients, will not take a lowball offer, and will go to trial if a fair settlement offer is not made.

Insurance companies also know which lawyers will roll over and take whatever offer the insurance company makes. Insurance companies call these people "settlement lawyers." Insurance companies do not respect ambulance chasers who constantly appear in loud advertisments on TV and who do not regularly take cases to jury trial. Think about it. An insurance company has nothing to worry about if they know that your lawyer has a reputation of settling and not going to trial.

You and the insurance company have the same ability to research lawyers and find one who has an excellent reputation for ethics and legal ability. Martindale Hubbell™ is the leading source for information about attorneys. It has published a legal directory since

1868 and currently provides profiles and ratings for over 1,500,000 lawyers and law firms in the United States, Canada and 160 other countries. You can search lawyers by name by going to www.martindale.com. Martindale Hubbell rates lawyers in two areas: legal ability and ethics. The rating consists of two letters, AV, BV, or CV. The A, B or C rating is the same as grade cards in school. The V rating refers to whether the attorney meets very high ethical standards.

If Martindale Hubbell does not list a rating for an attorney, there is a reason. First, the lawyer may not have practiced long enough (or long enough in one state) for a rating to have been established. This is common for lawyers who have practiced less than ten years or for lawyers who have practiced in one state and subsequently moved to a different state. Second, no rating will be listed if the lawyer's legal ability is considered a D or F. Third, no rating will be listed if the lawyer does not meet ethical standards.

> **Martindale Hubbell** (martindale.com) is the leading source for information about attorneys
>
> **AVVO** (avvo.com) also provides helpful information, including ratings based on reviews by clients and other lawyers.

So, if you are looking at a lawyer who has practiced 10 or more years in one state who has no rating from Martindal Hubbell, you should be seriously concerned. You do not want a lawyer who rates a C or worse or a lawyer who does not meet ethical standards.

The other place to look for lawyer ratings is www.avvo.com. AVVO™ provides ratings which are based on reviews by other lawyers and by clients. AVVO uses a bright red "ATTENTION!" warning for lawyers who have been disciplined by the state regulatory agency. That should tell you something about the lawyer, and it will definitely tell the insurance company something about you if you choose to hire such a person.

A lawyer's reputation rubs off on the client and either helps or hurts the client's claim. Consider the client who hires an attorney who advertises on TV with screeching tires, and who is widely known as an "ambulance chaser" or "settlement lawyer". Hiring that type of lawyer speaks volumes about the client to the insurance company valuing the claim and to a judge or jury evaluating your credibility.

Consider, on the other hand, the client who hires an attorney who is known for her integrity and legal excellence. Hiring this type of lawyer also speaks volumes about the client to the insurance company valuing the claim and to a judge or jury evaluating your credibility.

The third reason to hire a lawyer for a serious injury is that a good lawyer can increase the value of your case by being able to identify all of the potential parties against whom claims can be pursued, all of the potential claims, and all of the potential insurance coverage. As discussed earlier in this book, in a motor vehicle wreck where you were rear-ended by a drunk driver the drunk driver is the obvious defendant. However, there may also be claims against the bar which served him, the insurer and owner of the vehicle which was being driven if it wasn't his own car, the car manufacturer due to faulty airbags or other safety equipment, and the paramedic for putting an endotracheal tube down your esophagus instead of your trachea. Without an experienced lawyer you probably would not identify all of these potential claims and realistically would not be able to pursue all of these potential claims.

Fourth, an experienced lawyer will be able to collect and present the evidence which is necessary to win your case. The ambulance chaser will collect the medical records and bills. Depending on the requirements of your case, the good experienced trial lawyer will collect the records and bills and will also get reports from doctors about your injuries and anticipated future medical needs, evidence from your employer and a vocational expert about past and future lost income, may retain an expert to reconstruct a collision to prove fault, may retain experts to establish a product defect, etcetera.

By getting all of this evidence and presenting it to the responsible parties and their insurers early on in the case, the experienced lawyer shows those who are responsible that the lawyer has everything that is necessary to win at trial. By being ready for trial the insurance company is much more likely to make a fair settlement. We always tell clients to hope for the best but plan for the worst. Good experienced lawyers will obtain the evidence needed to win at trial so that they can get the case settled without having to go to trial.

Fifth, experienced trial attorneys can advocate for you. They have the ability to analyze the opposition's evidence which is against you, identify and demonstrate flaws in their evidence, and present evidence to support your claims and prove the extent of your damages. This is why some lawyers consistently win cases at trial and obtain significant settlements for their clients, and is why "settlement lawyers" do not. Insurance companies evaluating your claims know the difference.

Lawyers who handle injury cases typically handle them on a contingency or percentage fee. That means that the lawyer only gets paid if the lawyer wins the case for you and then the lawyer charges a percentage of the settlement or recovery. This sort of arrangement does a few things for you: First, it allows you to hire an attorney without coming up with money up front (known as a "retainer"), keeps you from getting a bill each month, and makes it so you do not have any financial risk. Second, this arrangement makes the lawyer work hard since he does not get paid unless he obtains a recovery for you. Third, it lets you get an attorney immediately after an injury without any additional expense. By being involved early on, the attorney can prevent many problems from occurring or can fix problems before they fester and cause more problems.

Typically attorneys charge one-third of a settlement, or a slightly higher percentage if the case is not settled and suit has to be filed or if the attorney has to take the case to trial. The contingency fee arrangement needs to be put in writing for you. This may seem like a lot of money, and in really small cases it may make sense not to hire a lawyer with whom you will have to share your settlement. But in a case involving real and significant injuries you will be better served with an experienced ethical lawyer than without because the lawyer will add value to your case.

A case in point is one which we took to trial a few years ago. In that case the client originally hired a TV lawyer who told her to try to settle for $25,000.00. When the insurance company offered nothing the TV lawyer dropped the case. The client was then referred to our office. We took the case to jury trial and obtained a verdict for our client of $247,200.00. So, consider the economics of hiring good ethical and diligent lawyers:

No Lawyer:	*TV Lawyer:*	*AV Rated Trial Lawyer:*
$0.00 offer	$25,000 recommendation (but no offer from insurer)	$247,200.00 verdict
_____	- $250.00 expenses	- $1,536.96 advanced expenses
$0.00 to client	x 2/3	x 2/3
	_____	_____
	$16,666.67 recommended (if settlement had been reached)	**$163,775.36 to client**
	$0.00 actual to client	

Another example is a case we tried to a jury in March 2014, just a month before the above case. Before hiring a lawyer the defendant paid some of the victim's medical bills but offered nothing to settle the case and even made a claim against the victim for damage to the defendant's property. We took the case to trial and obtained a verdict of $200,000.00

for the client against the defendant. Again, consider the economics of hiring good trial lawyers:

No Lawyer:	*AV Rated Trial Lawyer:*
$0.00 offer	$200,000.00
	- $6,235.55 advanced expenses
	x 2/3
$0.00 to client	
	$129,174.30 to client

Some cases do not turn out this extreme, but hiring a lawyer still makes sense most of the time. For example, a potential client with a very minor case contacted us in October 2013. She had tried to settle her claim for $15,000.00 without a lawyer but the insurance company would only offer her $2,000.00. She had not been able to get the case settled and the statute of limitations was just three days away when she finally was referred to our office. We filed suit to protect the statute of limitations and then got the case settled for the amount the client wanted, $15,000.00, in less than two months. Again consider the economics:

No Lawyer:	*AV Rated Trial Lawyer:*
$2,000.00 offer	$15,000.00
	- $310.75 advanced expenses
$2,000.00 to client	x 2/3
(if offer had been accepted)	
	$9,792.83 to client

So, by hiring an AV rated trial lawyer, the client netted 489% more than she was able to get without a lawyer—even after paying expenses and fees.

Of course, every case is different and the outcome of the case depends on the facts of that case. These are just a few examples of how, economically, it makes sense to retain an ethical and experienced lawyer in the event of a serious injury or death.

As you see in the above examples, there are also expenses. Lawyers usually advance the expenses associated with pursuing a case. Typical expenses include things like charges from medical providers for copies of records, filing fees, expert witness charges, court reporter charges, and the like.

Some lawyers make both fees and reimbursement for advanced litigation expenses contingent upon the recovery. This means that the lawyer only gets paid and only gets expenses reimbursed if the case is won. Other lawyers will charge you expenses regardless of whether the case is won or lost. Be careful about this, and be sure that this is addressed in your written attorney-client agreement. You do not want your lawyer to lose your case and then send you a bill for expenses.

Finally, some lawyers deduct expenses off the top of a settlement and only charge a fee on the net recovery. Other lawyers charge fees on the total settlement and take the expenses out of the client's net recovery. The rules of professional conduct in your state may address which way the expenses and contingent fees are supposed to be handled. The way that the expenses are deducted can make a big difference in a case with significant expenses and in a case with a small recovery, as shown in the below example:

$25,000.00 settlement	**$25,000.00 settlement**
- $5,000.00 expenses	x 2/3
x 2/3	- $5,000.00 expenses
$13,333.33 to client	**$11,666.67 to client**

Obviously, it is better for you if the expenses come off the top and the contingency fees are charged on the net recovery.

The long and short of it is that the best cases to handle without a lawyer are minor injury cases with minimal medical treatment and bills, and with no permanent injury or damage. This might be cases worth less than $5,000.00 where you have plenty of time to fall back and get an attorney if things go south.

But if you have a significant injury then an experienced, ethical lawyer is absolutely necessary. It is safe to say that the value of a good lawyer increases exponentially with the severity of your injuries and losses.

APPENDIX 1

AUTOMOBILE/TRUCK COLLISION COMPLAINT

This Complaint was used in a car versus truck collision case where the defendant truck driver had a medical history which created a risk to himself and others. It will help you identify potentially liable parties and theories of recovery.

This particular Complaint names three defendants including the driver for his conduct; the driver's employer under both vicarious liability and for it's own negligence in hiring, retention, and supervision; and the insurance company for the driver and employer.

This was filed in Federal Court based on diversity of citizenship jurisdiction. Since it was filed in Federal Court the Complaint was more detailed than many which are filed in state court.

**IN THE UNITED STATES DISTRICT COURT
FOR THE DISTRICT OF KANSAS**

███████████████ ,   )
)
            Plaintiff,   )
)
)
vs.   )   Case No. _____
)
CLEAN HARBORS ENVIRONMENTAL SERVICES,)
INC., ELWIN BROWN, and ZURICH AMERICA)
INS., CO.,   )
)
            Defendants.   )
_____)

COMPLAINT

COMES NOW the Plaintiff, ███████████████ , by and through her attorney, Matthew

L. Bretz, and for Plaintiff's cause of action against the Defendants states as follows:

1.   Plaintiff ███████████████ is an individual, resident, citizen and domiciliary of the

       State of Kansas, residing at ███████████████████████████ .

2.   Defendant Elwin Brown is an individual, resident, citizen and domiciliary of the State of

       Oklahoma, and may be served with process at his residence at ███████████████

       ████████████ .

3.   Defendant Clean Harbors Environmental, is a company existing under the laws of the State

       of Oklahoma, and is not a resident, citizen or domiciliary of the State of Kansas, and may be

       served with process by serving it registered agent for service of process, The Corporation

       Company, 120 North Robinson, Suite 735, Oklahoma City, Oklahoma 73102.

4.   Defendant Zurich American Ins. Co. is the insurance carrier for Defendants Elwin Brown and

       Clean Harbors Environmental Services, Inc., and is not a resident, citizen or domiciliary of

       the State of Kansas, and may be served with process by serving the Kansas Insurance

       Commissioner at 420 SW 9th Street, Topeka, Kansas 66612-1678.

-1-

5.   The jurisdiction of this Court is invoked pursuant to 28 U.S.C. § 1332, in that there is complete diversity of citizenship, and the amount in controversy exceeds the sum or value of $75,000.00, exclusive of interest and costs.

6.   On or about June 14, 2007, Defendant Elwin Brown negligently, recklessly, willfully, and with wanton disregard for the safety of others drove a tractor-trailer combination through a 20 mile-per-hour business district at 60 miles-per-hour and through a stop sign and flashing stop light.

7.   As a result of this unlawful conduct of Defendant Brown, the tractor trailer combination which he was driving struck the vehicle being operated by   which was lawfully stopped in the intersection awaiting a left turn.

8.   At all times material hereto, Defendant Elwin Brown was in the course and scope of his employment with Defendant Clean Harbors Environmental Services, Inc. As such, Defendant Clean Harbors Environmental Services, Inc., is vicariously liable for the negligent, willful, wanton, reckless and unlawful actions of Defendant Elwin Brown under the doctrine of respondeat superior.

9.   Upon reasonable opportunity for further investigation and discovery, Plaintiff also alleges that the conduct of Defendant Clean Harbors Environmental Services, Inc., was negligent, grossly negligent, wilful, wanton, reckless and unlawful in one or more of the following, or other, respects:

    A.   Violation of the Federal Motor Carrier Safety Regulations in one or more of the following, or other, respects:

        1.   Allowing Defendant Brown to drive without proper qualifications;

        2.   Conducting an inadequate background check and application investigation;

-2-

3.   Failing to properly update driving records;

4.   Failing to perform a proper annual driver review;

5.   Failing to keep an active file;

6.   Failing to keep proper log books;

7.   Failing to follow hours of service rules;

B.   Negligent hiring, retention or control.

C.   Failing to properly supervise and control Defendant Elwin Brown.

D.   Negligent entrustment.

10.   Defendant Zurich American Ins. Co. is the insurer for Defendants Clean Harbors Environmental Services, Inc., and Elwin Brown, and is therefore jointly liable for the damages caused by Defendants Clean Harbors Environmental Services, Inc., and Elwin Brown.

11.   Due to the reckless, grossly negligent, wilful and wanton conduct of the Defendants, Plaintiff seeks an award of punitive damages for the purpose of restraining and deterring Defendants and others from committing like wrongs of a willful, wanton and reckless nature.

12.   As a result of the negligent, grossly negligent, wilful, wanton, reckless and unlawful actions of the Defendants, Plaintiff has suffered, and will suffer in the future, permanent, severe and disabling injuries, medical expenses, surgical expenses, loss of income, loss of earnings capacity, physical pain, suffering, disability, disfigurement, mental and emotional stress, and other consequential damages.

13.   At all times material hereto, Plaintiff was lawfully married to ▨▨▨▨▨ ▨▨▨▨▨. Plaintiff also brings this action on behalf of her husband for loss of consortium.

WHEREFORE, Plaintiff prays for judgment against each of the Defendants in an amount in excess of $75,000.00, for costs of this action, and for such other and further relief as the Court deems just and equitable.

Respectfully submitted,

By: _s/ Matthew L. Bretz_
    Matthew L. Bretz, #15466
    1227 North Main Street
    P.O. Box 1782
    Hutchinson, KS 67504-1782
    (620) 662-3435
    (620) 662-3445 (fax)
    mbretz@bretzpilaw.com
    Attorney for Plaintiff

DESIGNATION OF PLACE OF TRIAL

Plaintiff hereby designates Kansas City, Kansas, as the place of trial in this matter.

By: _s/ Matthew L. Bretz_
        Matthew L. Bretz

REQUEST FOR JURY TRIAL

COMES NOW the Plaintiff, pursuant to applicable Kansas law, and respectfully makes demand for trial by jury of all issues herein joined.

By: _s/ Matthew L. Bretz_
        Matthew L. Bretz

APPENDIX 2

COMMERCIAL TRUCK INTERROGATORIES AND REQUESTS FOR PRODUCTION

The Interrogatories and requests for production which are attached were used in the case which is referenced in Appendix 1.

Interrogatories are written questions from one party in a lawsuit to another party to a lawsuit. In the written questions, a party can ask about virtually anything which is related in any way to the claims which are being made and the defenses which are being asserted. Courts generally limit the number of interrogatories which each party may submit to any other party.

Requests for production are, as the name suggests, requests from one party to another party to produce a document. They can also be used to request inspection of property. Requests for production are usually not limited, and frequently several sets of requests are sent as a case progresses and additional documents, records or other things are discovered.

The interrogatories and requests for production which are attached will help you identify what sort of things may be requested to help you identify various claims which can be made and evidence which might support each of the claims.

Each state has different rules which govern interrogatories and requests for production. These rules address timing for sending the requests, the number of requests which can be sent, to whom the requests can be sent, and other matters. If your case is in federal court, then the Federal Rules of Civil Procedure provide the rules which govern these requests and are the same regardless of which federal court in which your case is filed.

**IN THE UNITED STATES DISTRICT COURT
FOR THE DISTRICT OF KANSAS**

████████████████ ,	)	
Plaintiff,	)	
	)	
vs.	)	Case No.: 08 CV 2124
	)	
CLEAN HARBORS ENVIRONMENTAL SERVICES,	)	
INC., ELWIN BROWN, and ZURICH AMERICA	)	
INS., CO.,	)	
Defendants.	)	
	)	

**PLAINTIFF'S FIRST REQUEST FOR PRODUCTION OF DOCUMENTS
TO DEFENDANTS**

COMES NOW the Plaintiff and requests Defendants to produce the following

documents, articles and items of tangible nature within thirty (30) days after receipt of this

request pursuant to Fed.R.Civ.P 34.

1. All insurance claims and underwriting files pertaining to the subject matter of this

    lawsuit.

2. Original or true and correct copies of all policies of insurance, and corresponding

    declarations pages, for all policies of insurance which may provide coverage for this

    motor vehicle accident.

3. Original or true and correct copies of any and all photographs which depict damage to the

    vehicle which Elwin Brown was driving at the time of the accident.

4. Original or true and correct copies of any and all photographs which depict damage to the

    vehicle in which Plaintiff was an occupant at the time of the accident.

5. Original or true and correct copies of all repair estimates and repair bills for damage

    sustained by the vehicle which Elwin Brown was driving at the time of the accident.

6.   Original or true and correct copies of all repair estimates and repair bills for damage sustained by the vehicle in which Plaintiff was an occupant at the time of the accident.

7.   Original or true and correct copies of all photographs depicting Plaintiff.

8.   Original or true and correct copies of any recorded statement taken of Plaintiff.

9.   Original or true and correct copies of any recorded statement taken of Elwin Brown in this matter.

10.   Original or true and correct copies of any recorded statement taken of any other person in any way related to the motor vehicle accident which is the subject of this litigation, any witnesses to the subject motor vehicle accident, Plaintiff, and/or Plaintiff's injuries and damages.

11.   Original or true and correct copies of all medical records and reports pertaining in any way to Plaintiff.

12.   Original or true and correct copies of all employment records pertaining in any way to Plaintiff.

13.   All documents you intend to introduce as evidence at the time of trial.

14.   All documents you contend support the denials set forth in your Answer.

15.   All documents identified in Defendant's responses to Plaintiff's First Set of Interrogatories.

16.   Original or true and correct copies of Elwin Brown's driver's logs and related information and driver notes for June 14, 2007, and the preceding 30 days.

17.   Original or true and correct copies of all service orders and receipts for Elwin Brown for June 14, 2007, and the preceding 30 days.

18.   Original or true and correct copies of the bills of lading for the load which Elwin Brown

was driving on June 14, 2007, and for all other loads which he pulled during the preceding 30 days.

19. Original or true and correct copies of the manifest and waybills for the load which Elwin Brown was driving on June 14, 2007, and for all other loads which he pulled during the preceding 30 days.

20. Original or true and correct copies of any rental contracts involving the truck and trailer which were involved in the June 14, 2007, motor vehicle collision which is the subject of this suit.

21. Original or true and correct copy of the accident register for the June 14, 2007, motor vehicle collision which is the subject of this suit.

22. Original or true and correct copies of all vehicle maintenance records for the truck and trailer which were involved in the June 14, 2007, motor vehicle collision which is the subject of this suit, for June 14, 2007, and the preceding 30 days.

23. Original or true and correct copies of all insurance policies for the truck and trailer which were involved in the June 14, 2007, motor vehicle collision which is the subject of this suit.

24. Original or true and correct copies of all insurance policies which may provide coverage for Elwin Brown for the June 14, 2007, motor vehicle collision which is the subject of this suit.

25. Original or true and correct copies of all insurance policies which may provide coverage for Clean Harbors Environmental Services, Inc., for the June 14, 2007, motor vehicle collision which is the subject of this suit.

26. Original or true and correct color copies of all photographs of the scene, truck, trailer and

automobile which were involved in the June 14, 2007, motor vehicle collision which is the subject of this suit.

27. Original or true and correct copies of all lease and trip lease contracts applicable to the load which Elwin Brown was pulling on June 14, 2007.

28. Original or true and correct copies of all trip reports, maps and trip communications for Elwin Brown for June 14, 2007, and the preceding 30 days.

29. Original or true and correct copies of all vehicle repair invoices for the truck and trailer which Elwin Brown was driving on June 14, 2007, and the preceding 30 days.

30. Original or true and correct copies of all safety and training manuals and videotapes used by Clean Harbors Environmental Services, Inc., to train drivers including Elwin Brown.

31. Original or true and correct copies of all convictions or suspensions for traffic violations by Elwin Brown.

32. Original or true and correct copies of all manuals covering truck safety and driving standards used by Clean Harbors Environmental Services, Inc.

33. Original or true and correct copies of Elwin Brown's personnel file maintained by Clean Harbors Environmental, Inc.

34. Original or true and correct copies of Elwin Brown's medical file maintained by Clean Harbors Environmental, Inc.

35. Original or true and correct copies of Elwin Brown's human resources file maintained by Clean Harbors Environmental Services, Inc.

36. Original or true and correct copies of Elwin Brown's drug and alcohol testing records.

37. Original or true and correct copies of all personnel files for Elwin Brown which Clean Harbors Environmental obtained from previous employers.

38.   Original or true and correct copies of all Elwin Brown's results for any drug or alcohol testing before hired, after hired, and after the June 14, 2007, collision.

39.   Original or true and correct copies of all NTSC investigation reports related in any way to Elwin Brown.

40.   Original or true and correct copies of all delivery manifests for the load which Elwin Brown was driving on June 14, 2007, and for all other loads which he pulled during the preceding 30 days.

41.   Original or true and correct copies of all dispatch records for Elwin Brown for June 14, 2007, and for all other loads which Elwin Brown pulled during the preceding 30 days.

42.   Original or true and correct copies of all expense sheets and canceled checks for Elwin Brown for June 14, 2007, and for the preceding 30 days.

43.   Original or true and correct copies of all fuel receipts for Elwin Brown for June 14, 2007, and for the preceding 30 days.

44.   Original or true and correct copies of all credit card receipts and bills for Elwin Brown for June 14, 2007, and for the preceding 30 days.

45.   Original or true and correct copies of all debit card receipts for Elwin Brown for June 14, 2007, and for the preceding 30 days.

46.   Original or true and correct copies of the registration and title for the truck which Elwin Brown was driving on June 14, 2007.

47.   Original or true and correct copies of all pick up and delivery records for Elwin Brown for June 14, 2007, and for all other loads which Elwin Brown pulled during the preceding 30 days.

48.   A true and correct copy of both the front and back of Elwin Brown's CDL.

49. Original or true and correct copy of the truck and trailer license for the truck and trailer which were involved in the June 14, 2007, collision which is the subject of this suit.

50. Original or true and correct copy of Elwin Brown's driver's qualification file, including his medical certificates, and all other files pertaining to Elwin Brown.

51. Original or true and correct copy of the mission statement for Clean Harbors Environmental Services, Inc.

52. Original or true and correct copy of the safety policy and safety information for Clean Harbors Environmental Services, Inc.

53. Original or true and correct copy of the company-generated incident report of the report received by the dispatcher from Elwin Brown related to the June 14, 2007, collision which is the subject of this suit.

54. Original or true and correct color copies of all photographs taken by any camera supplied to Elwin Brown which are in any way related to the June 14, 2007, collision which is the subject of this suit.

55. Original or true and correct copies of all documents in Elwin Brown's trip envelope on June 14, 2007.

56. Original or true and correct copies of all 70 hour and other compliance audits of Elwin Brown.

57. Original or true and correct copies of all satellite tracking information for Elwin Brown for the six month period immediately preceding June 14, 2007.

58. Original or true and correct copies of all bills and statements from Com Data or similar expense/cash advance services used by Clean Harbors Environmental Services, Inc., related in any way to Elwin Brown.

59.   Original or true and correct copies of all information at any time contained in or retrieved from any onboard data record, including, but not limited to ECM or black boxes, for the truck which was being operated by Elwin Brown on June 14, 2007.

BRETZ LAW OFFICES, LLC

By_____
                Matthew L. Bretz, SC #15466
                Attorney for Plaintiff

IN THE UNITED STATES DISTRICT COURT
FOR THE DISTRICT OF KANSAS

███████████████ ,	)	
Plaintiff,	)	
	)	
vs.	)	Case No.: 08 CV 2124
	)	
CLEAN HARBORS ENVIRONMENTAL SERVICES,	)	
INC., ELWIN BROWN, and ZURICH AMERICA	)	
INS., CO.,	)	
Defendants.	)	
	)	

PLAINTIFF'S SECOND REQUEST FOR PRODUCTION OF DOCUMENTS
TO DEFENDANT ELWIN BROWN

COMES NOW the Plaintiff and requests Defendants to produce the following

documents, articles and items of tangible nature within thirty (30) days after receipt of this

request pursuant to Fed.R.Civ.P 34.

1.   A signed Medical Authorization allowing Plaintiff access to any and all medical records

for Defendant Elwin Brown, for the ten (10) years preceding the accident which is the

subject of these proceedings.

2.   Any and all medical records in Plaintiff's possession, custody or control, regarding any

general or special medical condition.

BRETZ LAW OFFICES, LLC

By_____
        Matthew L. Bretz, SC #15466
        Attorney for Plaintiff

IN THE UNITED STATES DISTRICT COURT
FOR THE DISTRICT OF KANSAS

██████████████████ ,	)	
Plaintiff,	)	
	)	
vs.	)	Case No.: 08 CV 2124
	)	
CLEAN HARBORS ENVIRONMENTAL SERVICES,	)	
INC., ELWIN BROWN, and ZURICH AMERICA	)	
INS., CO.,	)	
Defendants.	)	
_____	)	

PLAINTIFF'S THIRD REQUEST FOR PRODUCTION OF DOCUMENTS
TO DEFENDANT ELWIN BROWN

COMES NOW the Plaintiff and requests Defendants to produce the following

documents, articles and items of tangible nature within thirty (30) days after receipt of this

request pursuant to Fed.R.Civ.P 34.

1.   A signed Medical Authorization.

2.   Legible copies of documents produced by Defendants marked as documents: 175, 176, B-

       MC-1, B-MC-2, and B-MC-3 (Bates Numbered 420055, 420056, 460001, 460002, and

       460003).

3.   All cellular phone records and bills for Defendant Elwin Brown for June, 2007.

                           BRETZ LAW OFFICES, LLC

                    By_____
                           Matthew L. Bretz, SC #15466
                           Attorney for Plaintiff

IN THE UNITED STATES DISTRICT COURT
FOR THE DISTRICT OF KANSAS

▓▓▓▓▓▓▓▓▓▓▓▓ , Plaintiff,)))	
vs.)	Case No.: 08 CV 2124
)	
CLEAN HARBORS ENVIRONMENTAL SERVICES,) INC., ELWIN BROWN, and ZURICH AMERICA) INS., CO.,) Defendants.))	

PLAINTIFF'S FIRST SET OF INTERROGATORIES TO
DEFENDANTS

Pursuant to Fed.R.Civ.P 33, Plaintiff propounds to Defendants these Interrogatories to be answered within thirty (30) days after service hereof. Space is included for answers to the Interrogatories upon the original. These Interrogatories are deemed continuing in nature and require your additional response should additional information or changes in your answers come to your attention.

In each response to these Interrogatories, provide all information in your possession, custody or control. If you are able or willing to provide only part of the information sought, specify the reason for your inability or unwillingness to provide the remainder. In addition to supplying the information requested, you are to identify all documents that support your answer or make reference to the subject matter of each Interrogatory and your answer. Further, if any or all documents identified are no longer in your possession, custody or control, because of loss, destruction or any other reason, then provide the following with respect to each such document:

1.   Describe the nature of the document;

2.   State the date of the document;

3.   Identify the person who sent and received the original and any copies of the document;

4.   State in as much detail as possible the contents of the document; and

5.   State the manner of the disposition of the document.

If you decline to answer any portion of the Interrogatory, provide all information called for by the balance of the Interrogatory. If you object to any portion of the Interrogatory on any ground, provide all information called for which you concede is discoverable. These Interrogatories apply to information that you have or possess and any information that you, any agent, servant, employee, or investigator has or possesses on your behalf.

DEFINITIONS

"Document" -- as used herein, the term "document" means any medium upon which intelligence or information can be recorded or retrieved, and includes, without limitation, the original or copies of any written, recorded, or graphic matter, however produced or reproduced, including, but not limited to, any book, pamphlet, periodical, letter, correspondence, telegram, invoice, contract, purchase order, estimate, report, memorandum, interoffice communication, interoffice memorandum, working paper, record, study, paper, worksheet, cost sheet, estimating sheet, bid, bill, time card, work record, chart, index, data sheet, data processing card, data processing tape, recording, transcription thereof, graph, photograph, object or tangible things, and all other memorials of any conversation, meeting or conference, by telephone or otherwise, and any other writing or recording which is in your possession, custody or control, in the possession, custody or control of your agents or attorneys, or which was but is no longer in your possession, custody or control, which would constitute or contain evidence relating to any matter which is relevant to the subject matter of this proceeding.

"Identification" -- As used herein, the terms "identification", "identify", or "identity", when used in reference to a person or persons, means to state the name, address, and telephone number of each such person and the name of the current employer and place of employment of each such person. When used in reference to a document or documents, such terms mean to describe each such document by date, subject matter, name of each person who wrote, signed, initialed, dictated, or otherwise participated in the creation or obtaining of such document, the name of each addressee (if any) and, if it now exists, the name and address of each person having custody of such document. When used in reference to any act, event, occurrence, statement of conduct (hereinafter "act"), "identify", "state", and "describe" mean: (1) to describe the event(s) constituting such act; (2) to state the date when such act occurred; (3) to identify each person participating in such act; (4) to identify each other person, if any, present when such act occurred; (5) to identify each document which in any way refers to, discusses, analyzes, comments upon or otherwise relates to such act; and (6) to state whether each such document now exists.

"You" -- As used herein, the term "you" means "your" or "yourself", and refers to Defendant, and each of its agents, representatives, employees, servants, and attorneys and each person acting on his or her or its behalf.

"Representative" --   As used herein, the term "representative" means any and all agents, employees, servants, officers, directors, attorneys or any other persons acting or purporting to act on behalf of the person in question.

"Communication" -- As used herein, the term "communication" means any oral or written utterance, notation or statement of any nature whatsoever, by and to whomsoever made, including, but not limited to, correspondence, conversations, dialogues, discussions, interviews, consultations, agreements, and other understandings between or among two or more persons.

"Identification of Documents" -- With respect to each Interrogatory, in addition to supplying the requested information, you are to identify all documents which support, refer to, or evidence the subject matter of each Interrogatory and your answer thereto.

"Contention Interrogatories" -- When an Interrogatory requires you to "state the basis of" a particular claim, contention, allegation or defense, state in your answer the identity of each and every communication and each and every fact and each and every legal theory you believe supports, refers to or evidences such claim, contention or allegation.

"Or" -- As used herein, when the word "or" appears in an Interrogatory, it should not be read so as to eliminate any part of the Interrogatory, but, whenever applicable, it should have the same meaning as the word "and". For example, an Interrogatory which states "support or refer" should be read as "support and refer" if an answer which does both can be made.

INTERROGATORY NO. 1.   Identify each individual likely to have discoverable information relevant to the disputed facts alleged in the Complaint on file herein. Categorize the identity of such persons with knowledge of the disputed facts by reference to the paragraph number of the Complaint and the Answer.

ANSWER:

INTERROGATORY NO. 2.   Describe any policy of insurance (known or believed to exist by you, your agents, or your attorneys) which will or may provide any type of coverage to you for your liability toward Plaintiff for the accident described in the Complaint or in your Answer. For each such policy of insurance, provide: the name and address of the insurer of each such policy and the policy number, the name and address of each named insurer for each policy, the limits of coverage of each such policy as might be applied to Plaintiff, and whether or not all "excesses," "catastrophic," and "umbrella" policies known to exist are listed above and if not, why not.

ANSWER:

INTERROGATORY NO. 3. List the names, present or last known addresses, occupations, and places of employment of all agents, servants, employees, representatives, insurance adjusters, private investigators, or others (besides your present attorneys) who independently or on behalf of any party investigated the incident which is the subject matter of the litigation.

ANSWER:

INTERROGATORY NO. 4. List any photographs, tapes, transcripts, communications, videos, affidavits, court reporter statements, or other documentation of any statements taken from any witness or any party or individual with any relevant information obtained by you, your agents, or representatives, family members, or any other individual acting on your behalf. Include all notes reflecting statements by or conversations with any witness or person having knowledge of the events or injuries which are the subject of this litigation. For each such listed item, provide the following information: the name, business address, home address, phone number, and occupation of the particular witness or party from whom the statement, affidavit, transcript, tape, or note was taken, the name, address, phone number, place of employment, title, and supervisor of the person taking the statement, transcript, note, tape, or affidavit, the date each item was made, including date of each original statement or note and each subsequently made transcript copy or record, the name, address, place of employment, title, and phone number of the custodian of each listed item, the contents of each such item, document, or tape, and the detailed explanation of how and under what conditions the statement, affidavit, transcript, note, tape, or record was obtained and/or made.

ANSWER:

INTERROGATORY NO. 5. Other than photographs, statements, tapes, affidavits, or other documents already identified in answers to previous Interrogatories, list and identify any documentary evidence in your possession or known to you, your representatives, family members, or persons acting on your behalf that may be relevant to the issues involved in this action; including, but not limited to, diagrams, correspondence, charts, plats, graphs, books, notes, transcripts, photographs, tapes, videos, records, financial and corporate records. Please furnish sufficient descriptive data to identify each item including a date each was generated, the subject matter of each, the present location of each, and the names, address, and phone number of the person having control and/or custody of each item.

ANSWER:

INTERROGATORY NO. 6. Identify each person you expect to call as an expert witness at the trial of this case, and as to each expert so identified, state the subject matter on which the expert is expected to testify, the substance of the facts and opinions to which the expert is expected to testify, and a summary of the grounds for each opinion.

ANSWER:

INTERROGATORY NO. 7. If you contend that Plaintiff was negligent in any manner in causing or contributing to the accident which is the subject of this litigation, please state with specificity your contentions as to each negligent act, and state with specificity each and every fact which you believe supports your contention.

ANSWER:

INTERROGATORY NO. 8. If you believe that Plaintiff's injuries and/or damages are not of the nature or extent alleged, please state all facts which you believe support your contentions.

ANSWER:

INTERROGATORY NO. 9. Please state in detail your version of events that led up the occurrence which is the subject matter of this lawsuit.

ANSWER:

INTERROGATORY NO. 10. Describe all acts of negligence and theories of fault by any person (whether the Plaintiff or any other person or legal entity) which you contend caused or contributed to the accident and include for each such act of negligence or theory of fault all facts upon which you base such allegations of negligence or fault. If you do not contend that other persons (whether the Plaintiff or any other person or legal entity) were negligent or at fault for causing or contributing to the accident, then so state.

ANSWER:

STATE OF KANSAS, COUNTY OF RENO ss:

The undersigned, being of lawful age and being first duly sworn upon oath, states:
That he/she has read the above and foregoing Interrogatory and the answers thereto; that the answers are true and correct to the best of his/her knowledge, information and belief.

_____

SUBSCRIBED and SWORN TO before me this _____ day of _____, _____.

_____
Notary Public

**IN THE UNITED STATES DISTRICT COURT
FOR THE DISTRICT OF KANSAS**

▯▯▯▯▯▯▯▯▯▯▯ , Plaintiff, vs. CLEAN HARBORS ENVIRONMENTAL SERVICES, INC., ELWIN BROWN, and ZURICH AMERICA INS., CO., Defendants.	)))) Case No.: 08 CV 2124)))))))

**PLAINTIFF'S SECOND SET OF INTERROGATORIES TO
DEFENDANT ELWIN BROWN**

Pursuant to Fed.R.Civ.P 33, Plaintiff propounds to Defendants these Interrogatories to be answered within thirty (30) days after service hereof. Space is included for answers to the Interrogatories upon the original. These Interrogatories are deemed continuing in nature and require your additional response should additional information or changes in your answers come to your attention.

In each response to these Interrogatories, provide all information in your possession, custody or control. If you are able or willing to provide only part of the information sought, specify the reason for your inability or unwillingness to provide the remainder. In addition to supplying the information requested, you are to identify all documents that support your answer or make reference to the subject matter of each Interrogatory and your answer. Further, if any or all documents identified are no longer in your possession, custody or control, because of loss, destruction or any other reason, then provide the following with respect to each such document:

1. Describe the nature of the document;

2. State the date of the document;

3.   Identify the person who sent and received the original and any copies of the document;

4.   State in as much detail as possible the contents of the document; and

5.   State the manner of the disposition of the document.

If you decline to answer any portion of the Interrogatory, provide all information called for by the balance of the Interrogatory. If you object to any portion of the Interrogatory on any ground, provide all information called for which you concede is discoverable. These Interrogatories apply to information that you have or possess and any information that you, any agent, servant, employee, or investigator has or possesses on your behalf.

DEFINITIONS

"Document" -- as used herein, the term "document" means any medium upon which intelligence or information can be recorded or retrieved, and includes, without limitation, the original or copies of any written, recorded, or graphic matter, however produced or reproduced, including, but not limited to, any book, pamphlet, periodical, letter, correspondence, telegram, invoice, contract, purchase order, estimate, report, memorandum, interoffice communication, interoffice memorandum, working paper, record, study, paper, worksheet, cost sheet, estimating sheet, bid, bill, time card, work record, chart, index, data sheet, data processing card, data processing tape, recording, transcription thereof, graph, photograph, object or tangible things, and all other memorials of any conversation, meeting or conference, by telephone or otherwise, and any other writing or recording which is in your possession, custody or control, in the possession, custody or control of your agents or attorneys, or which was but is no longer in your possession, custody or control, which would constitute or contain evidence relating to any matter which is relevant to the subject matter of this proceeding.

"Identification" -- As used herein, the terms "identification", "identify", or "identity", when used in reference to a person or persons, means to state the name, address, and telephone number of each such person and the name of the current employer and place of employment of each such person. When used in reference to a document or documents, such terms mean to describe each such document by date, subject matter, name of each person who wrote, signed, initialed, dictated, or otherwise participated in the creation or obtaining of such document, the name of each addressee (if any) and, if it now exists, the name and address of each person having custody of such document. When used in reference to any act, event, occurrence, statement of conduct (hereinafter "act"), "identify", "state", and "describe" mean: (1) to describe the event(s) constituting such act; (2) to state the date when such act occurred; (3) to identify each person participating in such act; (4) to identify each other person, if any, present when such act occurred; (5) to identify each document which in any way refers to, discusses, analyzes, comments upon or otherwise relates to such act; and (6) to state whether each such document now exists.

"You" – As used herein, the term "you" means "your" or "yourself", and refers to Defendant, and each of its agents, representatives, employees, servants, and attorneys and each person acting on his or her or its behalf.

"Representative" – As used herein, the term "representative" means any and all agents, employees, servants, officers, directors, attorneys or any other persons acting or purporting to act on behalf of the person in question.

"Communication" – As used herein, the term "communication" means any oral or written utterance, notation or statement of any nature whatsoever, by and to whomsoever made, including, but not limited to, correspondence, conversations, dialogues, discussions, interviews, consultations, agreements, and other understandings between or among two or more persons.

"Identification of Documents" -- With respect to each Interrogatory, in addition to supplying the requested information, you are to identify all documents which support, refer to, or evidence the subject matter of each Interrogatory and your answer thereto.

"Contention Interrogatories" -- When an Interrogatory requires you to "state the basis of" a particular claim, contention, allegation or defense, state in your answer the identity of each and every communication and each and every fact and each and every legal theory you believe supports, refers to or evidences such claim, contention or allegation.

"Or" -- As used herein, when the word "or" appears in an Interrogatory, it should not be read so as to eliminate any part of the Interrogatory, but, whenever applicable, it should have the same meaning as the word "and". For example, an Interrogatory which states "support or refer" should be read as "support and refer" if an answer which does both can be made.

INTERROGATORY NO. 1. Identify by stating the name, address and telephone number, each and every mental or healthcare provider Elwin Brown has seen in the ten (10) years preceding the filing of this action. For each provider listed, please provide an explanation of treatment provided and dates.

ANSWER:

STATE OF KANSAS, COUNTY OF RENO ss:

The undersigned, being of lawful age and being first duly sworn upon oath, states:
That he/she has read the above and foregoing Interrogatory and the answers thereto; that the answers are true and correct to the best of his/her knowledge, information and belief.

_____

SUBSCRIBED and SWORN TO before me this _____ day of _____, _____.

_____
Notary Public

**IN THE UNITED STATES DISTRICT COURT
FOR THE DISTRICT OF KANSAS**

_____ , Plaintiff,	)))	
vs.	))	Case No.: 08 CV 2124
CLEAN HARBORS ENVIRONMENTAL SERVICES, INC., ELWIN BROWN, and ZURICH AMERICA INS., CO., Defendants.	))))))	

**PLAINTIFF'S THIRD SET OF INTERROGATORIES TO
DEFENDANT ELWIN BROWN**

Pursuant to Fed.R.Civ.P 33, Plaintiff propounds to Defendants these Interrogatories to be answered within thirty (30) days after service hereof. Space is included for answers to the Interrogatories upon the original. These Interrogatories are deemed continuing in nature and require your additional response should additional information or changes in your answers come to your attention.

In each response to these Interrogatories, provide all information in your possession, custody or control. If you are able or willing to provide only part of the information sought, specify the reason for your inability or unwillingness to provide the remainder. In addition to supplying the information requested, you are to identify all documents that support your answer or make reference to the subject matter of each Interrogatory and your answer. Further, if any or all documents identified are no longer in your possession, custody or control, because of loss, destruction or any other reason, then provide the following with respect to each such document:

1. Describe the nature of the document;

2. State the date of the document;

3.   Identify the person who sent and received the original and any copies of the document;

4.   State in as much detail as possible the contents of the document; and

5.   State the manner of the disposition of the document.

If you decline to answer any portion of the Interrogatory, provide all information called for by the balance of the Interrogatory. If you object to any portion of the Interrogatory on any ground, provide all information called for which you concede is discoverable. These Interrogatories apply to information that you have or possess and any information that you, any agent, servant, employee, or investigator has or possesses on your behalf.

DEFINITIONS

"Document" -- as used herein, the term "document" means any medium upon which intelligence or information can be recorded or retrieved, and includes, without limitation, the original or copies of any written, recorded, or graphic matter, however produced or reproduced, including, but not limited to, any book, pamphlet, periodical, letter, correspondence, telegram, invoice, contract, purchase order, estimate, report, memorandum, interoffice communication, interoffice memorandum, working paper, record, study, paper, worksheet, cost sheet, estimating sheet, bid, bill, time card, work record, chart, index, data sheet, data processing card, data processing tape, recording, transcription thereof, graph, photograph, object or tangible things, and all other memorials of any conversation, meeting or conference, by telephone or otherwise, and any other writing or recording which is in your possession, custody or control, in the possession, custody or control of your agents or attorneys, or which was but is no longer in your possession, custody or control, which would constitute or contain evidence relating to any matter which is relevant to the subject matter of this proceeding.

"Identification" -- As used herein, the terms "identification", "identify", or "identity", when used in reference to a person or persons, means to state the name, address, and telephone number of each such person and the name of the current employer and place of employment of each such person. When used in reference to a document or documents, such terms mean to describe each such document by date, subject matter, name of each person who wrote, signed, initialed, dictated, or otherwise participated in the creation or obtaining of such document, the name of each addressee (if any) and, if it now exists, the name and address of each person having custody of such document. When used in reference to any act, event, occurrence, statement of conduct (hereinafter "act"), "identify", "state", and "describe" mean: (1) to describe the event(s) constituting such act; (2) to state the date when such act occurred; (3) to identify each person participating in such act; (4) to identify each other person, if any, present when such act occurred; (5) to identify each document which in any way refers to, discusses, analyzes, comments upon or otherwise relates to such act; and (6) to state whether each such document now exists.

"You" -- As used herein, the term "you" means "your" or "yourself", and refers to Defendant, and each of its agents, representatives, employees, servants, and attorneys and each person acting on his or her or its behalf.

"Representative" -- As used herein, the term "representative" means any and all agents, employees, servants, officers, directors, attorneys or any other persons acting or purporting to act on behalf of the person in question.

"Communication" -- As used herein, the term "communication" means any oral or written utterance, notation or statement of any nature whatsoever, by and to whomsoever made, including, but not limited to, correspondence, conversations, dialogues, discussions, interviews, consultations, agreements, and other understandings between or among two or more persons.

"Identification of Documents" -- With respect to each Interrogatory, in addition to supplying the requested information, you are to identify all documents which support, refer to, or evidence the subject matter of each Interrogatory and your answer thereto.

"Contention Interrogatories" -- When an Interrogatory requires you to "state the basis of" a particular claim, contention, allegation or defense, state in your answer the identity of each and every communication and each and every fact and each and every legal theory you believe supports, refers to or evidences such claim, contention or allegation.

"Or" -- As used herein, when the word "or" appears in an Interrogatory, it should not be read so as to eliminate any part of the Interrogatory, but, whenever applicable, it should have the same meaning as the word "and". For example, an Interrogatory which states "support or refer" should be read as "support and refer" if an answer which does both can be made.

INTERROGATORY NO. 1. Identify by stating the name, address and telephone number, of each and every former employer for whom Elwin Brown engaged as a truck driver. For each employer listed, please provide the job title(s) held and the dates the position was held.

ANSWER:

INTERROGATORY NO. 2. Identify by stating the name, address and telephone number, of each and every former employer, in the past ten (10) years, for whom Elwin Brown engaged in work that did not include working as a truck driver. For each employer listed, please provide the job title(s) held and the dates the position was held.

ANSWER:

STATE OF KANSAS, COUNTY OF RENO ss:

The undersigned, being of lawful age and being first duly sworn upon oath, states:
That he/she has read the above and foregoing Interrogatory and the answers thereto; that the answers are true and correct to the best of his/her knowledge, information and belief.

_____

SUBSCRIBED and SWORN TO before me this _____ day of _____, _____.

_____
Notary Public

APPENDIX 3

COMMERCIAL TRUCK DEMAND/MEDIATION LETTER

This letter is a summary of the claims being pursued and the evidence supporting each of the claims. While this particular letter was used with a federal court judge for a mediation, the same sort of letter can be used as a demand letter to initiate settlement negotiations with an insurance company.

BRETZ LAW OFFICES, LLC
ATTORNEYS AT LAW

Matthew L. Bretz †
Mitchell W. Rice
Melinda G. Young ††

1227 North Main Street
P.O. Box 1782
Hutchinson, KS 67504-1782
(620) 662-3435
Fax (620) 662-3445
Mbretz@bretzpilaw.com

†Licensed in Kansas and California
††Licensed in Kansas and Iowa

August 28, 2009

The Honorable Magistrate Judge Donald W. Bostwick
403 U.S. Courthouse
401 N. Market
Wichita, KS 67202

RE: ████████████ v. Clean Harbors Environmental, et al
       08-CV-02124

Dear Judge Bostwick:

This matter has been scheduled for mediation with you on Thursday, September 3, 2009, starting at 9:30 a.m. I will be present along with my client, ████████████████.

LIABILITY

On June 14, 2007, at approximately 5:30 p.m., ████████████████ was driving westbound on US 24, in Hoxie, Sheridan County, Kansas. She had just left the grocery store and was heading downtown. As she approached the intersection, she turned on her turn signal and slowed to a stop so that she could allow oncoming eastbound traffic to clear the intersection before making a left turn onto southbound Main Street.

At the same time, a tractor-trailer combination being driven by Defendant Brown was traveling northbound on Main Street, traveling through the downtown business district. Shockingly, he was driving 65 miles per hour in a 20 mile an hour zone, and ran the flashing red light and the posted stop sign at the intersection US 24 and K23, striking ████ 's car in the driver's side.

After the collision Mr. Brown admitted to the investigating officer:

"D-1 stated he was northbound on K-23 traveling at 65 mph and did not realize he was in a town or that the speed limit was 20 mph."

Mr. Brown was determined to be at fault by the investigating officer due to his failure to yield the right of way, his total disregard and apparent contempt for traffic signs, signals or road markings, and due to his failure to give full time and attention. A copy of the Motor Vehicle Accident Report is enclosed for your review.

There were four disinterested witnesses to the collision who gave statements to the investigating Kansas Highway Patrol Trooper. The first witness was the Sheridan County Sheriff, Brian Fenner, who was off duty at the time of the collision. Sheriff Fenner reported:

> Witness #1 (Sheriff Fenner): "….I was driving west on Oak Street (US 24) and as I approached 11th and Oak I saw a red semi pulling a tank trailer run the stop sign on the south side and the semi hit a car that was in the intersection."

The other three witnesses confirmed how the collision occurred:

> Witness #2 (Rebecca Farber): "…..The car had slowed down and its front was about half away through the intersection just getting ready to turn. The semi came speeding up and rammed directly into the driver's side door."

> Witness #3 (Loren Biltoft): "I was coming into town from the west when I witnessed a tan car turning onto Main Street from Highway 24. Then a red semi tractor trailer ran the stop sign coming from the south on Main Street and hit the tan car………"

> Witness #4 (Shannon Bird): "I was on Highway 24 eastbound turning out of turn by Maders when I saw truck go through intersection at a high rate of speed………."

In reviewing the applicable jury instructions, it is clear that 100 percent of the liability rests with Mr. Brown and his employer, Clean Harbors Environmental. The jury instructions provide as follows:

> The laws of Kansas provide that the driver of any vehicle shall obey the instructions of any official traffic control device, unless otherwise directed by a traffic or police officer. P.I.K. 3d 121.09.

> The laws of Kansas provide that no person shall drive a vehicle at a speed greater than is reasonable under the conditions and hazards then existing. At the time and place and with the vehicle involved in this case, any speed in excess of 20 miles per hour was unlawful. In addition, the law provides that the driver of every vehicle shall drive at a safe and appropriate speed when traveling on any narrow or

winding narrow roadway. P.I.K. 3d 121.13.

The laws of Kansas provide that every driver of a vehicle approaching a stop sign shall stop at the point nearest the intersecting roadway where the driver has a view of approaching traffic on the intersecting roadway before entering it, if there is no crosswalk at the near side of the intersection. After having stopped, the driver shall yield the right of way to any vehicle in the intersection or approaching on another roadway so closely as to constitute an immediate hazard and to any pedestrian within an adjacent crosswalk. P.I.K. 3d 121.31.

It is the duty of the driver on a public highway to use ordinary care to keep his vehicle under proper control and drive within the range of his vision so that his vehicle may be stopped, slowed, or turned aside and thus avoid colliding with any other vehicle using the highway. P.I.K. 3d 121.02.

It is the duty of the driver of a motor vehicle on a public highway to keep a proper lookout for vehicles and objects in his line of vision which may affect his use of the highway. The law presumes that a driver will see those things which a person would and could see in the exercise of ordinary care under like or similar circumstances. P.I.K. 3d 121.03.

Further, it is clear that there was nothing which ▓▓▓▓▓▓▓▓▓▓ did which caused or contributed to the collision, and it is clear that there was nothing which she could have done to prevent the collision. The evidence establishes that she had come to a complete stop and was waiting for oncoming traffic to clear the intersection before turning onto southbound Main Street. The law applicable to ▓▓▓▓▓▓▓▓ provides:

Persons using a public street or highway have the right to assume that each will obey the law. Each is entitled to rely on this assumption until he or she has knowledge to the contrary. P.I.K. 3d 121.85.

It appears from the statements of the drivers and witnesses, the physical evidence, the laws of the State of Kansas, and the investigating officer's report, that liability rests solely with your insured.

MEDICAL CONDITION DEFENSE

When Defendants filed their Answer in this case, they alleged that Defendant Brown had a sudden, unexpected, temporary and partial loss of consciousness which caused the wreck, and alleged that they should not be liable. Thus, significant discovery has been conducted concerning Mr. Brown's medical history predating the collision.

-3-

Mr. Brown has a lengthy medical history. At his deposition Mr. Brown's primary physician, Dr. Daniels, testified that before the June, 2007, collision Mr. Brown had a history of chronic fatigue, shortness of breath, obesity, emphysema, chronic bronchitis (COPD), loss of more than one-third of his lung function in inhaling, loss of more than one-half of his lung function in exhaling, chest pain upon exertion, diabetes, high cholesterol, and TIAs. The TIAs had left Mr. Brown with partial facial paralysis and drooling. Moreover, when a sleep study had been ordered, Mr. Brown did not show. Dr. Daniels testified that he talked with Mr. Brown about all of these medical conditions multiple times.

In his deposition, Mr. Brown admitted that he knew he was diabetic, he knew he had chronic bronchitis, he knew he had plaque in his arteries, he knew he had coronary artery disease, he knew he had difficulty breathing, he knew he had congestive heart failure, and that he knew he had lung function problems. And while he knew about all of these medical problems which could cause a collision, he chose to drive anyway. In his deposition, Mr. Brown initially denied having daytime sleepiness. But then he was forced to admit that as well. (See p. 61 of his deposition, and p. 380005 from his medical records.)

Mr. Brown's decision to drive when he knew about all of these medical conditions and his problems with daytime sleepiness and chronic fatigue, seems quite similar to the person who knows he has been drinking and that he may not be safe to drive, but does it anyway. Essentially, it appears from his testimony and from the testimony of Dr. Daniels and Dr. Feverly that Mr. Brown recklessly disregarded his known medical conditions and decided to drive anyway – endangering everyone on the road and causing severe injuries to ▮▮▮▮▮▮▮▮▮▮▮▮▮ .

There is a real question about Mr. Brown's veracity. At the scene of the wreck he gave a statement to the EMT about how the collision occurred. He was quite specific about highway numbers, directions of travel, and so on. (See p. 45 from his deposition.) And while he made those statements at the scene about how the collision occurred, he later claimed he could not remember the accident. (See p. 59 from his deposition, and p. 370039 from his medical records.) He also falsely claimed that he was in "good health". (See pages 80, and 86-87) And he wasn't quite truthful about his seatbelt use. (See p. 88.)

So, it appears that the jury can find liability either way: either he knew what was going on and consciously chose to drive through the red light; or he knew that he had significant medical problems and that he posed a risk to others on the roadway, but consciously decided to drive anyway.

What is also interesting about his medical condition is his diabetes. While Mr. Brown admitted that he knew he has been a diabetic for more than ten years, he did not eat at all on June 14. His last food was on June 13, 2007, at 7 to 9pm, and had not eaten in 21 to 22 hours before the collision. (See Brown deposition at pp. 34-35.) Is it reasonable for a diabetic to not eat at all for 21 to 22 hours?

What is most interesting is the testimony of the defense expert, Dr. Feverly. Dr. Feverly admits that Mr. Brown was not qualified to drive a semi-tractor/trailer or to have a CDL license (p. 85), that the medications that Mr. Brown was taking which he did not disclose to the DOT examiner specifically disqualified Mr. Brown from having a DOT medical card (pp. 83-84, 86), and that the medical conditions about which Mr. Brown lied at the time of his DOT physical all increased the likelihood of him having a loss of consciousness and causing a collision exactly like the one which he had (pp.

77-82). These lies by Mr. Brown to the DOT medical examiner in February, 2007, included denying that he had high blood pressure, denying episodes of shortness of breath, denying having congestive heart failure, denying TIAs which had left him with partial facial paralysis and drooling, denying having diabetes, denying having daytime sleepiness and loud snoring.

As the defense's expert testified, he was "pissed" that Mr. Brown was driving prior to the subject collision. (p. 115) Of course, had Mr. Brown been honest with his DOT medical examiner, he would not have been allowed to drive.

Moreover, if Clean Harbors had done the type of investigation which our office has performed, i.e. simply getting Mr. Brown's records and looking at them, they should not have given Mr. Brown a truck to drive. Thus, the basis for our negligence claim against Clean Harbors for negligent hiring, retention and supervision.

Kansas courts do not appear to have addressed the issue of a medical condition defense in a situation where the defendant knew of the medical condition, but this issue has been addressed in other jurisdictions. In *McCall v. Wilder*, 913 S.W.2d 150 (Tenn. 1995), the court held that "liability may be imposed upon the driver who knows of the medically incapacitating disorder, and who poses an unreasonable risk of harm to others by driving under circumstances such that a reasonably prudent person could foresee an accident." *Id*. at 152. In *McCall*, the defendant suffered a seizure while driving, which cause the motor vehicle accident. *Id*. The defendant "had experienced seizures prior to the day of the accident" and he "knew he had a seizure disorder which caused loss of consciousness." *Id*. The defendant "took an unreasonable risk by driving his vehicle knowing he suffered from a seizure disorder which caused loss of consciousness." *Id*. It was argued, and the Court agreed, "[i]t was certainly foreseeable that an accident might occur if [the defendant] experienced a seizure while driving his vehicle." *Id*. The Court held that "[a] risk is unreasonable and gives rise to a duty to act with due care if the foreseeable probability and gravity of harm posed by defendant's conduct outweigh the burden upon defendant to engage in alternative conduct that would have prevented the harm." *Id*. at 153. The following factors were set forth by the Court to consider in determining whether a risk is an unreasonable one:

> [T]he foreseeable probability of the harm or injury occurring; the possible magnitude of the potential harm or injury; the importance or social value of the activity engaged in by defendant; the usefulness of the conduct to defendant; the feasibility of alternative, safer conduct and the relative costs and burdens associated with that conduct; the relative usefulness of the safer conduct; and the relative safety of alternative conduct.

Id. (citing Restatement (Second) of Torts, §§ 292, 293 (1964)). A "duty of reasonable care exists if defendant's conduct poses an unreasonable and foreseeable risk of harm to persons or property. *Id*.

Thus, in the present case, we fully expect that the "medical condition defense" will fail.

INJURIES, MEDICAL TREATMENT and DAMAGES

The force of the impact caused complete destruction of ▮▮▮▮▮▮▮▮▮▮ 's vehicle. The driver's side door caved in, trapping ▮▮▮▮▮▮▮▮▮ in her vehicle. The collision spun ▮▮▮▮ 's car around, and shoved it approximately 98 feet – about a third of the length of a football field. ▮▮▮ was pinned in the car and the steering wheel was shoved into her chest and abdomen. She had excruciating pain and difficulty breathing from a punctured and collapsed lung which had air and blood outside the lung causing both a pneumothorax and a hemothorax. Her feet were pinned beneath the dash, with her right foot under the brake pedal.

The emergency medical personnel could not immediately help ▮▮▮ because of the severity of damage to her vehicle. So she was not able to be provided any oxygen until 1:51p.m., more than 20 minutes after the collision.

The jaws of life were called to cut her free from the wreckage, and she was forced to endure pain from her injuries for nearly an hour before be able to receive medical care and pain relief. Once ▮▮▮ ▮▮▮▮▮▮▮▮ was freed from the vehicle, she was secured to a spine board for spinal protection. The EMS records reveal that ▮▮▮ was initially disoriented and unable to remember the collision. transferred to the Sheridan County Medical Complex for evaluation.

Upon her arrival at the hospital, ▮▮▮▮▮▮▮▮ remained in a disoriented state, not being able to tell staff what had just happened. Significant bilateral bruising was noted to her lower extremities and attempts to draw blood were unsuccessful due to the trauma and damage to her legs. X-rays were taken which verified fractures of the right ankle, a mid-shaft fracture of the left upper humerus with fracture fragments in the middle of the shaft, multiple rib fractures which had punctured her left lung, and a fracture of the sacral ala. Due to the lung injuries and the severity of her other injuries, it was necessary to emergently transfer her by air ambulance to Wesley Medical Center in Wichita, Kansas.

On June 15, 2008, ▮▮▮▮▮▮▮▮ underwent several surgical procedures to stabilize and attempt to repair her injuries. She first had an open reduction internal fixation for the bimalleolar right ankle fractures. Next she had an open reduction and internal fixation for the left humeral shaft fractures. Then she had an attempted, but ultimately unsuccessful, repair of the left radial nerve transection. Finally, she had a left glenohumeral arthrotomy. While in surgery it was also discovered that ▮▮▮▮▮▮▮▮▮ had subcutaneous air in the right shoulder.

In all, ▮▮▮ was in Wesley Medical Center from June 14, 2007, until June 20, 2007. However, when she was discharged from Wesley she was not allowed to return home. Rather, she had to go from Wesley Medical Center to Hays Rehabilitation Facility. She began inpatient physical therapy, occupational therapy and rehabilitative nursing on June 20, 2007. She completed inpatient rehabilitation on June 30, 2007.

CURRENT CONDITION

Despite heroic treatment efforts and surgeries and exhaustive therapy, ▮▮▮▮ continues to suffer from the debilitating effects of her injuries and ongoing pain. Her shoulder, arm and radial nerve injuries effect every aspect of her life. From the time she wakes up in the morning, to the time she goes to bed at night, she is never without pain and disability from the Defendants' reckless conduct. When the alarm goes off in the morning, she has to use a trapeze to sit up in bed and has to get completely up before she can even turn off the alarm.

To get out of bed and stand up, she has to rely on only one arm as her left arm cannot be used to push up from the side of the bed. Walking to the bathroom on her ankle which suffered bimalleolar fractures is difficult, especially first thing in the morning. She must now use a grab bar to lower herself onto the toilet, and to get up when she is finished.

Getting dressed and doing her hair is painful and difficult. As a result of the humeral shaft fracture, the radial nerve transaction, and the left glenohumeral arthrotomy, she has been left with almost no use of her left hand and very limited range of motion and strength in her left arm. Her arm is even shorter now as a length of bone from her upper arm had to be removed during one of her surgeries. The effect of this means that she cannot curl and blow dry her hair, squeeze toothpaste onto a toothbrush while holding both, hold a mirror and put on makeup, or anything else which requires the use of both hands.

When she goes to the kitchen for breakfast, she limps. When she gets to the kitchen, she cannot hold the refrigerator door open with her right hand and take things out with her left hand. She cannot get anything out of the upper cabinets because doing so requires lifting her left arm above her head and she does not have active range of motion in her shoulder to do so. She has difficulty in doing mundane tasks in the kitchen such as peeling a potato, apple, carrot or pear. She can lift very light items, but cannot lift a pot of water or remove a casserole or tray from the oven. This means that she cannot fix a meal for her husband or her daughters without help.

The difficulty in going to the basement to do laundry or to go to the family room is only exceeded by the difficulty in going back up stairs. The bimalleolar ankle fractures have resulted in significant loss of strength and motion in her right ankle. Complicating this is the left shoulder and radial nerve injury. So, when she tries to negotiate the stairs, she suffers.

Driving is also extremely difficult. Imagine, if you will, trying to close the driver's side car door when you cannot extend your arm or grasp the door with your left hand. Turning on the turn signal, likewise, is difficult and has to be done by reaching her right arm across and behind the steering wheel to actuate it. Driving, however, is not nearly as important now as it was before she was hit by the Defendants' semi at 65 miles per hour because now she has many problems going anywhere. It is painful to walk any distance, so she limits everyday tasks such as going to the grocery store or to town.

Instead of doing the activities of daily living which most of us take for granted, she now spends most of her time at home sitting. She does the home exercises which her physical therapist taught her to perform. These deal primarily with lifting a one-pound weight with her left arm, and trying to stretch her ankle.

The Defendants took the joy out of living. No longer can ▮▮▮ do anything without pain. She has the constant reminder of being hit and nearly killed. Walking into church is with a limp and pain. Volunteer work has been eliminated.

▮▮▮ can no longer work at her husband's medical clinic because she cannot type any longer. This means that she cannot do scheduling on the computer, cannot type medical progress notes, and cannot do billing. Prior to the collision, ▮▮▮ worked one day a week at her husband's clinic, ▮▮▮▮▮▮▮▮▮▮▮, so that the office clerk could have a four-day per week schedule. While ▮▮▮ was not paid directly for this, she and her husband saved $10.50 per hour by not having to pay the office clerk one day each week. This equates to lost income of $84.00 per week, or $4,368.00 per year. The lost wage component of this case has since ended because of a stroke which ▮▮▮▮▮▮▮▮▮▮ suffered which ended his medical career. Thus, our lost wage claim is for only approximately one year and will be abandoned at trial.

Her evenings are now spent at home, sitting. She cannot hold a hand of cards, so she and her husband cannot play bridge or pinochle with their friends. She cannot do much. And at the end of the day, she lowers herself back into bed using the trapeze and tries to sleep. But the pain in her shoulder wakes her up regularly when she turns or rolls over.

In short, the Defendants' conduct has wrecked not only ▮▮▮'s car, but her life. There is not a single aspect of her life that has not been changed because of Mr. Brown driving 65 in a 20 zone and not stopping or even slowing for the flashing red light and stop sign. And to the extent that a jury believes that Mr. Brown had a "sudden, unexpected, temporary and partial loss of consciousness", then ▮▮▮▮▮▮▮▮▮▮'s life has been destroyed because Mr. Brown lied to his DOT medical examiner so that he could get a medical card enabling him to put lives at risk.

To date, ▮▮▮▮▮▮▮▮▮▮'s medical expenses total $154,603.04. I have enclosed a medical summary and a medical expense summary for your review.

SETTLEMENT OFFER and PUNITIVE DAMAGES

Prior to suit being filed we offered to settle this matter for payment of $502,651.04. This settlement offer was based on $154,603.04 in medical bills, $48,048.00 in lost income, $250,000.00 for pain, suffering, disability and scarring, and $50,000.00 for loss of consortium. Not only was this offer not accepted, it was ignored. Thus, we filed suit.

After filing suit, we retained Dr. John Pazell and Donna Wade, RN, CNCLP, to address future medical needs and costs. Copies of their reports which detail $365,038.00 in future medical expenses are enclosed for your review. The defense has not deposed either of these experts and discovery is closed.

We also have retained Gary Baker, Ph.D., to address other economic damages. His report, detailing $48,982.00 in loss of services is enclosed.

While our pre-suit offer was based on the actual compensatory damages, we also offered to waive our claim for punitive damages. Punitive damages are based on the Defendants' reckless and wanton conduct. Kansas law provides as follows:

> An act performed with a realization of the imminence of danger and a reckless disregard or complete indifference to the probable consequences of the act is a wanton act. P.I.K. 103.03. See also Stevens v. Stevens, 231 Kan. 726, 730, 647 P.2d 1346 (1982); Bowman v. Doherty, 235 Kan. 870, 686 P.2d 112 (1984); Powell v. Havner, 817 F.Supp. 90, 93 (D. Kan. 1993).

P.I.K. 171.44 provides the legal basis for punitive damages in this situation where Mr. Brown was driving 65 in a 20 zone and ran a flashing red light and stop sign. P.I.K. 171.44 provides, in pertinent part:

> Punitive damages may be allowed in the jury's discretion to punish a defendant and to deter others from like conduct.

> If you find the defendant did one or more of the acts claimed by the plaintiff you should then determine whether clear and convincing evidence has been presented that the defendant acted in a wanton manner. If you determine punitive damages should be allowed, your finding should be entered in the verdict form. After the trial the court will conduct a separate hearing to determine the amount of punitive damages to be allowed.

In the present case, evidence of Mr. Brown's wanton and reckless conduct comes both from Mr. Brown and from the eye witnesses. First, Mr. Brown admitted that he was driving 65 miles per hour in a 20 mile an hour business district. Second, Mr. Brown ran a flashing red light and a posted stop sign. Third, the eye witnesses all have testified that Mr. Brown's driving was wanton and reckless – exposing   and every other citizen of Hoxie to great danger of injury or death. Fourth, if the collision was caused by a "sudden, unexpected, temporary and partial loss of consciousness", then punitive damages are warranted due to the intentional conduct of lying to the DOT medical examiner so that he could drive and put lives at risk.

There is also a punitive damages claim against Clean Harbors. In short, Clean Harbors recklessly did nothing to investigate whether Mr. Brown was safe to drive even though it is quite apparent from just looking at Mr. Brown and listening to him that he has significant health issues.

LOSS OF CONSORTIUM

As previously mentioned, [redacted]'s husband, [redacted] recently had a series of strokes. He was hospitalized following the strokes but has been released to home. [redacted] has also been left with significant limitations due to his strokes. He can walk, but must do so with a walker. He is not able to lift, carry, or walk stairs without significant problems. And because of her injuries, [redacted] is not able to provide the home assistance which he needs.

Their youngest daughter, [redacted], lives in Hays, Kansas, which is about 80 miles from Hoxie. [redacted] now travels to Hoxie to assist her mother and father with the myriad of things which neither one of them are able to do.

Given the cap on non-economic damages, at trial we will only include the economic component of loss of consortium.

CURRENT SUMMARY OF CLAIMS

Currently, there is evidence to support the following elements of damages:

Past medical expenses	$154,603.04
Future medical expenses	$365,038.00
Pain, suffering and disability	$250,000.00
Punitive damages	$???
Loss of services	$48,982.00 to ???
Total	$818,623.04 to ???

A mediation in this case previously was held with Dennis Gillen. Al Herrington appeared without any representative from Clean Harbors and without any representative from Zurich, both of whom are parties. A local independent adjuster was present as a place-sitter. After wasting seven hours, the defense offered a structure with a $150,000.00 cost which would pay $200,000.00 over time.

Following the first mediation, Tim Finnerty requested that a second mediation take place because he, likewise, believes that the first mediation was a waste of time without representatives from Clean Harbors and from Zurich, and because he values the case far in excess of what was offered at the mediation. We have reluctantly agreed to a second mediation but do not anticipate going below $600,000.00.

Finally, it should be noted that discovery is complete other than the depositions of two Clean Harbor employees who the Court has ordered Al Herrington to produce for telephonic depositions. To date, Mr. Herrington has refused to provide dates for their appearance. Thus, we anticipate filing an appropriate motion for sanctions if the case is not settled.

I look forward to the upcoming mediation and to hearing your thoughts concerning this case.

Sincerely,

Matthew L. Bretz

Enclosures
    Motor Vehicle Accident Report
    Highway Patrol photos
    Summary of medical records
    Summary of medical bills
    Feverly Deposition transcript
    Brown Deposition transcript
    Dr. John Pazell expert report
    Donna Wade, RN, expert report
    Gary Baker, Ph.D. expert report

APPENDIX 4
AUTOMOBILE/TRUCK COLLISION PETITION

The attached Petition was filed in a state court rather than in a federal court. State courts have different requirements for filing a suit.

This particular Petition includes claims for both conscious pain and suffering and for wrongful death. Depending on the state where the incident occurred you may have both a "survivor's action" and a "wrongful death" action, as described earlier in this book. The survivor's action is typically pursued by the estate of the person who died, and the wrongful death action is typically pursued by the decedent's heirs.

Each state has different rules about what claims may be pursued and about who may pursue each of the claims.

In this case you will note that both the truck driver and his employer were listed as defendants.

BRETZ LAW OFFICES
1227 N. Main
P.O. Box 1782
Hutchinson, Kansas 67504-1782
Phone (620) 662-3435
Fax (620) 662-3445

IN THE DISTRICT COURT OF PRATT COUNTY KANSAS
(Pursuant to K.S.A. Chapter 60)

THE ESTATE OF ░░░░░, deceased,) by and through its Administrator, ,) and ░░░░ , ,) ░░░ , and ░░░░ , heirs at law of) ░░░░ , deceased,) Plaintiffs,) vs.) HEC L. BOWEN and AMERICAN TRUCKING, INC.,) Defendants.)	Case No. : 06 CV 41

PETITION

COME NOW the Plaintiffs, and for their causes of action against the above-named Defendants, and in support thereof, states and alleges:

1. The Estate of ░░░░░ , has been duly opened in Pratt County, Kansas, and ░░░ ░░░ has been appointed as Administrator of the Estate.

2. Plaintiffs ░░░ , ░░░ , ░░░ , and ░░░ are individuals and residents of the State of Kansas, and are the heirs at law of ░░░ ░░░ , deceased.

3. Defendant Hec L. Bowen is an individual and resident of the State of Kansas, and may be personally served with process at his place of employment, American Trucking, Inc., at 105 South Main, Sawyer, KS 67134.

-1-

4.   Defendant American Trucking, Inc., is a Kansas Corporation and may be served with process by serving its resident agent, Mike Van Ranken, 105 South Main, Sawyer, KS 67134.

5.   This court has subject matter jurisdiction over the cause of action, and personal jurisdiction over the parties.

6.   Venue is proper in this Court pursuant to K.S.A. 60-603, K.S.A. 60-604, and K.S.A. 60-608.

7.   That the acts of the Defendants set forth herein happened within the State of Kansas.

8.   On or about July 21, 2005, Defendant Hec L. Bowen operated a motor vehicle owned by Defendant American Trucking, Inc., in a negligent, reckless, wilful and wanton manner, causing a collision which resulted in fatal injuries to ▮▮▮▮▮▮▮▮.

9.   At the time of the collision, Defendant Hec Bowen was driving a dump truck over the center of the roadway and around a curve.

10.   Defendant Hec Bowen knew or should have known that his actions would subject others to a serious risk of injury or death, yet he recklessly disregarded the known probable consequences of his actions and drove blindly around the curve, over the center, without knowing whether or not someone was in the oncoming lane.

11.   Defendant Hec Bowen's conduct, in violation of statutory law, was negligence per se.

12.   Defendant Hec Bowen was further negligent in failing to provide care to ▮▮▮▮▮▮▮ at the scene of the collision, and in making false statements to law enforcement.

13.   At the time of the collision, Defendant Hec Bowen was working in the course and scope of his employment with American Trucking, Inc. As such, American Trucking, Inc., is vicariously liable for the negligence of Defendant Hec Bowen.

14.   Defendant American Trucking was also negligent in failing to properly maintain its vehicle, negligent hiring, negligent retention, negligent training, and in other respects.

-2-

15.   The sole and proximate cause of Plaintiffs' damages was the negligence of Defendants.

16.   The Estate of ▓▓▓▓▓▓ brings this action for his conscious pain and suffering, for ▓▓▓▓▓▓ 's funeral bills, and for property damage to ▓▓▓▓▓▓ 's truck which was destroyed in the collision.

17.   ▓▓▓▓▓▓ , ▓▓▓▓▓▓ , ▓▓▓▓▓▓ , and ▓▓▓▓▓▓ bring this action for the wrongful death of ▓▓▓▓▓▓ .

WHEREFORE, Plaintiff prays for judgment against the above-named Defendants for an amount in excess of $75,000.00, plus costs, and for such other and further relief as the Court deems just and equitable.

Respectfully submitted,

By: _____
Matthew L. Bretz, SC #15466
Attorney for Plaintiffs

REQUEST FOR JURY TRIAL

COME NOW the Plaintiffs, pursuant to applicable Kansas law, and respectfully make demand for trial by a jury of twelve (12) persons of all issues herein above joined.

BRETZ LAW OFFICES

By: _____
Matthew L. Bretz, SC#15466
Attorney for Plaintiffs

APPENDIX 5
AUTOMOBILE WRECK COMPLAINT

This case was filed in Federal Court in California based on diversity of citizenship.

It may not be necessary to be as detailed as this Complaint, but the detail was included in order to inform the court about the facts supporting our theory of liability against the defendant since our client failed to yield the right of way while pulling out from a stop sign. Without the added detail there was a concern that the federal judge would think that there was no potential liability on the defendant who hit our client when she pulled out from the stop sign.

California has pure comparison of fault, as discussed in Part One, Section IX, of this book. So we did not have to worry about getting kicked out of court based on a 50% or more finding of fault against our client. The focus in the case had to be on demonstrating as much fault as possible on the defendant driver who was accelerating at a high rate of speed, swerving in and out of traffic, and then demonstrated no compassion for the young lady which he hit.

BRETZ & YOUNG
1227 North Main Street
P.O. Box 1782
Hutchinson, Kansas 67504-1782
Phone (620) 662-3435
Fax (620) 662-3445

**IN THE UNITED STATES DISTRICT COURT
FOR THE CENTRAL DISTRICT OF CALIFORNIA**

_____,)
            Plaintiff,   )
)
vs.   )   Case No.:
)
MORDECHAI FERDER,   )
            Defendant.)
)

COMPLAINT

COMES NOW the Plaintiff, _____, by and through her attorney, Matthew L. Bretz, and for Plaintiff's causes of action against the Defendant, states as follows:

1.   Plaintiff _____ is an individual and citizen of the State of Kansas.

2.   Defendant Mordechai Ferder, is an individual and citizen of the State of California, and may be served with process at his residential address, _____

3.   Defendant is a citizen of the State of California and Plaintiff is a citizen of the State of Kansas. There is complete diversity of citizenship, and the matter in controversy exceeds, exclusive of interest and costs, the sum specified by 28 U.S.C. § 1332.

4.   On September 4, 2011, Mordechai Haim Ferder was the driver of a 2011 Mercedes-Benz CL63 in Irvine, California.

5.   At the same time, _____ was headed to church with a friend and was traveling eastbound on Concordia East and stopped at a stop sign. Upon stopping at the stop sign

Plaintiff looked to her left and saw a silver vehicle traveling southbound on Ridgeline at a normal speed and at a distance which allowed her to make a safe left turn onto northbound Ridgeline.

6. After Plaintiff checked to make sure that it was safe for her to proceed with her left turn, Defendant turned his vehicle from westbound University onto southbound Ridgedale and accelerated at a great rate speed then changed lanes to go around the much slower moving silver vehicle and also around a bicyclist, and then struck the vehicle which was being driven by Plaintiff.

7. At the time of impact, Defendant was driving 60 to 70 miles per hour in a 50 mph zone and was driving in a manner which demonstrated an extreme indifference to the safety of other drivers and bicyclists in the area. Defendant's conduct, in violation of statute, was negligent *per se.*

8. Following the collision Defendant's son reported to the police who investigated the collision that his father was "driving real fast".

9. An eyewitness to the collision, Katelyn Fike, reported that she was stopped on University and observed Defendant turn onto the No. 2 lane of Ridgedale, swerve into the No. 1 lane to go around a bicyclist, then swerve back into the No. 2 lane and accelerate at a high rate. Ms. Fike reported that the rate of acceleration was so great that she could hear the engine of Defendant's vehicle "rev".

10. Another eyewitness to the collision, Stephen Bryer, reported that Defendant accelerated at a high rate of speed through the left turn onto southbound Ridge and traveled at a high rate of speed until the collision occurred. Mr. Bryer reported that Defendant was driving approximately 60 miles per hour at the time of impact, even though it was a 50mph zone.

11.   As a result of the negligent conduct of Defendant, Plaintiff ▮▮▮▮▮ has suffered severe and permanent injuries. The injuries included, but were not limited to a concussion, fracture of the bilateral superior and inferior pubic rami, fracture of the left sacrum, left pneumothorax, pulmonary contusions and blunt chest trauma.

12.   The injuries suffered by ▮▮▮▮▮ have caused, and in the future will cause pain, suffering, discomfort, disability, distress, embarrassment, medical and surgical bills, loss of income, scarring, and loss of her ability to continue work as a swimwear model.

WHEREFORE, Plaintiff prays for judgment against each of the Defendants in an amount in excess of $75,000.00, for costs of this action, and for such other and further relief as the Court deems just and equitable.

Respectfully submitted,

/s Matthew L. Bretz
Matthew L. Bretz, CA Bar No. 156376
1227 North Main Street
P.O. Box 1782
Hutchinson, KS 67504-1782
(620) 662-3435 Phone
(620) 662-3445 Fax
matt@byinjurylaw.com

REQUEST FOR JURY TRIAL

COMES NOW the Plaintiff and respectfully makes demand for trial by jury of all issues herein joined.

/s Matthew L. Bretz
Matthew L. Bretz, CA Bar No. 156376

-3-

APPENDIX 6
AUTOMOBILE WRECK COMPLAINT

This case arose from a one vehicle wreck which occurred in Germany. The driver lost control on an exit ramp and rolled the vehicle into a ditch.

The case was filed in Federal Court in Illinois since the driver of the vehicle was an Illinois resident and since there was diversity of citizenship. Illinois allows both the driver of a vehicle and the owner of a vehicle to be named as defendants. Many states do not allow the owner of the vehicle to be named as a defendant if the owner was not driving.

The Complaint also includes a claim for loss of consortium, which is addressed in Part One, Section VI. B. Some states require the loss of consortium claim to be pursued by the injured spouse, and other states require the non-injured spouse to be named as a plaintiff in order to pursue the loss of consortium claim.

Bretz Law Offices, LLC
1227 North Main Street
Hutchinson, KS 67504-1782
(620) 662-3435
Fax (620) 662-3445

IN THE UNITED STATES DISTRICT COURT
FOR THE NORTHERN DISTRICT OF ILLINOIS

▮▮▮▮ and ▮▮▮▮ ▮▮▮ ,	)	
Plaintiffs,	)	
	)	
vs.	)	Case No.: 12 CV 09995
	)	
HANNAH C. KOBIT and ROSS MEADE,	)	
Defendants.	)	
	)	

FIRST AMENDED COMPLAINT

COME NOW the Plaintiffs, ▮▮▮▮ and ▮▮▮▮ , by and through their attorney, Melinda G. Young, and for Plaintiffs' causes of action against the Defendants, states as follows:

1.   Plaintiff ▮▮▮▮ is an individual and citizen of the State of Kansas.

2.   Plaintiff ▮▮▮▮ is an individual and citizen of the State of Kansas.

3.   Defendant Hannah C. Kobit is an individual and citizen of the State of Illinois and may be served with process at her residential address of ▮▮▮▮ ▮▮▮▮ .

4.   Defendant Ross A. Meade is an individual and citizen of the State of Maryland and may be served with process at his residential address ▮▮▮▮ .

5.   Defendants are citizens of the State of Illinois and Maryland, respectively, and Plaintiffs are citizens of the State of Kansas. There is complete diversity of citizenship, and the matter in

controversy exceeds, exclusive of interest and costs, the sum specified by 28 U.S.C. § 1332.

6. This Court has personal jurisdiction over the parties and subject matter jurisdiction pursuant to 28 U.S.C. § 1332.

COUNT I

7. On January 11, 2011, ▓▓▓▓▓▓▓▓ was a passenger in a motor vehicle which was being driven by Hannah Kobit and which was owned by Defendant Ross Meade.

8. At the time of the wreck which is the subject of this action, Defendant Hannah Kobit was an agent of the owner of the subject vehicle, Defendant Ross Meade.

9. Defendant Kobit was negligent in operating the vehicle in one or more of the following, or other, respects:

    A. Failing to pay full time and attention

    B. Driving too fast for the existing conditions

    C. Failing to take appropriate evasive and corrective maneuvers

    D. Driving too fast given the distance illuminated by her headlights

    E. Failing to keep the vehicle under control

    F. Driving far in excess of the posted speed limits

10. As a result of her negligence the Defendant lost control of the vehicle while attempting to exit at the intersection of B19 and B303 in Geldersheim, Germany, causing the vehicle to go off the road, into a ditch, through a culvert, over a yield sign, out of the ditch, and then through two medians.

11. As a result of the Hannah Kobit's negligence and the resulting wreck, Plaintiff ▓▓▓▓ ▓▓▓▓ has suffered severe, permanent and disabling injuries.

-2-

12.   's injuries include but are not limited to a fractured T11 vertebra, rib fractures, cervical spine injuries, thoracic spine injuries, lumbar spine injuries, loss of consciousness, traumatic brain injury, post concussion syndrome, balance problems, and dizziness.

13.   At the time of the motor vehicle wreck   was a member of the Military Police at the rank of SSG in the United States Army with eleven years of service.

14.   As a result of the injuries suffered by   in the subject wreck,   has been notified by the United States Army that he is physically unfit for duty and that he therefore is being medically discharged from the Army.

15.   As a result of the negligence of Defendant Hannah Kobit, Plaintiffs   and   have suffered and will suffer in the future significant medical, surgical and hospital charges, loss of income and benefits, pain, suffering, mental anguish and disability, and other consequential damages.

COUNT II

16.   Plaintiffs refer to and incorporate herein by reference all of the allegations set forth in paragraphs 1 through 15 of this First Amended Complaint.

17.   At the time of the motor vehicle wreck which is the subject of this action Plaintiff   lawfully married to   .

18.   As a result of the injuries suffered by   , Plaintiff   has suffered and will suffer in the future a loss of consortium.

19.   Accordingly, Plaintiffs also bring this action for loss of consortium suffered by   .

-3-

WHEREFORE, Plaintiffs ██████████ and ██████████ each pray for judgment against the Defendants in an amount in excess of $75,000.00, for costs of this action, and for such other and further relief as the Court deems just and equitable.

Respectfully submitted,

/s Edward A. Czapla
Edward A. Czapla, IL ARDC No. 6202297
1300 East Woodfield Road, Suite 205
Schaumburg, IL 60173
(847) 240-9010 Phone
(847) 240-9062 Fax
ed@grauerlaw.com

/s Melinda G. Young
Melinda G. Young, KS Bar No. 24309
1227 N. Main Street
P.O. Box 1782
Hutchinson, KS 67504-1782
(620) 662-3435 Phone
(620) 662-3445 Fax
melinda@bretzpilaw.com

REQUEST FOR JURY TRIAL

COMES NOW the Plaintiff, pursuant to applicable law, and respectfully makes demand for trial by jury of all issues herein joined.

/s Melinda G. Young
Melinda G. Young, KS Bar No. 24309
1227 N. Main Street
P.O. Box 1782
Hutchinson, KS 67504-1782
(620) 662-3435 Phone
(620) 662-3445 Fax
melinda@bretzpilaw.com

APPENDIX 7
PRODUCT LIABILITY PETITION

This is a petition from a product liability case arising from a motorcycle wheel failure. The petition will give you an idea about the different potential parties who may be involved in the design, manufacture, distribution and sale of a product, and will also give you an idea about the different claims which may arise from a dangerous or defective product.

Most product liability claims are based on state law, rather than federal law, so this particular Petition was filed in the appropriate state court format.

Sometimes cases can be filed in either state or federal court and an injured person or her family can make decisions before filing suit to pick the most advantageous venue for filing the suit and going to trial. Many state courts have different legal standards for the admissibility of testimony from expert witnesses, and we determined that state court had the best evidentiary rules for experts in this case.

Our client in this case was from Tennessee. The client initially hired a Tennessee lawyer who missed the Tennessee statute of limitations. The client was eventually referred to our office and we were able to get around the statute of limitations error based on a choice of law argument.

IN THE DISTRICT COURT OF SHAWNEE COUNTY, KANSAS
(Pursuant to K.S.A. Chapter 60)

<table>
<tr><td>█████████ by and through her
Conservator, █████████,
Plaintiff,

vs.

HARLEY-DAVIDSON MOTOR COMPANY
GROUP, LLC., BOST BROTHERS, LLC, dba
BOST HARLEY-DAVIDSON OF NASHVILLE, fka
C&S HARLEY-DAVIDSON, INC., C&S HARLEY
DAVIDSON OF NASHVILLE, L.P., dba BOST
HARLEY-DAVIDSON, D.I.D DAIDO KOGYO CO.,
LTD., DAIDO CORPORATION OF AMERICA, and
LEE HULL and KANDI HULL dba L&K
MOTORCYCLE TRIKES & TRAILERS,
Defendants.</td><td>)
)
)
)
)
)
)
)
)
)
)
)
)
)
)
)
)</td><td>

Case No.: 08 C 1723</td></tr>
</table>

SECOND AMENDED PETITION

COMES NOW the Plaintiff, █████████, by and through her attorney, Matthew L. Bretz, and for Plaintiff's cause of action against the Defendants states as follows:

1. Plaintiff █████████ is an individual, resident, citizen and domiciliary of the State of Tennessee.

2. Defendant Harley-Davidson Motor Company Group, LLC., is a corporation existing under the laws of the State of Wisconsin, with a principal place of business in Wisconsin, and may be served with process by serving its registered agent for service of process, C T Corporation System, 8040 Excelsior Drive, Suite 200, Madison, WI 53717.

3. Defendant Bost Brothers, LLC[1], dba Bost Harley-Davidson of Nashville, fka C&S Harley-

---

[1]Bost Brothers, LLC, dba Bost Harley-Davidson of Nashville, fka C&S Harley Davidson, Inc., and C&S Harley Davidson of Nashville, L.P., dba Bost Harley-Davidson, are collectively referred to hereinafter as "Bost Harley-Davidson".

Davidson, Inc., is a Tennessee Limited Liability Company, with a principal place of business in Tennessee, and may be served with process by serving its registered agent for service of process, Nestor & Company, C.P.A.'s, 4705 Alabama Avenue, Nashville, Tennessee 37209.

4. Defendant C&S Harley Davidson of Nashville, L.P., dba Bost Harley-Davidson is a Tennessee Limited Partnership, and may be served with process by serving its registered agent for service of process, John W. Nelley, Jr., 315 Deaderick Street, Nashville, Tennessee 37238.

5. Defendant D.I.D Daido Kogyo Co., Ltd., is a Japanese corporation, and may be served with process pursuant to the Hague Service Convention.

6. Daido Corporation of America is a Delaware corporation, and may be served with process by serving its registered agent for service of process, C T Corporation System, 800 South Gay Street, Suite 2021, Knoxville, Tennessee 37929-9710.

7. Defendants Lee Hull and Kandi Hull are doing business as "L&K Motorcycle Trikes & Trailers", and are individuals and residents of the State of Tennessee, and may be served with process at their residential address, ▮▮▮▮▮▮▮▮▮▮▮▮▮▮▮.

8. This Court has subject matter jurisdiction, and personal jurisdiction over the parties pursuant to K.S.A. 60-308(b).

9. Venue is proper in this district pursuant to K.S.A. 60-604 and K.S.A. 60-605, as the cause of action arose in Shawnee County, Kansas.

10. On or about August 20, 2004, ▮▮▮▮▮▮▮ purchased a Harley-Davidson motorcycle, VIN 1HD1FFW125Y604372 from Boswell's Harley-Davidson Sales, Inc.[2]

---

[2] A true and correct copy of the sales contract is attached hereto as Exhibit "1".

-2-

11. The subject motorcycle was designed, manufactured, distributed, and placed in the stream of commerce by Defendant Harley-Davidson Motor Company Group, Inc.

12. The subject motorcycle was a touring motorcycle, and was purchased for the particular purpose of using it for touring, including the particular purpose of carrying a passenger on both short and long cross-country trips.

13. In May, 2005, ▒▒▒▒▒▒▒ was driving the subject motorcycle, returning from a trip to Myrtle Beach, South Carolina, when the rear wheel on the motorcycle developed problems.

14. ▒▒▒▒▒▒▒ took the motorcycle to Bost Harley-Davidson for inspection and repairs.

15. Upon inspection, Bost Harley-Davidson found that the rim of the rear wheel on the motorcycle had split.

16. Upon finding that the rim had split, Defendants Harley-Davidson Motor Company Group, LLC, and Bost Harley-Davidson replaced the wheel under warranty provided by Defendant Harley-Davidson Motor Company Group, LLC.

17. The wheel was replaced on or about May 27, 2005, as shown on the Work Order Reprint attached hereto as Exhibit "2".

18. Bost Harley-Davidson sent the wheel and rim which had failed to Harley-Davidson Motor Company Group, LLC.

19. By replacing the wheel and rim, and by sending the wheel and rim to Defendant Harley-Davidson Motor Company Group, LLC, Defendants all knew or should have known that there was or was likely to be a defect in the warranty-replacement wheel and rim.

20. On or about July, 2005, ▒▒▒▒▒▒▒ purchased an L&K Classic Trailer, model number 54001, from Defendants Lee and Kandi Hull, dba L&K Motorcycle Trikes & Trailers, for

the stated particular purpose of pulling it behind the subject motorcycle on cross-country motorcycle trips.

21. On or about August 18, 2007, Plaintiff ▮▮▮▮▮▮▮ was a passenger on the subject motorcycle which was pulling the L&K trailer on I70, in Shawnee County, Kansas, near Topeka, Kansas.

22. As ▮▮▮▮▮▮▮ was riding on the motorcycle, the rim of the rear wheel split causing the tire to come off the rim and causing the motorcycle to crash.[3]

23. The defective and unreasonably dangerous condition in the rim which caused the motorcycle to crash was present at the time the wheel was replaced on or about May 27, 2005, but was not known to ▮▮▮▮▮▮▮ or ▮▮▮▮▮▮▮ until after the catastrophic crash on August 18, 2007.

24. Defendant D.I.D Daido Kogyo Co., Ltd., manufactured the wheel and rim which split causing the motorcycle to crash.

25. Defendant Daido Corporation of America imported the wheel and rim to the United States and sold it to Defendant Harley-Davidson Motor Company Group, LLC.

26. Defendant Harley-Davidson Motor Company Group, LLC, was the manufacturer and seller of the original wheel and warranty-replacement wheel and rim which split causing the motorcycle to crash.

27. Defendant Bost Harley-Davidson was the seller of the warranty-replacement wheel and rim which split causing the motorcycle to crash.

28. As a result of the split in the rear wheel and the crash, ▮▮▮▮▮▮▮ has suffered, and

---

[3]A true and correct copy of the Motor Vehicle Accident Report is attached hereto as Exhibit "3".

will suffer in the future, severe, permanent and disabling injuries.

29. As a further result of the split in the rear wheel and the crash, ▓▓▓▓▓▓▓ has suffered, and will suffer in the future, pain, suffering, disabilities, disfigurement, mental anguish, medical expenses, hospitalization expenses, surgical expenses, nursing home and long-term care expenses, loss of time, and loss of income.

30. ▓▓▓▓▓▓▓ has been suffering from a legal disability which tolls any statute of limitations at all times since August 18, 2007.

31. At the time of the injury, the motorcycle and wheel and trailer were being used or consumed within the State of Kansas in the ordinary course of trade or use.

NEGLIGENCE

32. Plaintiff incorporates by reference as though fully set forth herein all of the allegations of this Petition.

33. The subject motorcycle wheel rim was not supposed to split while traveling on the highway.

34. The subject motorcycle wheel rim would not have split while traveling on the highway had it been designed without negligence.

35. The subject motorcycle wheel rim would not have split while traveling on the highway had it been manufactured without negligence.

36. The subject motorcycle wheel rim would not have split while traveling on the highway had it been tested without negligence.

37. The subject motorcycle wheel rim would not have split while traveling on the highway had it been inspected without negligence.

38. Motorcycle wheel rims do not split while traveling on the highway absent negligence in the design of the wheel rim.

39. Motorcycle wheel rims do not split while traveling on the highway absent negligence in the manufacture of the wheel rim.

40. Motorcycle wheel rims do not split while traveling on the highway absent negligence in testing of the wheel rim.

41. Motorcycle wheel rims do not split while traveling on the highway absent negligence in inspection of the wheel rim.

42. At all times material to the design, manufacture, testing and inspection of the subject motorcycle and its component parts including the wheel and rim, the motorcycle, wheel and rim were in the exclusive control of one or more of the Defendants.

43. Plaintiff asserts the doctrine of *Res ipsa loquitur.*

44. Defendants were negligent in one or more of the following, or other, manners:

    a. Design of the motorcycle, wheel and rim;

    b. Manufacture of the motorcycle, wheel and rim;

    c. Production of the motorcycle, wheel and rim;

    d. Assembly of the motorcycle, wheel and rim;

    e. Testing of the motorcycle, wheel and rim;

    f. Warnings for the motorcycle, wheel and rim;

    g. Instructions for the motorcycle, wheel and rim;

    h. Labeling for the motorcycle, wheel and rim; or

    i. Sale of the trailer for the particular purpose of being pulled behind the subject motorcycle if it could not safely been used for that purpose.

45.   The negligence of the Defendants was the proximate and actual cause of the injuries suffered by ███████████, as more fully described herein.

BREACH OF WARRANTY

46.   Plaintiff incorporates by reference as though fully set forth herein all of the allegations of this Petition.

47.   Pursuant to the UCC-Sales (Tenn. Code Ann. 47-2-314 and K.S.A. 84-2-314(2)(c)) Defendants impliedly warranted that the motorcycle and all of its component parts, including the wheel and rim, were fit for the ordinary purposes for which such goods are used.

48.   Pursuant to the UCC-Sales (Tenn. Code Ann. 47-2-315 and K.S.A. 84-2-315) Defendants impliedly warranted that the motorcycle and all of its component parts, including the wheel and rim, were fit for the particular purpose of using it for touring, including the particular purpose of carrying a passenger on both short and long cross-country trips.

49.   Defendants had reason to know of the buyer's particular purpose for the motorcycle and its component parts.

50.   Defendants Lee and Kandi Hull, dba L&K Motorcycle Trikes & Trailers had reason to know of the buyer's particular purpose for the trailer.

51.   ███████████ relied on Defendants' expertise in furnishing goods suitable for these particular purposes.

52.   Defendants had reason to know of ███████████'s reliance.

53.   At all times material hereto, ███████████ was a resident in the household of ████

-7-

██████ and is, therefore, a third party beneficiary of the implied warranties of merchantability and of fitness for particular purpose under the UCC-Sales (Tenn. Code Ann. 47-2-318 and K.S.A. 84-2-318).

54. Defendants breached the implied warranties of merchantability and of fitness for particular purpose, and the express written warranty.

55. As a result of Defendants' breach of the implied warranties of merchantability and of fitness for particular purpose and the express warranty, Plaintiff has suffered consequential damages as defined in the UCC-Sales (Tenn. Code Ann. 47-2-715 and K.S.A. 84-2-715(2)(b)).

KANSAS PRODUCT LIABILITY ACT

56. Plaintiff incorporates by reference as though fully set forth herein all of the allegations of this Petition.

57. Defendants are all "product sellers" as defined by K.S.A. 60-3302(a).

58. Defendant Bost Harley-Davidson is a "retailer" as used in K.S.A. 60-3302(a).

59. Defendant Harley-Davidson Motor Company Group, LLC, is a "manufacturer" as defined by K.S.A. 60-3302(b) in that it is engaged in the business of selling products and it designs, produces, makes, fabricates, constructs or remanufactures the relevant product or component part of a product before it sale to a user or consumer, and holds itself out as the manufacturer.

60. Defendants Harley-Davidson Motor Company Group, LLC, D.I.D Daido Kogyo Co., Ltd., and Daido Corporation of America are all "manufacturers" as defined by K.S.A. 60-3302(b).

61. Plaintiff asserts a "product liability claim", as defined in K.S.A. 60-3302, against each of the Defendants.

62. The motorcycle and its component parts, including the wheel and rim, were unreasonably dangerous and defective.

63. Upon information and belief, Plaintiff alleges that the trailer was unreasonably dangerous and defective when used for its stated particular purpose of being pulled by the subject motorcycle.

64. Defendants had knowledge of the defect in the subject motorcycle and its component parts, including the wheel and rim, as evidenced by their knowledge of at least one prior incident where the wheel rim split and had to be replaced.

65. Defendants could have discovered the defect in the subject motorcycle and its component parts, including the wheel and rim, while exercising reasonable care.

66. All of the Defendants, except Bost-Harley Davidson, were "manufacturers" of the defective product or product components.

67. Plaintiff brings this claim or action for harm caused by the manufacture, production, making, construction, fabrication, design, formula, preparation, assembly, installation, testing, warnings, instructions, marketing, packaging, storage and/or labeling of the subject products.

68. Plaintiff brings this action based on strict liability in tort, negligence, breach of express or implied warranty, breach of or failure to discharge a duty to warn or instruct, and all other substantive legal theories.

69. Plaintiff brings this action for the harm suffered by her and which will be suffered in the future, including her personal physical injuries and mental anguish and accompanying medical, hospitalization, surgical, nursing home and long-term care expenses, loss of time and loss of income.

WHEREFORE, Plaintiff prays for judgment against each of the Defendants in an amount in excess of $75,000.00, for costs of this action, and for such other and further relief as the Court deems just and equitable.

Respectfully submitted,

By:_____
         Matthew L. Bretz, #15466
         1227 North Main Street
         P.O. Box 1782
         Hutchinson, KS 67504-1782
         (620) 662-3435
         (620) 662-3445 (fax)
         matt@bretzpilaw.com
         Attorney for Plaintiff

REQUEST FOR JURY TRIAL

COMES NOW the Plaintiff, pursuant to applicable Kansas law, and respectfully makes demand for trial by jury of all issues herein joined.

By:_____
         Matthew L. Bretz

-10-

APPENDIX 8

PRODUCT LIABILITY INTERROGATORIES AND REQUESTS FOR PRODUCTION

The Interrogatories and Requests for Production which are attached were used in the product liability case which is referenced in Appendix 7.

Interrogatories are written questions from one party to a lawsuit to another party to a lawsuit. In the written questions a party can ask about virtually anything which is related in any way to the claims which are being made and the defenses which are being asserted. Courts generally limit the number of interrogatories which each party may submit to any other party. In this case, however, there were multiple defendants so we were able to submit more interrogatories than the standard amount.

Requests for production are, as the name suggests, requests from one party to another party to produce a document. They can also be used to request inspection of property. Requests for production are usually not limited, and frequently several sets of requests are sent as a case progresses and additional documents, records or other things are discovered.

The interrogatories and requests for production which are attached will help you identify what sort of things may be needed in a product liability case with claims of negligence, breach of warranty, and statutory product liability.

IN THE DISTRICT COURT OF SHAWNEE COUNTY, KANSAS
(Pursuant to K.S.A. Chapter 60)

███████████ by and through her	)	
Conservator, ██████████,	)	
Plaintiff,	)	
	)	
vs.	)	Case No. 08 C 1723
	)	
HARLEY-DAVIDSON, INC., BOST BROTHERS, LLC,	)	
dba BOST HARLEY-DAVIDSON OF NASHVILLE, fka	)	
C&S HARLEY-DAVIDSON, INC., C&S HARLEY	)	
DAVIDSON OF NASHVILLE, L.P., dba BOST	)	
HARLEY-DAVIDSON, D.I.D DAIDO KOGYO CO.,	)	
LTD., and DAIDO CORPORATION OF AMERICA,	)	
Defendants.	)	

PLAINTIFF'S FIRST REQUEST FOR PRODUCTION OF DOCUMENTS
TO DEFENDANT HARLEY-DAVIDSON, INC.

COMES NOW the Plaintiff and requests Defendant Harley-Davidson, Inc., to produce the

following documents, articles and items of tangible nature within thirty (30) days after receipt of this

request.

1.   An exemplar wheel from the same lot or batch as the wheel which was on the motorcycle at

   the time of the August 18, 2007, accident.

2.   An exemplar wheel from the same lot or batch as the wheel which was on the motorcycle at

   the time that the motorcycle was originally sold to ██████████ .

3.   An exemplar rim from the same lot or batch as the rim which was on the motorcycle at the

   time of the August 18, 2007, accident.

4.   An exemplar rim from the same lot or batch as the rim which was on the motorcycle at the

   time that the motorcycle was originally sold to ██████████ .

5.   Original or true and correct copies of any tests or examinations conducted on the wheel

which was on the motorcycle at the time that the motorcycle was originally sold to ▓ ▓ and which was replaced on or about May 27, 2005.

6. Original or true and correct copies of any tests or examinations conducted on the rim which was on the motorcycle at the time of the August 18, 2007, accident.

7. Original or true and correct copies of any tests or examinations conducted on the motorcycle which is the subject matter of this lawsuit.

8. Original or true and correct copies of any manufacturer's specification(s) regarding the type of material used for the wheel which is the subject matter of this lawsuit.

9. Original or true and correct copies of any manufacturer's specification(s) regarding the type of material used for the rim which is the subject matter of this lawsuit.

10. Original or true and correct copies of any manufacturer's specification(s) regarding the chemical composition of the wheel which is the subject matter of this lawsuit.

11. Original or true and correct copies of any manufacturer's specification(s) regarding the chemical composition of the rim which is the subject matter of this lawsuit.

12. Original or true and correct copies of any manufacturer's specification(s) regarding any heat treatment used on the wheel which is the subject matter of this lawsuit.

13. Original or true and correct copies of any manufacturer's specification(s) regarding any heat treatment used on the rim which is the subject matter of this lawsuit.

14. Original or true and correct copies of any manufacturer's specification(s) regarding the strength material properties of the material used for the wheel which is the subject matter of this lawsuit.

15. Original or true and correct copies of any manufacturer's specification(s) regarding the strength material properties of the material used for the rim which is the subject matter of this

lawsuit.

16. Original or true and correct copies of any manufacturer's specification(s) regarding the fatigue and fracture material properties of the material used for the wheel which is the subject matter of this lawsuit.

17. Original or true and correct copies of any manufacturer's specification(s) regarding the fatigue and fracture material properties of the material used for the rim which is the subject matter of this lawsuit.

18. Original or true and correct copies of any manufacturer's three-dimensional solid model of the wheel which is the subject matter of this lawsuit, including, but not limited to, CAD renderings.

19. Original or true and correct copies of any manufacturer's three-dimensional solid model of the rim which is the subject matter of this lawsuit, including, but not limited to, CAD renderings.

20. Original or true and correct copies of any documents which are described in your responses to Plaintiff's Interrogatories.

21. Original or true and correct copies of any notice, including, but not limited to, correspondence, demand letter, settlement offer, legal action, formal complaints, warranty claims, formal petitions, demands, notices, investigation reports, e-mails, claims, or reports, and complaints, claims, or reports made via telephone, and any other complaint, claim, inquiry, report or other transmission of information. claims, notices or other reports made regarding wheels or rims, including, but not limited to, legal action, formal complaints, investigation reports, e-mail complaints, claims, or reports, and complaints, claims, or reports made via telephone.

22.   Original or true and correct copies of any invoices, receipts, sales contracts, or other documents or records regarding the sale of the wheel which is the subject of this lawsuit.

23.   Original or true and correct copies of any invoices, receipts, sales contracts, or other documents or records regarding the sale of the rim which is the subject of this lawsuit.

24.   Original or true and correct copies of any invoices, receipts, sales contracts, or other documents or records regarding the sale of the motorcycle which is the subject of this lawsuit.

25.   All documents you intend to introduce as evidence at the time of trial.

26.   All documents you contend support the denials set forth in your Answer.

27.   All documents identified in Defendant's responses to Plaintiff's First Set of Interrogatories.

BRETZ LAW OFFICES, LLC

By_____
            Matthew L. Bretz, SC #15466
            Attorney for Plaintiff

BRETZ LAW OFFICES, LLC
1227 N. Main
P.O. Box 1782
Hutchinson, Kansas 67504-1782
Phone (620) 662-3435
Fax (620) 662-3445

IN THE DISTRICT COURT OF SHAWNEE COUNTY, KANSAS
(Pursuant to K.S.A. Chapter 60)

▓▓▓▓▓▓▓ by and through her)	
Conservator, ▓▓▓▓▓▓▓▓▓▓▓,)	
Plaintiff,)	
)	
vs.)	Case No.: 08 C 1723
)	
HARLEY-DAVIDSON MOTOR COMPANY)	
GROUP, LLC., BOST BROTHERS, LLC, dba)	
BOST HARLEY-DAVIDSON OF NASHVILLE, fka)	
C&S HARLEY-DAVIDSON, INC., C&S HARLEY)	
DAVIDSON OF NASHVILLE, L.P., dba BOST)	
HARLEY-DAVIDSON, D.I.D DAIDO KOGYO CO.,)	
LTD., DAIDO CORPORATION OF AMERICA, and)	
LEE HULL and KANDI HULL dba L&K)	
MOTORCYCLE TRIKES & TRAILERS,)	
Defendants.)	
)	

PLAINTIFF'S SECOND REQUEST FOR PRODUCTION OF DOCUMENTS TO DEFENDANT HARLEY-DAVIDSON MOTOR COMPANY GROUP, LLC

COMES NOW the Plaintiff and requests Defendant Harley-Davidson Motor Company Group, LLC, to produce the following documents, articles and items of tangible nature within thirty (30) days after receipt of this request.

28. Original or true and correct copies of all Materials and Processes Group Laboratory Reports for all smoothie rims which have suffered a fracture. Please include all portions of such reports, including, but not limited to, background, testing, discussion, views of wheel and fracture surfaces, high magnification inspection images, microstructure images, chrome

-1-

condition images, and all photographs of such smoothie rims.

29. Original or true and correct copies of all tests or examinations conducted on all smoothie rims which have suffered a fracture.

30. Original or true and correct copies of all materials and Processes Group Laboratory Reports for all smoothie rims which have been replaced under warranty.

31. Original or true and correct copies of all tests or examinations conducted on all smoothie rims which have been replaced under warranty.

32. Original or true and correct copies of any and all records in which the cause of the fracture of the smoothie wheel identified in documents H-D 0110-0118 was addressed.

33. Original or true and correct copies of any and all records in which prevention of fractures in smoothie wheels is addressed.

34. Original or true and correct copies of any notice, including, but not limited to, correspondence, demand letter, settlement offer, legal action, formal complaints, warranty claims, formal petitions, demands, notices, investigation reports, e-mails, claims, or reports, and complaints, claims, or reports made via telephone, and any other complaint, claim, inquiry, report or other transmission of information, claims, notices or other reports made regarding smoothie rims, including, but not limited to, legal action, formal complaints, investigation reports, e-mail complaints, claims, or reports, and complaints, claims, or reports made via telephone.

BRETZ LAW OFFICES, LLC

By_____
　　　　　　Matthew L. Bretz, SC #15466
　　　　　　Attorney for Plaintiff

-2-

BRETZ LAW OFFICES, LLC
1227 N. Main
P.O. Box 1782
Hutchinson, Kansas 67504-1782
Phone (620) 662-3435
Fax (620) 662-3445

IN THE DISTRICT COURT OF SHAWNEE COUNTY, KANSAS
(Pursuant to K.S.A. Chapter 60)

▓▓▓▓▓▓▓▓▓▓▓▓▓▓ by and through her) Conservator, ▓▓▓▓▓▓▓▓▓▓▓▓,) Plaintiff,))	
vs.)	Case No.: 08 C 1723
)	
HARLEY-DAVIDSON MOTOR COMPANY) GROUP, LLC., BOST BROTHERS, LLC, dba) BOST HARLEY-DAVIDSON OF NASHVILLE, fka) C&S HARLEY-DAVIDSON, INC., C&S HARLEY) DAVIDSON OF NASHVILLE, L.P., dba BOST) HARLEY-DAVIDSON, D.I.D DAIDO KOGYO CO.,) LTD., DAIDO CORPORATION OF AMERICA, and) LEE HULL and KANDI HULL dba L&K) MOTORCYCLE TRIKES & TRAILERS,) Defendants.)	

PLAINTIFF'S THIRD REQUEST FOR PRODUCTION OF DOCUMENTS
TO DEFENDANT HARLEY-DAVIDSON MOTOR COMPANY GROUP, LLC

COMES NOW the Plaintiff and requests Defendant Harley-Davidson Motor Company Group, LLC, to produce the following documents, articles and items of tangible nature within thirty (30) days after receipt of this request.

35. All records of all smoothie wheels which have been replaced under warranty in the ten (10) years preceeding the date of this request.

36. All records of all smoothie wheels which have been replaced in the ten (10) years preceeding the date of this request.

-1-

37.   All records related to any and all changes to the design of the smoothie wheel at any time in the preceeding five (5) years.

38.   All internal communications at Harley-Davidson Motor Company Group, LLC concerning changes in the design of the smoothie wheel.

39.   All internal communications at Harley-Davidson Motor Company Group, LLC concerning the reasons for changes in the design of the smoothie wheel.

BRETZ LAW OFFICES, LLC

By_____
            Matthew L. Bretz, SC #15466
            Attorney for Plaintiff

IN THE DISTRICT COURT OF SHAWNEE COUNTY, KANSAS
(Pursuant to K.S.A. Chapter 60)

▓▓▓▓▓▓▓ by and through her	)
Conservator, ▓▓▓▓▓▓▓,	)
Plaintiff,	)
	)
vs.	) Case No. 08 C 1723
	)
HARLEY-DAVIDSON, INC., BOST BROTHERS, LLC,	)
dba BOST HARLEY-DAVIDSON OF NASHVILLE, fka	)
C&S HARLEY-DAVIDSON, INC., C&S HARLEY	)
DAVIDSON OF NASHVILLE, L.P., dba BOST	)
HARLEY-DAVIDSON, D.I.D DAIDO KOGYO CO.,	)
LTD., and DAIDO CORPORATION OF AMERICA,	)
Defendants.	)
	)

PLAINTIFF'S FIRST SET OF INTERROGATORIES TO
DEFENDANT HARLEY-DAVIDSON, INC.

Pursuant to K.S.A. 60-233, Plaintiff propounds to Defendant Harley-Davidson, Inc, these

Interrogatories to be answered within thirty (30) days after service hereof. Space is included for

answers to the Interrogatories upon the original. These Interrogatories are deemed continuing in

nature and require your additional response should additional information or changes in your

answers come to your attention.

In each response to these Interrogatories, provide all information in your possession,

custody or control. If you are able or willing to provide only part of the information sought,

specify the reason for your inability or unwillingness to provide the remainder. In addition to

supplying the information requested, you are to identify all documents that support your answer

or make reference to the subject matter of each Interrogatory and your answer. Further, if any or

all documents identified are no longer in your possession, custody or control, because of loss,

destruction or any other reason, then provide the following with respect to each such document:

1.   Describe the nature of the document;

-1-

2.   State the date of the document;

3.   Identify the person who sent and received the original and any copies of the document;

4.   State in as much detail as possible the contents of the document; and

5.   State the manner of the disposition of the document.

If you decline to answer any portion of the Interrogatory, provide all information called for by the balance of the Interrogatory. If you object to any portion of the Interrogatory on any ground, provide all information called for which you concede is discoverable. These Interrogatories apply to information that you have or possess and any information that you, any agent, servant, employee, or investigator has or possesses on your behalf.

DEFINITIONS

"Document" -- as used herein, the term "document" means any medium upon which intelligence or information can be recorded or retrieved, and includes, without limitation, the original or copies of any written, recorded, or graphic matter, however produced or reproduced, including, but not limited to, any book, pamphlet, periodical, letter, correspondence, telegram, invoice, contract, purchase order, estimate, report, memorandum, interoffice communication, interoffice memorandum, working paper, record, study, paper, worksheet, cost sheet, estimating sheet, bid, bill, time card, work record, chart, index, data sheet, data processing card, data processing tape, electronic record, e-mail, recording, transcription thereof, graph, photograph, object or tangible things, and all other memorials of any conversation, meeting or conference, by telephone or otherwise, and any other writing or recording which is in your possession, custody or control, in the possession, custody or control of your agents or attorneys, or which was but is no longer in your possession, custody or control, which would constitute or contain evidence relating to any matter which is relevant to the subject matter of this proceeding.

"Identification" -- As used herein, the terms "identification", "identify", or "identity", when used in reference to a person or persons, means to state the name, address, and telephone number of each such person and the name of the current employer and place of employment of each such person. When used in reference to a document or documents, such terms mean to describe each such document by date, subject matter, name of each person who wrote, signed, initialed, dictated, or otherwise participated in the creation or obtaining of such document, the name of each addressee (if any) and, if it now exists, the name and address of each person having custody of such document. When used in reference to any act, event, occurrence, statement of conduct (hereinafter "act"), "identify", "state", and "describe" mean: (1) to describe the event(s) constituting such act; (2) to state the date when such act occurred; (3) to identify each person participating in such act; (4) to identify each other person, if any, present when such act occurred; (5) to identify each document which in any way refers to, discusses, analyzes, comments upon or otherwise relates to such act; and (6) to state whether each such document now exists.

"You" -- As used herein, the term "you" means "your" or "yourself", and refers to Defendant, and each of its agents, representatives, employees, servants, and attorneys and each person acting on his or her or its behalf.

"Representative" -- As used herein, the term "representative" means any and all agents, employees, servants, officers, directors, attorneys or any other persons acting or purporting to act on behalf of the person in question.

"Communication" -- As used herein, the term "communication" means any oral or written utterance, notation or statement of any nature whatsoever, by and to whomsoever made, including, but not limited to, correspondence, conversations, dialogues, discussions, interviews,

-3-

consultations, agreements, and other understandings between or among two or more persons.

"Identification of Documents" -- With respect to each Interrogatory, in addition to supplying the requested information, you are to identify all documents which support, refer to, or evidence the subject matter of each Interrogatory and your answer thereto.

"Contention Interrogatories" -- When an Interrogatory requires you to "state the basis of" a particular claim, contention, allegation or defense, state in your answer the identity of each and every communication and each and every fact and each and every legal theory you believe supports, refers to or evidences such claim, contention or allegation.

"Or" -- As used herein, when the word "or" appears in an Interrogatory, it should not be read so as to eliminate any part of the Interrogatory, but, whenever applicable, it should have the same meaning as the word "and". For example, an Interrogatory which states "support or refer" should be read as "support and refer" if an answer which does both can be made.

"The Product" -- As used herein, when the term "the product" appears in an Interrogatory, it shall mean the product which caused injury or damage to the plaintiff as alleged in the plaintiff's pleadings and described as the rim which was on the rear wheel of the motorcycle at the time of the August 18, 2007, accident which is described in the First Amended Petition.

"Similar Products" -- As used herein, when the term "similar products" appears in an Interrogatory, it shall mean products other than "the product" which are essentially and substantially similar to "the product" with regard to design specifications, material composition, make and model and which were either designed, manufactured, assembled, packaged, sold, distributed, advertised, installed, serviced, prepared, maintained or in any way handled by the defendant.

"Comparable Products" -- As used herein, when the term "comparable products" appears

-4-

in an Interrogatory, it shall mean products other than "the product" or "similar products" which have likeness as to design, specifications, dimensions or material composition or have the same general uses as "the product" or "similar products".

"The Motorcycle" -- As used herein, when the term "the motorcycle" appears in an Interrogatory, it shall mean the motorcycle which was involved in the accident alleged in the plaintiff's pleadings and described as VIN No. 1HD1FFW125Y604372.

"Similar Motorcycles" -- As used herein, when the term "similar motorcycles" appears in an Interrogatory, it shall mean motorcycles other than "the motorcycle" which are substantially similar to "the motorcycle" with regard to design specifications, material composition, make and model and which were either designed, manufactured, assembled, packaged, sold, distributed, advertised, installed, serviced, prepared, maintained or in any way handled by the defendant.

"Comparable Motorcycles" -- As used herein, when the term "comparable motorcycles" appears in an Interrogatory, it shall mean motorcycles other than "the motorcycle" or "similar motorcycles" which have likeness as to design, specifications, dimensions or material composition or have the same general uses as "the motorcycle" or "similar motorcycles".

"Notice" -- As used herein, when the term "notice" appears in an Interrogatory, it shall mean any communication or transmission of information, including, but not limited to, correspondence, demand letter, settlement offer, legal action, formal complaints, warranty claims, formal petitions, demands, notices, investigation reports, e-mails, claims, or reports, and complaints, claims, or reports made via telephone, and any other complaint, claim, inquiry, report or other transmission of information.

"Wheel" – As used herein, when the term "wheel" appears in an Interrogatory, it shall mean the wheel and all component parts, including, but not limited to the tire, rim, spokes, hub

-5-

and axle.

"Rim" – As used herein, when the term "rim" appears in an Interrogatory, it means the

rim itself and not the rest of the component parts of a "wheel".

INTERROGATORY NO. 1. Identify each individual likely to have discoverable information relevant to the disputed facts alleged in the First Amended Petition on file herein, and categorize the identity of such persons with knowledge of the disputed facts by reference to the paragraph number of the Petition and the Answer.

ANSWER:

INTERROGATORY NO. 2. State with particularity the involvement of each of the following Defendants in the design, manufacture, inspection, testing, assembly, packaging, distribution, import, distribution, advertising, and/or warnings for the rim which was on the motorcycle at the time of the August 18, 2007, accident.

A.   Harley-Davidson, Inc.

B.   Bost Brothers, LLC

C.   Bost Harley-Davidson of Nashville

D.   C&S Harley-Davidson, Inc.

E.   C&S Harley Davidson of Nashville, L.P.

F.   Bost Harley-Davidson

G.   D.I.D Daido Kogyo Co. ,LTD.,

H.   Daido Corporation of America

ANSWER:

INTERROGATORY NO. 3. State with particularity the involvement of each of the following Defendants in the design, manufacture, inspection, testing, assembly, packaging, distribution, import, distribution, advertising, and/or warnings for the rim which was on the motorcycle at the time it was originally sold to ▓▓▓▓▓▓▓, and which was replaced on or about May 27, 2005.

    A.   Harley-Davidson, Inc.

    B.   Bost Brothers, LLC

    C.   Bost Harley-Davidson of Nashville

    D.   C&S Harley-Davidson, Inc.

    E.   C&S Harley Davidson of Nashville, L.P.

    F.   Bost Harley-Davidson

    G.   D.I.D Daido Kogyo Co. ,LTD.,

    H.   Daido Corporation of America

ANSWER:

INTERROGATORY NO. 4. With respect to the rim which was on the motorcycle at the time it was originally sold to ▓▓▓▓▓▓▓, and which was replaced on or about May 27, 2007, please state the following:

    A.   When did you become aware that there was alleged to be a problem with the rim?

    B.   What were you told concerning the alleged problem with the rim?

    C.   Identify the person(s) and entities that you informed about the alleged problem with the rim?

    D.   Identify all documents and other materials in which you communicated the existence of the alleged problem with the rim to any other person, persons and/or entities.

    E.   Identify all documents and other materials which pertain to any testing on the subject rim.

    F.   What testing, if any, did you do to determine what had caused the problem or alleged problem with the rim?

-7-

    G.   What, if anything, was done to prevent problems from occurring in the future with similar rims?

    H.   What, if anything, did you communicate to   concerning the rim and potential future problems with the rim which was provided to replace the original rim?

ANSWER:

INTERROGATORY NO. 5. Are you aware of any rims on motorcycle wheels which have suffered cracks, tears, breaks, fractures, failures, or other alleged problems whatsoever, other than the rim which was on the motorcycle when it was originally sold to and the rim which was on the motorcycle at the time of the August 18, 2007, accident? If so, please identify the following:

    A.   When you became aware of such cracks, tears, breaks, fractures, failures, or other alleged problems.

    B.   The owner of the rim at the time of the crack, tear, break, fracture, failure or other alleged problem.

    C.   The attorneys, if any, involved.

    D.   What, if any, defect was found or alleged to have been present in the rim?

    E.   What testing, if any, was done on the subject rim?

    F.   What, if anything, was done to prevent future cracks, tears, breaks, fractures, failures, or other alleged problems from occurring in the future?

    G.   The current location of the rim.

    H.   All expert reports pertaining to the rim.

    I.   The injuries alleged to have been suffered as a result of the crack, tear, break, fracture, failure or other alleged problem.

ANSWER:

INTERROGATORY NO. 6. If you contend that any person or entity other than you was negligent in any way which caused or contributed to Plaintiff's injuries and damages, please:

A.   Identify such other person or entity.

B.   State the resident agent for service of process for such other person or entity.

C.   Provide a complete description of the way in which such person or entity was negligent and caused or contributed to Plaintiff's injury.

ANSWER:

INTERROGATORY NO. 7. If Defendant Harley-Davidson Inc. has "notice" from anyone of any kind of problem regarding the product, similar products, comparable products, the motorcycle, similar motorcycles, or comparable motorcycles, please state:

A.   The names and addresses of the person or persons who gave such notice,

B.   A complete description of such notice,

C.   A complete description of any action taken by Defendant Harley-Davidson Inc. to resolve the issue.

ANSWER:

INTERROGATORY NO. 8. Please describe and explain each and every word, marking, number or other symbol, including the meanings and references of such words, markings, numbers or other symbols, appearing on the rim which was on the motorcycle at the time it was originally sold to ▮▮▮▮▮▮▮▮ , and include the following:

A.   The place of manufacture of the rim,

B.   The date of manufacture of the rim,

C.   The lot or batch of which the rim was a part,

D.   Any tests or examinations conducted on the rim.

ANSWER:

-9-

INTERROGATORY NO. 9. Please describe and explain each and every word, marking, number or other symbol, including the meanings and references of such words, markings, numbers or other symbols, appearing on the rim which was on the motorcycle at the time of the August 18, 2007, accident, and include the following:

    A.   The place of manufacture of the rim,

    B.   The date of manufacture of the rim,

    C.   The lot or batch of which the rim was a part,

    D.   Any tests or examinations conducted on the rim.

ANSWER:

INTERROGATORY NO. 10. If you made or caused to be made any alterations or changes in the rim which was on the motorcycle at the time of the August 18, 2007, accident subsequent to the date of manufacture or assembly, please describe in complete detail each such change or alteration made in the product, including, for each such alteration or change, such information as:

    A.   The date of the change or alteration,

    B.   An exact description of the change or alteration, including the procedure by which the change or alteration was accomplished,

    C.   The reason for making the change or alteration,

    D.   The name and address of the person or persons who made the change or alteration.

ANSWER:

INTERROGATORY NO. 11. Please state what precautions, if any, were taken by you prior to the alleged occurrence to prevent injuries or damage to any user of the rim.

ANSWER:

STATE OF _____, COUNTY OF _____ ss:

    The undersigned, being of lawful age and being first duly sworn upon oath, states:
    That he/she has read the above and foregoing Interrogatory and the answers thereto; that the answers are true and correct to the best of his/her knowledge, information and belief.

                                        _____

SUBSCRIBED and SWORN TO before me this _____ day of _____, _____.

                                        _____
                                        Notary Public

APPENDIX 9
FORD EXPLODING GAS TANK ARTICLE

The attached article provides a history of Ford's exploding gas tanks and the thought process involved in pursuing a product liability claim. The exploding gas tank cases are a prime example of how zealous and ethical trial lawyers can make this world a safer place for all of us to live.

Reprinted with permission from the author, Christopher Leggett.

THE FORD PINTO CASE:
THE VALUATION OF LIFE AS IT APPLIES
TO THE NEGLIGENCE-EFFICIENCY ARGUMENT

Christopher Leggett

Law & Valuation
Professor Palmiter
Spring, 1999

Abstract

The cases involving the explosion of Ford Pinto's due to a defective fuel system design led to the debate of many issues, most centering around the use by Ford of a cost-benefit analysis and the ethics surrounding its decision not to upgrade the fuel system based on this analysis.

ISSUE

Should a risk/benefit analysis be used in situations where a defect in design or manufacturing could lead to death or seriously bodily harm, such as in the Ford Pinto situation?

RULE

There are arguments both for and against such an analysis. It is an economically efficient method which has been accepted by courts for numerous years, however, juries may not always agree, so companies should take this into account.

ANALYSIS

Although Ford had access to a new design which would decrease the possibility of the Ford Pinto from exploding, the company chose not to implement the design, which would have cost $11 per car, even though it had done an analysis showing that the new design would result in 180 less deaths. The company defended itself on the grounds that it used the accepted risk/benefit analysis to determine if the monetary costs of making the change were greater than the societal benefit. Based on the numbers Ford used, the cost would have been $137 million versus the $49.5 million price tag put on the deaths, injuries, and car damages, and thus Ford felt justified not implementing the design change. This risk/benefit analysis was created out of the development of product liability, culminating at Judge Learned Hand's BPL formula, where if the expected harm exceeded the cost to take the precaution, then the company must take the precaution, whereas if the cost was liable, then it did not have to. However, the BPL formula focuses on a specific accident, while the risk/benefit analysis requires an examination of the costs, risks, and benefits through use of the product as a whole. Based on this analysis, Ford legally chose not to make the design changes which would have made the Pinto safer. However, just because it was legal doesn't necessarily mean that it was ethical. It is difficult to understand how a price can be put on saving a human life.

There are several reasons why such a strictly economic theory should not be used. First, it seems unethical to determine that people should be allowed to die or be seriously injured because it would cost too much to prevent it. Second, the analysis does not take into all the consequences, such as the negative publicity that Ford received and the judgments and settlements resulting from the lawsuits. Also, some things just can't be measured in terms of dollars, and that includes human life. However, there are arguments in favor of the risk/benefit analysis. First, it is well developed through existing case law. Second, it encourages companies to take precautions against creating risks that result in large accident costs. Next, it can be argued that all things must have some common measure. Finally, it provides a bright line which companies can follow.

I. Introduction

In May of 1968, the Ford Motor Company, based upon a recommendation by then vice-president Lee Iacocca, decided to introduce a subcompact car and produce it domestically. In an effort to gain a large market share, the automobile was designed and developed on an accelerated schedule. During the first few years sales of the Pinto were excellent, but there was trouble on the horizon.

A. Grimshaw v. Ford Motor Company[1]

In May 1972, Lily Gray was traveling with thirteen year old Richard Grimshaw in a 1972 Pinto when their car was struck by another car traveling approximately thirty miles per hour. The impact ignited a fire in the Pinto which killed Lily Gray and left Richard Grimshaw with devastating injuries. A judgment was rendered against Ford and the jury awarded the Gray family $560,000 and Matthew Grimshaw $2.5 million in compensatory damages. The surprise came when the jury awarded $125 million in punitive damages as well. This was subsequently reduced to $3.5 million.[2]

B. The Criminal Case[3]

Six month following the controversial Grirnshaw verdict, Ford was involved in yet another controversial case involving the Pinto. The automobile's fuel system design contributed (whether or not it was the sole cause is arguable) to the death of three women on August 10, 1918 when their car was hit by another vehicle traveling at a relatively low speed by a man driving with open beer bottles, marijuana, caffeine pills and capsules of "speed."[4] The fact that Ford had chosen earlier not to upgrade the fuel system design became an issue of public debate as a result of this case. The debate was heightened because the prosecutor of Elkart County, Indiana chose to prosecute Ford for reckless homicide and criminal recklessness.

Some felt the issues raised in the Ford Pinto cases were an example of the "deep pocket" company disregarding consumer safety in pursuit of the almighty dollar. Others feel they are an example of runaway media coverage blowing a story out of proportion.[5] Regardless of opinion, the Ford Pinto case is a tangled web of many complex legal and ethical issues.

To determine if the proper result was achieved in this case, one has to evaluate and weigh these many issues. The central issue in deciding whether Ford should be liable for electing not to redesign a defective product in order to maximize its bottom line, one must analyze the so-called "cost/benefit" analysis Ford used to defend this decision. Within the scope of this paper, this cost/benefit issue (and associated sub-issues) will be the focus of discussion. Other issues, such as the ethics involved in Ford's decision, the choice of prosecuting Ford criminally, whistle-blowing, the assignment of punitive damages and the Court of Appeals decision reducing the damages are all important issues of this case that will not be the focus herein.

II. Facts

A. Incident Facts

On August 10, 1978, three teenage girls stopped to refuel the 1973 Ford Pinto sedan they were driving. After filling up, the driver loosely reapplied the gas cap which subsequently fell off as they headed down U. S. Highway 33. Trying to retrieve the cap, the girls stopped in the right lane of the highway shoulder since there was no space on the highway for cars to safely pull off the roadway. Shortly thereafter, a van weighing over 400 pounds and modified with a rigid plank for a front bumper was traveling at fifty five miles an hour and stuck the stopped Pinto. The two passengers died at the scene when the car burst into flames. The driver was ejected and died shortly thereafter in the hospital. Inspecting the van shortly after the accident, the police found open beer bottles, marijuana and caffeine pills inside.[6]

The subsequent proceedings were rather surprising. Based on the facts of the case, it seemed that any one of a number of parties could be liable in a civil action or prosecuted criminally. The obvious target seemed to be the driver of the van. It seems he could have been prosecuted for criminal homicide or the families of the victims could have pursued a civil action, in light of the fact the driver possessed several controlled substances at the time of the accident.

A second potential party open to a civil suit was the Indiana Highway department. It was their design which left no safe stopping place along Highway 33 where cars could pull over for emergencies. In fact, the road was so dangerous that the Elkart County Citizens' Safety Committee had previously written a letter to the department asking that the road design be modified to provide safe stopping place for emergencies.[7] It is also conceivable, the driver of the Pinto could have been found negligent for stopping a car in the middle of the highway.

The first surprise of the resulting litigation carne when Indiana state prosecutor filed suit against Ford Motor Company for criminal recklessness and reckless homicide.[8] The famous and highly publicized legal battle was underway. Some have argued the prosecution acted unethically from day one, gathering and hiding evidence from the defendant and concealing information about the condition of the van driver.[9] Whether true or not, the following litigation caused damage that would take Ford years to recover from.

B. Questionable Design

The controversy surrounding the Ford Pinto concerned the placement of the automobile's fuel tank. It was located behind the rear axle, instead of above it. This was initially done in an effort to create more trunk space. The problem with this design, which later became evident, was that it made the Pinto more vulnerable to a rear-end collision. This vulnerability was enhanced by other features of the car. The gas tank and the rear axle were separated by only nine inches. There were also bolts that were positioned in a manner that threatened the gas tank. Finally, the fuel filler pipe design resulted in a higher probability that it would to disconnect from the tank in the event of an accident than usual, causing gas spillage that could lead to dangerous fires. Because of these numerous design flaws, the Pinto became the center of public debate.

These design problems were first brought to the public's attention in an August 1977 article in Mother Jones magazine. This article condemned the Ford Motor Company and the author was later given a Pulitzer Prize.[10] This article originated the public debate over the risk/benefit analysis used by the Ford Motor Company in their determination as to whether or, not the design of the Pinto fuel tank be altered to reduce the risk of fire as the result of a collision.

The crux of the public debate about The Ford Motor Company was the decision not to make improvements to the gas tank of the Pinto after completion of the risk/benefit analysis. Internal Ford documents revealed Ford had developed the technology to make improvements to the design of the Pinto that would dramatically decrease the chance of a Pinto "igniting" after a rear-end collision.[11] This technology would have greatly reduced the chances of burn injuries and deaths after a collision. Ford estimated the cost to make this production adjustment to the Pinto would have been $11 per vehicle.[12] Most people found it reprehensible that Ford determined that the $11 cost per automobile was too high and opted not to make the production change to the Pinto model.

C. Risk/Benefit Analysis

In determining whether or not to make the production change, the Ford Motor Company defended itself by contending that it used a risk/benefit analysis. Ford stated that its reason for using a risk/benefit analysis was that the National Highway Traffic Safety Administration (NHTSA) required them to do so.[13] The risk/benefit approach excuses a defendant if the monetary costs of making a production change are greater than the "societal benefit" of that change. This analysis follows the same line of reasoning as the negligence standard developed by Judge Learned Hand in United States vs. Carroll Towing in 1947 (to be discussed later). The philosophy behind risk/benefit analysis promotes the goal of allocative efficiency. The problem that arose in the Ford Pinto and many other similar cases highlights the human and emotional circumstances behind the numbers which are not factored in the risk/benefit analysis.

The Ford Motor Company contended that by strictly following the typical approach to risk,/benefit analysis, they were justified in not making the production change to the Pinto model. Assuming the numbers employed in their analysis were correct, Ford seemed to be justified. The estimated cost for the production change was $11 per vehicle. This $11 per unit cost applied to 11 million cars and 1.5 million trucks results in an overall cost of $137 million.

The controversial numbers were those Ford used for the "benefit" half of the equation. It was estimated that making the change would result in a total of 180 less burn deaths, 180 less serious burn injuries, and 2,100 less burned vehicles. These estimates were multiplied by the unit cost figured by the National Highway Traffic Safety Administration. These figures were $200,000 per death, $67,000 per injury, and $700 per vehicle equating to the total "societal benefit" is $49.5 million. Since the benefit of $49.5 million was much less than the cost of $137 million, Ford felt justified in its decision not to alter the product design. The risk/benefit results indicate that it is acceptable for 180 people to die and 180 people to burn if it costs $11 per vehicle to prevent such casualty rates. On a case by case basis, the argument seems unjustifiable, but looking at the bigger picture complicates the issue and strengthens the risk/benefit analysis logic.

III. History and Development of Product Liability

A. Introduction

When defendants were found liable for only intentional harms, these harms fell under the category of absolute liability. Over time, courts added liability to some accidental harms. In order for a court to determine there was no liability in a conflict, it had to be ascertained whether or not the accident was "truly unavoidable."[14] Technological advances created societal harms that were never before contemplated by courts. The truly unavoidable standard became a grayer area that was undefined and unreliable. Eventually, as industry rapidly advanced further, it became impossible and unreasonable to describe any accident as unavoidable.[15] Still, courts seemed unwilling to shift to the theory of absolute liability, as it seemed to strict. However, with the courts finding fewer and fewer harms "unavoidable", another level had to be found between unavoidable accidents and strict liability.[16]

B. The Ordinary Care Standard

In the mid 1800s, courts began the evolution of moving away from what they once considered an important decision--whether a harm was a result of an action "on trespass" or a harm as a result of an action "on the case."[17] The first landmark decision moving away from this distinction and thinking was Brown v. Kendall[18] in 1850. In the decision, Chief Justice Shaw acknowledged moving away from this traditional distinction and to consideration of whether a harm was "willful, intentional, or careless."[19] Not only did this decision move away from the strict "all or nothing" standard, it established the fluctuating standard of "ordinary care." Judge Shaw explained the use of this new standard:

> "In using this term, ordinary care, it may be proper to state that
> what constitutes ordinary care will vary with the circumstances
> of cases. In general, it means that kind and degree of care,
> which prudent and cautious men would use, such as required
> by the exigency of the case, and such as is necessary to guard
> against probable danger."[20]

In essence Judge Shaw had created a "moving" standard of negligence that varied from situation to situation depending on the extent of care used, rather than the inflexible extremes discussed above. This new standard was not just a flat decision of whether an actor used due care in a situation, but whether the actor should have recognized the danger before taking the risk. Courts also required a defendant's actions be related to the harm incurred. In Crain v. Petrie,[21] the court stated that "damages must appear to be the legal and natural consequences arising from the tort.[22] Courts also considered whether the defendant should have taken some kind of preventive measure in advance that could have foreseeable prevented the harm.[23]

These many factors the court considered boiled down into one main question: Was the accident truly avoidable or the fault of the defendant?[24] The Brown court stated,

> "If, then, in doing this act, using due care and all proper

> precautions necessary to the exigency of the case, to avoid the
> hurt to others, in raising his stick..., he accidentally hit the
> plaintiff in his eye and wounded him, this was the result of the
> pure accident, or was involuntary, and unavoidable, and
> therefore the action would not lie."[25]

This thinking was followed in similar cases and decisions of the time.[26] As stated above, this thinking moved the court from cut-and-dried ideas of negligence to ones that fluctuated and had to be examined on a case by case basis. If an accident seemed to be unavoidable and part of every day life there would be no action for recovery.

As technology progressed, courts began to find less and less accidents "unavoidable." In Huntress v. Boston & Main R.R.,[27] the court found the defendant negligent even though it took all necessary precautions. When a pedestrian was killed walking across the railroad tracks and the locomotive engineer had used all possible precautions in conducting the train, the defendant was still found to be negligent. The court stated that the railroad company should have foreseen the plaintiff's poor appreciation of the risk and that whether more precautions were necessary was a question for the jury.[28] As the power of design and invention advanced, so did the courts' perception of the power to prevent accidents.[29] It seemed the courts had almost moved to the extreme of absolute liability. With this evolution, the courts were faced with a new problem. Should defendants be found liable in almost every situation because of new technological 'advancements? This created a new theory of negligence, one of balancing risks and benefits. In the early 1900s the courts evolved from just determining if an accident were unavoidable (as most at this point were considered to be) to what the costs were to avoid this accident in some fashion. The first attempt to consider this question and create a new standard was in a 1919 case, Adams v. Bullock.[30]

In Adams, a young boy was playing with a rod when it struck the defendant's trolley wires that had been strung under a railroad bridge where the boy was walking. The court reversed a judgment for the plaintiff, claiming that the company had taken all reasonable precautions to avoid the accident. Judge Cardozo's opinion made use of the traditional analysis and verbiage of the avoidable/unavoidable analysis. However, he discussed the "duty to adopt all reasonable precautions.[31] Furthermore, Judge Cardozo stated that the defendant had acted with the area of normal provision.[32]

C. The Introduction of the Balancing Approach

Although Judge Cardozo concluded that the accident was not foreseeable and therefore unavoidable, the Adams case laid the groundwork for a "balancing" approach to negligence. The balancing approach assumes that if an accident has a very low probability, and there is a cost associated with preventing it, a defendant is not liable if he does not take precautionary measures. By stating that absent a "gift of prophecy the defendant could not have predicted the point upon the route where such an accident would occur," Judge Cardozo indicated that giving every possibility the ultimate amount of protection would be too costly compared to the risk of injury.[33] He further stated that guards everywhere would have prevented the injury but this would prove to be much too costly, and "guards here and there are of little value.[34] This decision was the harbinger of the balancing standard and cost/benefit analysis; a weighing of the risk of harm and the overall costs of avoiding it.

At the turn of the century, courts began focusing on this "balancing" method to determine liability. Costs, risks, and probability began to make their way into decisions. Courts began to compare degrees of risks and costs of harms with the benefits of activities on society. The trend moved toward placing the burden on society in instances where the benefit outweighed the risk or the risk was less than the cost to avoid it.[35] In cases such as this, the ``risk initiator" was assigned no liability. This balancing act seemed to be a tolerable middle ground between the old negligence liability standard and the extreme standard of absolute liability.

With courts struggling to define the middle ground during this time of technological advancement, they faced the same questions legal systems faced in similar times such as the industrial revolution and the growth of railroads. As the advancements created new products and the profits that went with them, courts had to decide what levels of risk society could tolerate and who should bear the costs when harms actually occurred.[36]

D. The "BPL" Formula

With the evolution of the negligence standard incorporating risks and costs, courts sought a middle ground that would not leave defendants open for unreasonable liability suits but which also would not leave victims uncompensated when damages had occurred. In the 1947 decision of United States v. Carroll Towing Co.,[37] Judge Learned Hand boiled the theory of negligence down to an algebraic equation. In Carroll Towing, a barge named the "Anna C" was tied up to a pier along with a flotilla of other barges. A tug, the "Carroll," owned by the Carroll Towing Company attempted to move from one barge in the same area to another. During this time, the "Anna C" broke away from the pier and floated down the river where it collided with a tanker and sank. Since there was no bargee on board the "Anna C," no one informed the "Carroll" that the "Anna C" was leaking. Because of this, the "Anna C" sank and its cargo was lost. Under admiralty law, if the defendants could prove that plaintiff's negligence contributed to the loss, they would be excused from paying a portion of the damage.[38] The defendant's argument was based on the fact that since there was no bargee present, the plaintiff was also liable. However, there was no general rule as to whether the presence of a bargee would make the owner of the barge liable for lost cargo and injuries to other boats.

Judge Hand attempted to quantify a criteria to determine when leaving a barge unattended was negligence and when it was not. He decided that this would be determined by a weighing of the factors discussed above. Judge Hand transformed the "balancing act" utilized in prior decisions. In his opinion, he wrote:

> "Since there are occasions when every vessel will break from her moorings, and since, if she does, she becomes a menace to those about her; the owner's duty, as in other similar situations, to provide against resulting injuries is a function of three variables: (1) The probability that she will break away; (2) the gravity of the resulting injury, if she does; (3) the burden of adequate precautions. Possibly it serves to bring this notion into relief to state it.in algebraic terms: if the probability be called P; the injury, and the burden, B; liability depends upon whether B is less than L multiplied by P."[39]

Under the theory that Judge Hand developed in Carroll, a party is found negligent and liable for the damages resulting from his actions if B<PL. "B," the burden of adequate precautions, is the accident avoidance cost. "P" is the probability the defendant's actions will result in an accident. "L" is the cost of that accident if it did occur. "PL" is the risk of the activity, the expected liability of the discounted accident cost.[40] The negligence standard had been formalized into algebraic terms. If the expected harm exceeded the cost to take precaution, the defendant was obligated to take the precaution, and if they did not, would be held liable. If the cost was larger than the expected harm, the defendant was not expected to take the precaution. If there was an accident, he was not found liable. Based on the facts of Carroll Towing, the defendant was found liable. Judge Hand felt the expected harm (the probability of the accident, multiplied by the cost of the accident) was greater than the justification for a one and a half day absence of a bargee.[41]

E. Risk/Utility Analysis

Risk/utility analysis then developed out of the same balancing reasoning, applied to determine liability in the area of product design. In these types of cases, courts must determine whether a manufacturer should be held liable if goods are "imperfect" as a result of production or distribution. In past cases, courts had difficulty in this area. In Greenman v. Yuba Power Products, Inc.,[42] a 1963 case, the court stated that the defendant was not able to see the possibility for injury until after the injury occurred and by traditional negligence standards should be found not liable.[43] This type of conclusion troubled the courts, since the burden on the plaintiff seemed almost insurmountable.

There were a number of reasons why this type of finding was unfair. First and foremost, companies' manufacturing operations are the party in control of the product from its inception. Manufacturing divisions have a chance to monitor design and distribution and therefore seems the logical party to be held liable if the design of its product leads to an injury. However, it seems illogical for the consumer to bear the burden of a harm it had absolutely no control over. Also, requiring manufacturers to be liable for their products makes them take more precautionary measures, the cost of which can be spread out in the price of its products to the consumers who make use of them.[44] The problem was the same, however. Where is the middle ground between the earlier standard and absolute liability and how is it defined?

The first step in finding this middle ground in manufacturing liability cases was to remove requirements of warranty and privity of contract that manufacturers used to escape liability in the past.[45] In Greenman, the court stated that removing the obstacles earlier set by warranty law put manufacturer's liability in the correct realm. This area was "not one governed by the law of contract warranties but by the law of strict liability in tort ... A manufacturer is strictly liable in tort when an article he places in the market... proves to have a defect that causes injury to a human being."[46] The obvious question therefore was, what is a "defective product"?[47]

The definition provided by section 402A of the Second Restatement of Torts assigned strict liability to products with "a condition not contemplated by the ultimate consumer, which will be unreasonably dangerous to him ... Many products cannot possibly be made entirely safe for all consumption, and any food or drug necessarily involves some harm, if only from overcomsumption."[48] Obviously, there was intended to be some leeway short of strict liability for manufacturers, but there was still no clear answer as to what was defective and what was not.[49]

Attempting to end the frustration and quantify "defective product," courts started to turn to a risk-utility balancing similar to Judge Learned Hand's "BPL Formula." This evolved into a balancing of the benefits of the product against the risks and the cost of avoidance. In Caterpillar Tractor Co. v. Beck,[50] the court stated the jury could be instructed a product is defectively designed if "the plaintiff proves that the product's design proximately caused injury and the defendant fails to prove in the light of relevant factors, that on balance the benefits of the challenged design outweigh the risk of the danger inherit in .such design."[51] In Turner v. General Motors Corp,[52] the court stated that "a defectively designed product is one that is unreasonably dangerous as designed, taking into consideration the utility of the product and the risk involved in its use."[53]

After long debate, the courts have settled upon this risk/benefit analysis. For a defendant to be found liable, its product must be determined to be defective. A defect can take three forms: a defect in design (as was alleged against the Ford Motor Company), a defect in manufacture, or a defect in warning. In Ford's case, if the design is found to be defective, the company would be held liable. The question remains, what makes a design defective?

While not stated neatly in algebraic terms, such as in the BPL analysis, this entails a balancing of utility and risks. This standard is not easily quantified and must be decided on a case-by-case basis by juries. They must decide in each instance whether the risks associated with the product are reasonable for society to absorb given the benefits of the product. Therefore, the duty of the jury is not to decide whether the conduct of the manufacturer is reasonable, but whether the product, after the full ramifications are revealed, is reasonable. The difference is that risk/utility analysis requires a determination of the costs, risks and benefits of society's use of the product as a whole, while the 13PL cost/benefit analysis entailed determining the costs and benefits of preventing the particular accident. In the end, the risk-utility's primary duty is to establish a threshold of acceptable risk that every good must equal or exceed, a threshold that can rise with changing social and commercial experience.[54] This leads to a economically efficient use of resources and overall wealth maximization.

F. Ford's Risk/Benefit Analysis

The main controversy surrounding the Ford Pinto case was The Ford Motor Company's choices made during development to compromise safety for efficiency and profit maximization. More specifically, it was Ford's decision to use the cost/benefit analysis detailed in section 11 to make production decisions that translated into lost lives. During the initial production and testing phase, Ford set "limits for 2000" for the Pinto. That meant the car was not to exceed $2000 in cost or 2000 pounds in weight. This set tough limitations on the production team. After the basic design was complete, crash testing was begun. The results of crash testing revealed that when struck from the rear at speeds of 31 miles per hour or above, the Pinto's gas tank ruptured. The tank was positioned according to the industry standard at the time (between the rear bumper and the rear axle), but studs protruding from the rear axle would puncture the gas tank.

Upon impact, the fuel filler neck would break, resulting in spilled gasoline. The Pinto basically turned into a death trap. Ford crash tested a total of eleven automobiles and eight resulted in potentially catastrophic situations. The only three that survived had their gas tanks modified prior to testing.[55]

Ford was not in violation of the law in any way and had to make the decision whether to incur a cost to fix the obvious problem internally. There were several options for fuel system redesign. The option most seriously considered would have cost the Ford Motor Company and additional $11 per vehicle.[56] Under the strict $2000 budget restriction, even this nominal cost seemed large. In addition, Ford had earlier based an advertising campaign on safety which failed miserably. Therefore, there was a corporate belief, attributed to Lee Iacocca himself, of "safety doesn't sell."[57]

Ultimately, the Ford Motor Company rejected the product design change. This was based on the cost-benefit analysis performed by Ford (see Exhibit One). Using the NHTSA provided figure of $200,000 for the "cost to society" for each estimated fatality, and $11 for the production cost per vehicle, the analysis seemed straightforward. The projected costs to the company for design production change were $137 million compared to the project benefits of making the design change which were approximately $49.5 million. Using the standard cost/benefit analysis, the answer was obvious--no production changes were to be made.

Exhibit One: Ford's Cost/Benefit Analysis

Benefits and Costs Relating to Fuel Leakage Associated with the Static Rollover Test Portion of FMVSS 208

Benefits

Savings: 180 burn deaths, 180 serious burn injuries, 2100 burned vehicles
Unit Cost: $200,000 per death, $67,000 per injury, $700 per vehicle
Total Benefit: 180 x ($200,000) + 180 x ($67,000) + 2100 x ($700)
= $49.5 Million

Costs

Sales: 11 million cars, 1.5 million light trucks
Unit Cost: $11 per car, $11 per truck
Total Cost: 11,000,000 x ($11) + 1,500,000 x ($I 1) = **$137 Million**

From Ford Motor Company internal memorandum: "Fatalities Associated with Crash--Induced Fuel Leakage and Fires." Source: Douglas Birsch and John H. Fielder, THE FORD PINTO CASE: A STUDY IN APPLIED ETHICS. BUSINESS, AND TECHNOLOGY. p. 28.1994.

IV. The Negligence Efficiency Argument

A. Ford's Decision

The Ford Motor Company's use of the risk/benefit analysis was the central issue of the suits filed against the company. Many pieces of evidence, including a number of internal Ford documents indicate the risk/benefit analysis was the main reason for Ford's decision not to make design changes to increase vehicle safety. However, before discussion of the risk/benefit analysis it should be noted there were secondary concerns which supported Ford's decision not to upgrade the fuel system design: (1) As stated above, Ford had based an earlier advertising campaign around safety, which failed. The company realized this was not a primary factor in car sales; (2) the bad publicity involved with a recall would be too much negative publicity to overcome. If this unquantifiable factor were included in the cost/benefit analysis the difference may have been overwhelming. Even though it was not a factor included in the analysis, Ford wanted to avoid it at any cost; (3) At the time of the product design and crash tests, the law did not require them to redesign the fuel system; and, (4) It was customary in the automotive industry to place the gas tank and between the rear axle and bumper.

Although case law has shown that business custom is not an excuse to escape liability, custom combined with the risk/benefit analysis would lead to the same result.[58] With these factors influencing the decision in the background, the primary factor was Ford's risk/benefit analysis of making the changes. The question is: Should a risk/benefit analysis be used in all circumstances, and was it the proper framework to use in this situation? If so, it seems that the correct decision was made. Examining this question after-the-fact, it certainly seems like a poor decision.

B. The Numbers

The Ford Motor Company's risk/benefit analysis indicated costs would be 2.5 times larger than the resulting benefits. It is apparent why Ford chose no to go ahead with the fuel tank adjustment. However, basing this decision on just the numbers with no consideration of any other factors falls short of a comprehensive analysis of the action. chose not to go ahead with the fuel tank adjustment. To do a complete job of analyzing Ford's decision, the variables inside the equation must be examined. On the cost side of the equation, the most questioned variable during the case was the cost per vehicle used by Ford. The manufacturer claimed making adequate changes to the fuel system would have cost $11 per vehicle. Some evidence indicated that these potential costs may have been much lower, maybe as low as $5 per vehicle.[59] Even with this lower cost and all other factors remaining the same, the costs still would have exceeded the benefits, although the difference would have been much less substantial (see Exhibit 2). In fact, will all other variables remaining the same, the cost per vehicle would have had to be as low as $3.96 to make the benefits "break even" with the costs (see Exhibit 3). However, if the costs were around $5 per vehicle, the Ford Motor Company would not have had as strong a risk/benefit argument as with the $11 figure provided.

Exhibit Two: Ford's Cost/Benefit Analysis at $5.08 Per Fuel Tank Replacement

Benefits

Savings: 180 burn deaths, 180 serious burn injuries, 2100 burned vehicles
Unit Cost: $200,000 per death, $67,000 per injury, $700 per vehicle
Total Benefit: 180 x ($2,00,000) + 180 x ($67,000) + 2100 x ($700) = **$49.5 Million**

Costs

Sales: 11 million cars, 1.5 million light trucks
Unit Cost: $5.08 per car, $5.08 per truck
Total Cost: 11,000,000 x ($5.08) + 1,500,000 x ($5.08) = **$63.5 Million**

Exhibit Three: The Break Even Point of the Cost/Benefit Analysis

Benefits

Savings: 180 burn deaths, 180 serious burn injuries, 2100 burned vehicles
Unit Cost: $200,000 per death, $67,000 per injury, $700 per vehicle
Total Benefit: 180 x ($200,000) + 180 x ($67,000) + 2100 x ($700)
= $49.5 Million

Costs

Sales: 11 million cars, 1.5 million light trucks
Unit Cost: $5.08 per car, $5.08 per truck
Total Cost: 11,000,000 x ($3.96) + 1,500,000 x ($3.96) = **$49.5**
Million
Therefore, if the cost to replace the fuel tank was $3.96 per vehicle, the costs and benefits would equal each other out (all other things remaining the same).

The "benefit side" of the equation contains the most controversial number of the analysis--the value of a human life. Ford estimated no alterations to the gas tank design would result in 180 deaths, 180 burn victims and 2100 burned vehicles. In retrospect, these estimates are slightly low. It is hard to determine the exact number of victims because every victim did not file a claim, but these numbers were reasonable estimations at the time. Ford used $200,000 as the "cost" or "lost benefit" for each fatal burn injury, 567,000 for each burn injury and $700 for each burned vehicle. The number quantifying the price of a value life ($200,000) is what makes this problem so difficult. It is hard to decide what a life is worth, but most people feel the value of theirs is greater than $200,000. While this $200,000 figure was the most controversial of the equation, it was not determined by Ford. In 1972, the National Highway Traffic Safety Administration (NHTSA) provided the auto industry with the number $200,725 as the value to be utilized in risk/ benefit analysis such as was done by Ford (see Exhibit 4).[60]

Exhibit Four: What is a Life Worth?
Societal Cost Components for Fatalities
1972 NHTSA Study

Component	1971 Costs
Future Productivity Losses	
Direct	$ 132,000
Indirect	$ 41,300
Medical Costs	
Hospital	$ 700
Other	$ 425
Property Damage	$ 1,500
Insurance Administration	$ 4,700
Legal and Court	$ 3,000

Employer Losses	$ 1,000
Victim's Pain and Suffering	$ 10,000
Funeral	$ 900
Assets (Lost Consumption)	$ 5,000
Miscellaneous	$ 200
Total Per Fatality	**$ 200,725**

Source: Douglas Birsch and John H. Fielder, THE FORD PINTO CASE: A STUDY IN APPLIED ETHICS, BUSINESS. AND TECHNOLOGY, p. 26, 1994.

Following the standard for negligence established by Judge Learned Hand in Carroll Towing, or the risk/utility standard established for manufacturer's liability, the decision was well founded. The costs to Ford to make this change, which would have been borne by the consumer, was 2.5 times higher (using the original numbers) than the benefit to society. Some negative publicity may have been expected, but certainly Ford did not anticipate being found criminally negligent. In fact, it would seem Ford had a strong argument against any liability whatsoever. The decision in the liability suit with the award of punitive damages was a surprise to the Ford Motor Company, much less the criminal prosecution. How could such a decision be rendered after Ford Motor Company had followed the standard set by the courts themselves? The answer lies in the fact that the "benefit" side of the equation included the benefit of saving lives, and putting a value on this variable is not as defensible as putting a value on the benefit of saving an inanimate object, such as a vehicle.

V. The Negligence-Efficiency Debate

A. Introduction

The Ford Motor case has spurned the arguments for and against the use of risk/benefit analysis because of its foundation of economic efficiency. The Ford Motor Company case has spurred this argument. In 1972, Judge Richard Posner's article on the negligence-efficiency theory seemed to be the "starting point" for this argument and was both highly praised and highly criticized. The essence of this article is summarized in the following excerpt: "We lack a theory to explain the social function of the negligence concept ... This article attempts to formulate and test such a theory.... The essential clue, I believe, is provided by Judge Learned Hand's famous formulation of the negligence standard.... In a negligence case, Hand said, the judge (or jury) should attempt to measure three things: the magnitude of the loss if an accident occurs; the probability of the accident's occurring; and the burden of taking precautions that would avert it. If the product of the first two terms exceeds the burden of precautions, the failure to take those precautions is negligence. Hand was adumbrating, perhaps unwittingly, an economic meaning of negligence.... If the cost of safety measures.... exceeds the benefit in accident avoidance to be gained by incurring that cost, society would be better off, in economic terms, to forego accident prevention.... Furthermore, overall economic value or welfare would be diminished ... by incurring a higher accident-prevention cost to avoid a lower accident cost."[61]
Thus, the economic efficiency of negligence argument was born. While many economists have agreed and praised this article, it has been equally criticized by those not taking the "economic point of view." I will first discuss some of the many arguments against this economic efficiency point of view in light of the Ford Pinto case. Following is a further elaboration of Posner's view and defense of his position.

B. Arguments Against Negligence-Efficiency

1. Ethics

Taking an ethical approach to the Ford Pinto case makes accepting the risk/benefit analysis performed by the Ford Motor Company difficult. In making what seems to be the correct decision based on numbers, Ford is essence adopted a policy of allowing a certain number of people to die or be injured even though they could have prevented it. When taken on a case-by-case basis the decision seems to be a blatant disregard for human life. From a human rights perspective, Ford disregarded the injured individual's rights and therefore, in making the decision not to make adjustments to the fuel system, acted unethically.[62]

2. Act Utilitarianism

A second problem with strictly applying the risk/benefit framework is that it does not seem to take into account all of the consequences of Ford's decision. This position is considered the "act utilitarian' point of view. The act utilitarian approach evaluates each action separately and the consequences that arise from it.[63] This analysis would include any "harms" or "benefits" incurred by any people involved in the case. In utilizing this approach, it seems there are many factors that the Ford Motor Company did not account for in its risk/benefit analysis. When taking the situation from this perspective, it seems like the harms of not changing the fuel system outweighed the benefits. Not included in the previous risk/benefit analysis was the millions of dollars in settlements in unreported cases that never saw the courtroom. It is almost a sure bet that the settlement numbers were more on a per-case basis than the average numbers used for lost life per accident. Also, the bad publicity and reputational damage suffered by Ford over the next few years for being the cause of these lawsuits is hard to quantify, but the harm was considerable.[64] >From the utilitarian point of view, the harms and the benefits are far closer together than Ford determined in its analysis. In addition, if this was figured after-the-fact the harms far outweighed the benefits. This would be due to the cost of having to recall the 1971-1976 Pintos after the fact and the extreme bad publicity (much worse than could have been expected) that the Ford Motor Company suffered through for years after all litigation was settled.

3. Health and Safety Regulation Exception

Critics argue there are several other related, yet distinct reasons why the Ford Motor company, as well other companies finding themselves in similar positions, should be condemned for relying on a risk/benefit analysis to make decisions based on consumer safety. In the areas of safety and health regulation, there are instances where it may not be wise to undertake a certain decision even though the benefits do not outweigh the costs.[65] This idea is imbedded somewhere between the utilitarian point of view and ethical point of view, discussed above. That is, the issue of whether the benefits outweigh the costs should not govern our moral judgment. There are some cases where a company must "do the right thing." While this may seem an argument based on emotion, there seem to be certain instances where these kind of considerations must be made. For instance, when governmental officials decide what level of pollution is allowable they take into effect certain vulnerable people--such as asthmatics or the elderly--and set the standard higher although the average citizen would not be affected by a lower one. This decision escapes the risk/benefit analysis. The higher standard is set so that the rights of the minority are not sacrificed for the needs of the majority. This kind of decision, much like automobile safety, are in the realm of specially valued things. For these, many will argue, risk/benefit analysis should not apply.[66]

4. Expressing Terms in Dollar Values

In order to perform a risk/benefit analysis, all costs and benefits must be expressed in some common measure. This measure is typically in dollars, as the Ford Motor Company used in its analysis. This can prove difficult for things that are not commonly bought and sold on the open market. This is mainly the case for environmental policy, such as permissible levels of air pollutants, as in the example above.[67] The Ford Pinto case provides an extreme example. It questions how to value human life.

Economists have attempted to quantify, non-quantifiable items using varying methods with varying success.[68] Since individuals have unique tastes and values they are willing to pay different amounts for products and resources. This valuation system often receives high criticism. People's willingness to pay for something can also vary widely depending upon other circumstances. Based on these reasons, attempts to quantify something such as a human life can be very difficult and is the most debated aspect of the Ford Pinto case.

There are numerous things which individuals consider "priceless." For instance, most people would claim that they would not sell their right to vote or their freedom of speech for any amount of money.[69] Therefore, to tell someone that there is a certain price for their life is a preposterous notion. Therefore when taken on a case-by-case basis it is impossible for an individual to grasp the concept. There are numerous things which individuals consider "priceless." For instance, most people would claim that they would not sell their right to vote or their freedom of speech for any amount of money. Moreover, would a parent be able to put a value on the life of a child? Obviously, the notion that, on an individual basis, a person would take a certain amount of money for their life is ludicrous. To tell someone that $200,725 is a sufficient trade-off for their life, as argued in the Ford Pinto case, illustrates this point.

Economists, however, do not agree with the "priceless" concept. To them, to trade one unit of anything, even a life, for an infinite quantity of all other goods is an equally preposterous notion. It can be argued that everything can be priced or have a value laid upon it. To take this theory down to an individual level reduces the strength of this notion.

In Ford's case, the $200,725 value of a human life was provided to the company by the National Highway Traffic Safety Administration. The criticism for the value can not be laid upon Ford. The criticism is in using a number, or in other words using the risk/benefit analysis, in this situation at all. To compound the problem, Ford seemed to blindly follow the dictated numbers without giving any extra consideration to the fact that it in fact was a human life they were quantifying.

5. No Wealth Maximization

Related to the lack of "markets" or "prices" for a life is the idea of wealth maximization. The foundation of the risk/benefit analysis is the theory of economic efficiency and an underlying principle for efficiency is wealth maximization. If legal decisions are based on efficiency, then nothing will be wasted and the wealth of the country will be at its maximum.[70] However, in order to conduct an efficiency analysis, everything must have a price--returning to the reoccurring problem. Since the reliance on prices is necessary and not merely contingent, the system of wealth maximization cannot tell us anything about right conduct where no prices exist. Prices are, in part, the result of demand and demand is the result of prior entitlements. Consequently, wealth maximization cannot generate an initial set of entitlements."[71]

Along the same lines, efficiency theory assumes that wealth maximization is the goal of law, which is not the case. The goal of law is the indefinable term. "justice."[72] Judges and juries do not attempt to make decisions based on wealth maximization, they base their decisions on justice. This difference can be seen in the special rules for rescue, handicapped citizens, and whether the insane are found liable for their torts.[73]

6. Externalities

Another potential problem with the risk,/benefit approach is the fact that it does not take externalities into effect. This is a topic with which the law of torts often has trouble. However, it cannot be ignored just because it is hard to compute.[74] Victims are permitted to recover for pain and suffering and the cost/benefit analysis seems to ignore this point. It is yet another one of the variables that is almost impossible to estimate, much less pinpoint. In addition, this is another area where the lack of a market is influential. Minimization of social costs differs from the minimization of private costs precisely because there is an absence of complete markets, and this absence is exactly what makes measurements so difficult.[75]

7. Activity Frequency

If a company or a court were to accurately analyze the costs and benefits of an activity, it must calculate the number of times the potential victim engages in the activity.[76] Taking out the number of times the activity is engaged in reduces the damages. This calculation is often unobtainable, especially in Ford's case in terms of automobile use. Professor Polinsky, in his book, An Introduction to Law and Economics explains, "In practice it is usually not feasible to include the level of participation in the activity has an aspect of the standard of care. For example, it would be virtually impossible for a court to determine bow many miles a particular person drives each. year since that person might drive a different car that is shared with other family members or he might drive different cars owned by the household. If the injurer's level of participation in the activity is omitted from the standard of care, than a negligence rule generally will lead him to participate in the activity to an excess degree. The reason for this is straightforward, if the care he exercises meets the standard of care, be will not be liable for any damages. In practice, the negligence rule is likely to be inefficient for this reason.[77]

8. Negligence is Predictable: Victims Often Lose

Finally, the cost/benefit analysis and economic efficiency reasoning is argued to be a skewed framework because it does not take into account the fact that injured parties are at a disadvantage. While the law attempts to place the plaintiff and defendant on equal ground, it is impossible to accomplish. The plaintiff must prove the negligence, a difficult task. The negligence-efficiency theory does not account for plaintiffs who cannot afford to bring a lawsuit to trial or those who cannot establish negligence although it exists. With the adoption of the negligence-efficiency theory, it is predictable that victims are going to lose more than. They are going to win.[78]

9. Conclusion

Obviously there are a number of arguments against the use of cost/benefit analysis and the negligence-efficiency theory. Most of these arguments are separate but related and .revolve around the fact that there are no markets or prices for human life. It will be forever debated whether it is possible to set a price or value on a life to use in these calculations and whether this leads to an economically efficient outcome In the case of Grimshaw, the jury was obviously appalled with Ford's attempt to apply the NHTSA's calculation to risk/benefit standard. Was this a sign of this standard's inefficiency or was it just a sign of an ineffective jury?

C. For Negligence-Efficiency

For as many arguments as there are against risk/benefit analysis, there are as many claiming it is economically efficient and therefore the correct standard. In defense of the Ford Motor Company, this standard developed over many years of caselaw, as detailed earlier in this paper. This negligence standard and the use of risk/benefit analysis for product liability had been accepted by courts for years before the Pinto controversy. There was no reason for Ford to believe that this was not the standard that should be used in making its decision. Ford's automatic decision once it "ran the numbers" confirms the fact that they did not question the idea of using this analysis. In addition, there are many arguments in support of this sort of analysis other than just the fact that this was the standard at the time.

1. Risk/benefit Analysis is "Instinctively Done"

In 1972, Judge Richard Posner wrote an article entitled, "A Theory of Negligence," claiming all tort law furthers economic efficiency. He claims that while judges do not write opinions in terms of welfare economics, there has always been an effort to decide cases on this basis. "People can apply the principles of economics intuitively--and thus 'do' economics without knowing they are doing it."[79] Therefore, Posner claims that the Carroll Towing decision was not a novel concept, it just expressed in algebraic terms what court had long been applying.[80]

2. Maximization of Social Resources

For defendants, such as the Ford Motor Company, who create risks of harm that may be suffered by others, the risk-benefit standard for negligence provides incentives to take precautions to avoid or minimize risks that can be avoided more cheaply than the cost of the precautions. By holding a defendant liable for injuries that could have been avoided at less cost than the accident, a risk-benefit test acts as a deterrent to curb risks that are worth avoiding, while allowing a defendant to take actions or avoid precautions that are not worth deterring. Deterring conduct that results in greater accident costs than the benefits of the conduct minimizes the total costs of accidents and accident precaution. Therefore, it seems this tort "policy" serves the goal of maximizing societal resources.[81]

To understand the efficiency theory of the risk-benefits analysis, one other point must be explained. In a products liability design defects case, use of the discussed liability standard requires identification of an alternative design that would have prevented the accident. One must be able to compare the additional costs created by the alternative design, in relation to the existing design, with the costs of the injuries that the alternative design could prevent.[82] In the Pinto case, Ford obviously undertook this analysis, examining the additional $11 cost per unit of changing the fuel system design.

3. Economic Feasibility of Valuing Non-Economic Items

The decision to use a risk/benefit analysis does not necessarily result in the strict utilitarianism as suggested by some critics.[83] Most all detractors of cost/benefit analysis center their argument around the idea that placing a value on "non-economic" items, such as a human life, does not lead to economic efficiency. Proponents of the system claim their risk/benefit analysis is nothing more than what it claims to be--an effort to find some common measure for things that are not easily comparable, yet must be compared. While this may seem crass--comparing lives to dollars--some comparison must be made and all the factors in the equation must be brought down to a common denominator for the comparison to take place. Other instances arise where lives are traded against lives, just not brought down to the dollar amount that took place in the Ford Pinto case. In the choice between hospital beds and preventive treatment, lives are traded against lives.[84] It is when the analysis is taken down to an individual level that it becomes problematic. Economists dispel the related argument just as easily. The idea that if one can quantify "non-economic" items, there are certain "specially valued" things that cannot be priced. It is true that different individuals value certain things differently, but simply because an individual deems something has "special value" does not mean that they are unaffected by economic factors. One may specially value a personal relationship, but how often he calls this person is influenced by long-distance rates. One may specially value music or watching sporting events, but still can be affected by the price of records and tickets to the Kennedy Center or the price for watching events on cable or a ticket to the ball game.[85]

4. Efficiency Does Not Equal Immoral

Critics look at risk/benefit analysis in cases such as the Ford Pinto case as a depravity of morality. The idea is that everyone has the "right" to a safe and healthy workplace, or the "right" to expect product they purchase to be safe.[86] Those who subscribe to this philosophy feel there are some "moral" decisions that must be made no matter what the fiscal impacts may be or what the risk,/benefit relationship dictates. Proponents of the risk/benefit analysis counter this "ethical" argument with the idea that these are not either/or decisions being made, but rather gradations of risk.[87] That is, Ford is not sacrificing all safety features of the Pinto, it is a question of to what degree Ford feels safety features are necessary. It could be argued that the safety question was answered for them prior to the risk/benefit analysis when Ford's earlier advertising campaign based on safety failed. Decisions involving gradation of risks are made every day, just not under such strict scrutiny. Obviously, highways would be safer if the speed were restricted to 25 miles per hour on all roads. However, this must be balanced with the "price" of slower traffic. in choosing 55 or 65 as the speed limit, we are sacrificing lives to make travel quicker and less costly. Therefore, the Ford Motor Company is not morally void for choosing between levels of safety. Auto manufacturers do this every day.

5. No Standard for Using an "Ethical Balancing"

All of the arguments against the use of risk/benefit analysis seem to center around the "ethical argument." Instead of a monetary system, sire should adopt an ethical system that balances conflicts between certain unspecified duties and rights according to "deliberate reflection.[88] While placing dollar amounts on these items is admittedly arbitrary, the "ethical" method would open a much larger debate. Who would be in charge of this ethical reflecting and on whose behalf would these decisions be made? There would be no clear limits for the actions of regulatory agencies. What public values would rise above these vague guidelines? Finding or arriving at a consensus for this ethical standard is virtually impossible.

6. Conclusion

In conclusion, all of the arguments against Judge Posner's negligence-efficiency argument center around valuing human life. Is it possible to set a price for all things, especially a human life? Is it ethically correct to attempt to do such a thing? Should a company be allowed to use this standard to determine whether to "upgrade" an automobile. The answer to all of these questions is yes. The use of the risk/benefit analysis maximizes overall economic value and general welfare. In fact, these choices are subconsciously made by individuals, companies and governmental agencies on an everyday basis. Judge Posner argues this standard was used long before Judge Learned Hand first expressed it in algebraic terms in Carroll Towing. While criticizing the numbers or values used by the Ford Motor Company in the risk/benefit analysis may be valid, the use of the risk/benefit analysis itself cannot be questioned.

VI. Conclusion

Through years of case law, the negligence and products liability standard has evolved. Many will argue that courts have "subconsciously" used cost/benefit analysis for many decades, especially with the old "reasonable man" standard. However, Judge Hand finally established this standard in Carroll Towing, explicit acknowledging the "BPL" formula. Judge Posner gave the standard a ringing endorsement in an article in 1972, defending it on economic efficiency grounds. Since that time it has been the source of hot debate.

While not absolutely perfect, the risk/benefit standard for negligence advances overall economic value and welfare, is economically efficient, and therefore is the correct standard to apply (or at least the best option). Criticism of the standard almost always occurs when looking at the standard on an individual case-by-case basis. Critics and laypeople have a difficulty valuing non-economic entities as is required by the formula. Approaching it in this manner, it seems insulting to place a monetary value on a life. This is where the efficiency standard ran into trouble in the Ford Pinto case. One must realize these "valuations" and determinations are part of everyday public policy. In determining safety and environmental standards, a choice must be made as to what level these areas should be regulated.

The Ford Motor Company was not wrong in applying this risk/benefit standard. While the numbers the company used in its analysis may be questioned, the decision to employ the framework which resulted in the decision not to redesign the fuel system shouldn't be. Ford ran into the; trouble of taking this framework and having to justify it on a individual case basis, as a result of the lawsuits. In addition, the Ford Motor Company was an attractive defendant to find liable. The jury's disgust with the deep--pocketed defendant and the troubling value of a life concept was evidenced by the ridiculous punitive damage award initially granted to the plaintiff Obviously, one cannot assume a jury will understand the economic efficiency of the risk/benefit analysis. Even if they do, who knows what they will decide anyway? This fact raises the question--If the Hand risk/benefit formula is truly used to decide negligence cases as Judge Posner claims, why isn't the jury instructed about it.[89]

In conclusion, this framework is economically efficient and the proper one to apply. However, companies beware. The result of the Ford Pinto case indicate there is a belief held by most of the public that it is wrong for a corporation to make decisions which may sacrifice the lives of its customers in order to reduce the company's cost or increase its profits.[90] With this widespread attitude among those who make up juries, trial lawyers would not be wise; to defend cases on the economic analysis of why it was not efficient to redesign a faulty model. Instead, trial lawyers argue that the alternative design compromises the product's function or creates different risks in the product, but not that the costs of the alternative design outweigh the injury or death toll that may be avoided.[91] These options did not seem plausible in Ford's case, which spelled trouble. Therefore, while it may be valid economic efficiency reasoning, the Ford Motor Company and others are forced to think twice before utilizing a risk/benefit analysis in their decision making process.

1. Grimshaw v. Ford Motor Co., 1 19 Cal.App.3d 757, 174 Cal. Rptr. 348 (1981).

2. In the resulting suits against Ford, the jury--after deliberating for eight hours--awarded the Gray family wrongful death damages of $560,000; Grimshaw was awarded over $2.5 million in compensatory damages and $125 million in punitive damages as well. The trial judge reduced the punitive damage award to $3.5 million as a condition for denying a new trial. Two years after the court of appeals affirmed these results in all respects, the state supreme court then denied a hearing. See Gary T. Schwartz, The Myth of the Ford Pinto Case, 43 Rutgers L. Rev. 1013, 1015 (1991).

3. State v. Ford Motor Co., Cause No. 11-431 (1980).

4. See Malcom E. Wheeler, Product Liability, Civil or Criminal -- The Pinto Litigation, ABA, Tort and Insurance Law Journal, 14, 1981.

5. See Douglas Birsch and John H. Fielder, THE FORD PINTO CASE: A STUDY IN APPLIED ETHIC'S, BUSINESS, AND TECHNOLOGY, 1994.

6. See Wheeler, supra note 4, at 15.

7. Id.

8. The prosecutor of Elkhart County, Indiana, chose to seek an indictment against Ford Motor Company for reckless homicide and criminal recklessness, claiming that the cause of the deaths was the design of the Pinto and Ford's failure to "remove the car from the highways" before August 10, 1978. See Wheeler, supra note 4, at 15.

9. The prosecutor obtained information against the van driver for possession of amphetamines. Rather than promptly proceeding to judgment and sentencing on that charge, he kept those charges hanging over the van driver's head until after March 1980, when the driver had testified against Ford and the trial of Ford had ended. Moreover, the pills reported as amphetamines in the official police report were later analyzed and determined to be caffeine pills:, but that information was concealed from Ford's lawyers until after the driver took the stand at trial, and the charge of

possessing amphetamines was kept pending throughout the trial. See Wheeler, supra note 4, at 15.

10. Mark Dowie, Pinto Madness, Mother Jones 18 (Sept./Oct. 1977).

11. Goodyear had developed a bladder and demonstrated it to the automotive industry. On December 2, 1970, Ford Motor Company ran a rear-end crash test on a car with the rubber bladder in the gas tank. The tank ruptured, but no fuel leaked. On January 15, 1971, Ford again tested the bladder and it worked. Mark Dowie, Pinto Madness, Mother Jones, Sept./Oct. 1977, at 20.

12. The total purchase and installation cost of the bladder would have been $5.08 per car. Mark Dowie, Pinto Madness, Mother Jones, Sept./Oct. 1977, at 20.

13. Ford contended that its reason for making the cost/benefit analysis was that the National Highway Traffic Safety Administration required them to do so. Moreover, Ford said that the NHTSA supplied them with the $200,000 as the figure for the value of a lost life. Richard A. Posner, TORTS: CASES AND ECONOMIC ANALYSIS 725 (1983).

14. Barbara Ann White, Risk-Utility Analysis and the Learned Hand Formula: A Hand That Helps or a Hand That Hides?, 32 Ariz. L. Rev. 77, 81 (1990).

15. "A perfect locomotive engine, properly equipped and properly run, will not ordinarily throw out sufficient sparks to destroy adjoining property." Judson v. Giant Powder Co., 107 Cal. 549, 500, 40 P. 1021, 1023 (1985).

16. See White, supra note 12, at 82.

17. Id. at 88.

18. Brown v. Kendall., 60 Mass. (6 Cush.) 292 (1850).

19. Id. at 294-95 (emphasis added).

20. Id. at 296.

21. Crain v. Petrie, 6 Hill 522 (ICY. Sup. Ct. 1844).

22. Id. at 524.

23. See White, supra note 12, at 90.

24. The inquiry into defendant's knowledge and actions was framed in a way to determine if the harm was really the result of a convolution of events rather than defendant's conscious deeds. 1fd. at 90.

25. 60 Mass. (6 Cush.) 292, 297 (1850).

26. In Vincent v. Stinehour, 7 Vt. 62 (1835), the court stated, "If the horse, upon a sudden surprise, run away with his rider, and runs against a man and hurts him, this is not battery. Where a person , in doing an act which it is his duty to perform, hurts another, hs is not guilty of battery .... A soldier, in exercise, hurts his companion--no recovery can be had against him.... If the act which occasioned the injury to the plaintiff was wholly unavoidable, and no degree of blame can be imputed to the defendant, the conduct of the defendant was no unlawful."'
Similarly, in Lehigh Bridge v. Lehigh Coal & Navig. Co., 4 Rawle 8 (Pa. 1833), the court stated, "The defendant had the ... right to erect the damn at the particular place ... and if chargeable with no want of attention to its probable effect, is not answerable for consequences which it was impossible to foresee and prevent. Where a loss happens exclusively from an act of Providence, it will not be pretended that it out to be borne by him whose superstructure was made the immediate instrument of it.

27. Huntress v. Boston & Main R. R., 66 N. H. 185, 34 A. 156 (1870).

28. Id. at 191-192, 34 A. at 157.

29. In Butcher v. Vaca Valley & Clear Lake R.R, 67 Cal. 518, 8 P. 174 (1885), the California Supreme Court decided that a presumption of negligence was raised by evidence that, theoretically, a railroad engine could be made that would not provide fire- causing sparks. Therefore, the court found that the railroad engine's production of sparks was, in fact, prima facie proof of defendant's negligence. In Giraudi v. Electric Imp. Co., 107 Cal. 120, 40 P. 108 (1895), a restaurant employee went on the roof to repair a sign during a heavy thunderstorm. He inadvertently came in contact with a power line that he knew was there. The court upheld a jury verdict against the power company, stating that electricity was dangerous and that the defendant had to take the utmost standard of care.

30. Adams v. Bullock, 227 N.Y. 208, 125 N.E. 93 (1919).

31. Id. at 210, 125 N.E. at 93.

32. Id.

33. Id.

34. Id. at 211, 125 N.E. at 94.

35. See White, supra note 12, at 83.

36. Id. at 85.

37. United States v. Carroll Towing, 159 F.2d 169 (2d Cir. 1947).

38. David W. Barnes and Lynn A. Stout, CASES AND MATERIALS ON LAW AND ECONOMICS 93 (1992).

39. Id. at 94.

40. Id. at 95.

41. Carroll Towing Co., 159 F.2d 169 (2d Cir. 1947).

42. Greenman v. Yuba Power Products, Inc., 59 Cal.2d 57, 377 P.2d 897, 27 Cal. Rptr. 697 (1963).

43. Id.

44. See White, supra note 12, at 106.

45. In MacPherson v. Buick Motor Company, 217 N.Y. 382, 111 N.E. 1050 (1916), Judge Cardozo removed the requirement of privity of contract that prevented the ultimate purchaser from suing the manufacturer in tort for harms arising out of the use of his product. Prior to this decision, the manufacturer was liable only to the immediate purchaser who was usually a middle man and not the ultimate user. The demise of the requirement of privity, however, did not alleviate the plaintiff's evidentiary problems of proving defendant's negligent behavior. Until the landmark decision of Greenman v. Yuba Power Products, Inc., 59 Cal..2d 57, 377 P.2d 897, 27 Cal. Rptr. 697 (1963), substantial legal loopholes enabled manufacturers to avoid liability for harms the courts clearly wanted to impose.

46. Greenman, 59 Cal.2d 57, 377 P.2d 897, 27 Cal. Rptr. 697 (1963).

47. The court stated, "A manufacturer is strictly in tort when an article he places on the market .... proves to have a. defect that causes injury to a human being." Id.

48. RESTATEMENT (SECOND) OF TORTS § 402A, comment g (1965).

49. See White, supra note 12, at 108.

50. Caterpillar Tractor Co. v. Beck, 593 P.2d 886 (Alaska 1979).

51. Id. at 886. (emphasis added).

52. Turner v. General Motors Corp., 584 SW.2d 844 (Tex. 1979).

53. Id. at 847 n.1. (emphasis added).

54. See White, supra note 12, at I 11.

55. Dennis A. Gioia, Pinto Fires and Personal Ethics: A Script Analysis of Missed Opportunities, JOURNAL OF BUSINESS ETHICS 11, 381 (1992).

56. One document that was not sent to Washington by Ford was a "Confidential" cost analysis Mother Jones was able to obtain, showing that crash fires could be largely prevented for considerably less than $11 a car ... The total purchase and installation cost of the bladder would have been $5.08. Dowie,Pinto Madness, MOTHER JONES 18 (Sept./Oct. 1977).

57. See Gioia, supra note 53, at 382.

58. See, e. g., The T.J. Hooper, 60 F.2d 737 (2d Cir. 1932): The court acknowledged that at the time of an accident, custom in the tug industry was not to carry radios to check weather reports.. Even though this was the case, it found a tug line liable: "But here there was no custom at all as to receiving sets; some had them, some did not; the most that can be urged is that they had not yet become general ... We hold the tugs (liable) because had they been properly equipped, they would have gotten the weather reports."

59. See Dowie, supra note 54.

60. Id.

61. Posner, A Theory of Negligence, 1 J. LEGAL STUD. 29, 29, 32-34 (1972).

62. See Birsch, supra note 3, at 159.

63. Id. at 160.

64. Id. at 161.

65. Id. at 129.

66. See Birsch, supra note 3, at 129.

67. Id.

68. Economists have tried to develop methods for imputing a person's "willingness to pay" for such things, their approach generally involving a search for bundled goods that care traded on markets and that vary as to whether they include a feature that is, by itself; not marketed. Thus, fresh air is not marketed, but houses in different parts of Los Angeles that are similar except for the degree of smog are. Id.

69. Id. at 133.

70. Frank J. Vandall, Judge Posner's Negligence Efficiency Theory: A Critique, 35 EMORY L.J. 383, 391 (1986).

71. Coleman, Efficiency, Utility, and Wealth Maximization, 8 HOFSTRA L. Rev. 509, 526 (1980).

72. See 2 F. HARPER & F. JAMES, THE LAW OF TORTS 743 (1956).

73. See Vandall, supra. note 68, at 199.

74. Rizzo, Law Amid flux: The Economics of Negligence and Strict Liability in Tort, 9 J. LEGAL STUD. 291, 299 (1980).

75. See Vandall, supra note 68, at 389.

76. Id. at 402.

77. A. POLINSKY, AN INTRODUCTION TO LAW AND ECONOMICS 123-26, at 46-47 (1983)

78. See Vandall, supra note 68, at 405.

79. See generally William M. Landes & Richard A. Posner, The Economic Structure of Tort Law, 23 (1987).

80. Michael D. Green, Negligence = Economic Efficiency: Doubts, 75 Tex. L. Rev. 1605, 1607 (1997).

81. Id. at 1608.

82. Id.

83. Id.

84. Id. at 1609.

85. Id.

86. See Birsch, supra note 3, at 137.

87. Id. at 139.88. Id. at 138.

89. See Green, supra note 78, at 1631.

90. Id. at 1642.

91. Id.

Source: https://users.wfu.edu/palmitar/Law&Valuation/Papers/1999/Leggett-pinto.html

APPENDIX 10
NURSING HOME PETITION—ASSAULT

This Petition was filed in state court arising from the sexual assault and murder of our clients' mother in a nursing home.

The facts of the case were particularly offensive. The nursing home's lack of security and lack of any meaningful response to multiple assaults in the community and at its own facility was appalling.

The petition demonstrates how the survivor's claim is made by an estate and the wrongful death claim is made by the heirs in a nursing home case.

The petition filed in this case was very fact-intensive because the suit was against the nursing home who failed to protect its resident rather than against the murderer who was sitting in prison. The fact-intensive allegations were made to demonstrate the knowledge the nursing home had or should have had about assaults on elderly women in the community, giving rise to a higher duty to protect the nursing home's residents.

Bretz Law Offices, LLC
1227 N. Main
P.O. Box 1782
Hutchinson, KS 67504-1782
(620) 662-3435
Fax (620) 662-3445

IN THE DISTRICT COURT OF RENO COUNTY KANSAS
(Pursuant to K.S.A. Chapter 60)

ESTATE OF ███████████ , and ███████████ ,   )
███████████ ,   )
      and ███████████ , heirs at law of ███████████)
███████,   )
                              Plaintiffs,   )
)
vs.   )   Case No.: 09 CV 38
)
BUHLER SUNSHINE HOME, INC., SUNSHINE   )
VILLA, INC., and KEITH PANKRATZ,   )
                              Defendants.   )
)
_____)

FIRST AMENDED PETITION

COME NOW the Plaintiffs, by and through their attorney, and state and allege as follows:

1. The Estate of ███████ has been duly opened in Reno County, Kansas, and ███████ has been appointed and qualified as administrator.

2. Plaintiff ███████ is a resident and citizen of the State of Kansas.

3. Plaintiff ███████ is a resident and citizen of the State of Kansas.

4. Plaintiff ███████ is a resident and citizen of the State of Kansas.

5. Plaintiff ███████ is a resident and citizen of the State of Kansas.

6. Plaintiff ███████ is a resident and citizen of the State of California.

7. Defendant Buhler Sunshine Home, Inc., is a Kansas corporation that is authorized to do business in the State of Kansas, and may be served with process by serving its registered

Page 1 of 7

agent, Nick Rempel, 212 West 8th, Buhler, Kansas 67522.

8. Defendant Sunshine Villa, Inc., is a Kansas corporation that is authorized to do business in the State of Kansas, and may be served with process by serving its registered agent, Richard I. Heim, 412 West Ave. C, Wichita, Kansas 67203.

9. Defendant Keith Pankratz is a resident and citizen of the State of Kansas, and may be served with process at his residence, ███████████████████████.

10. This court has subject matter jurisdiction over the cause of action, and personal jurisdiction over the parties.

11. Venue is proper in this Court pursuant to K.S.A. 60-603 and K.S.A. 60-604.

12. Plaintiffs █████████████████████████████████ and ████████ are the children and heirs at law of ████████.

13. At all times material hereto, ████████ was a resident at Buhler Sunshine Home, Inc. and/or Sunshine Villa, Inc.

14. At all times material hereto, Defendant Keith Pankratz was the Administrator of Buhler Sunshine Home, Inc. and Sunshine Villa, Inc.

15. Defendants Buhler Sunshine Home, Inc. and Sunshine Villa, Inc. are vicariously liable for the actions and omissions of Keith Pankratz under the doctrine of respondeat superior.

16. On or about March 21, 2008, at approximately 5:30a.m. to 6:00a.m., ████████ awoke and found a man in her bed. The man told her to calm down. The man identified himself as "Mark Koehn". The man kissed and touched her, and indicated that he wanted to have sex with her. ████████ refused and the man got out of her bed and started to pull his pants down. ████████ again told him no and to get out. The man left. The man was later identified as Marvin Gifford, Jr., herinafter referred to as "Gifford".

17. This action does NOT assert a claim for liability or a claim for damages arising out of the March 21, 2008, incident.

18. The March 21, 2008, incident was reported by ███████████ to her children.

19. After being informed about the March 21, 2008, incident, ██████████ reported the same to Keith Pankratz, the Administrator at Buhler Sunshine Home, Inc. and Sunshine Villa, Inc. Upon reporting this information to Keith Pankratz, Mr. Pankratz stated that he knew some Koehn's in town, asked whether ██████████ was in her right mind or having problems with dimentia, and stated that there was nothing he could do about it.

20. It was later learned that Keith Pankratz actually knew Mark Koehn and that he had lied by omission by failing to acknowledge that he knew Mark Koehn.

21. Defendant Pankratz later lied stating that he had reported the incident to the police two times when, in truth, he had not.

22. Defendants negligently failed to investigate the attack, negligently failed to provide additional security at the facility, negligently failed to report the attack to police and other authorities, negligently failed to contact other law enforcement entities in the area to determine whether there had been other attacks on elderly women, negligently failed to notify other residents and staff members of the attack and need for heightened security, and were negligent in other respects.

23. Around this same period of time and for a number of years prior to this time, there were several other assaults on women in the area of which Defendants Pankratz and Buhler Sunshine Home, Inc. and Sunshine Villa, Inc. knew or should have known.

24. In April, 2000, Gifford was caught by the McPherson Police Department while peeking into the window of a residence at a female.

25. On January 21, 2005, Gifford rang the door bell at the residence of a 71-year-old woman who lived alone in McPherson. When she answered the door, he was masturbating.

26. On October 20, 2005, Gifford tapped on a window of a McPherson residence where a 76 year old woman lived by herself. He stood outside the window, with his pants pulled down and masturbated. He asked the elderly woman if she wanted to take a picture of "it."

27. On December 3, 2005, Gifford knocked on the door of a 73 year old McPherson woman who lived alone. When she answered the door, he was wearing a Halloween mask. The elderly woman sprayed him in the face with hair spray.

28. On December 17, 2005, Gifford was arrested by the McPherson Police Department for grabbing the leg of a 76 year old woman who lived by herself. The victim reported to the police that Gifford had previously been to her residence on June 6, 2004, and had knocked on a window and told her to go to the front door. When she had opened the door he was masturbating.

29. On February 22, 2008, 92 year old   reported to a staff member at the Good Samaritan Village in Hutchinson, Kansas, that a white male, later identified as Gifford, knocked on her door where she lived alone, and then opened the door and entered her apartment.

30. On March 22, 2008, 87 year old   reported to staff at the Good Samaritan Village in Hutchinson, Kansas, that at approximately 5:45 a.m. her door bell rang, and then someone began pounding on the door.

31.   , age 95, reported to staff at the Good Samaritan Village that on March 22, 2008, her son and daughter-in-law's dog began barking at about 6:00 a.m and that a man dressed in dark clothing was seen, and that the next morning they discovered the window

Page 4 of 7

screen had been cut. ▓▓▓▓ further reported that there had been three or four prior incidents where someone had knocked on her door at the nursing home during the middle of the night.

32. On March 30, 2008, 90 year old ▓▓▓▓ reported that an unknown white male, later identified as Gifford, entered the door of her assisted living apartment at the Mennonite Friendship Manor in South Hutchinson, Kansas, and physically attacked her, anally sodomized her with his finger, and tried to strangle her with his hands.

33. ▓▓▓▓, 83 years old, reported that on an unknown date prior to Daylight Savings time, at approximately 7:00 a.m., her doorbell rang and then her door opened and there was a man, later identified as Gifford, who entered her apartment at Good Samaritan Village, in Hutchinson, Kansas.

34. On April 6, 2008, at approximately 6:00 a.m. 62 year old ▓▓▓▓ was attacked in her home, suffering injuries to her neck from strangulation and to her nose and rectal area.

35. On May 17, 2008, two elderly women, ages 85 and 90, reported that someone came to the doors of their apartments at Mennonite Friendship Manor in South Hutchinson and constantly rang their door bells.

36. On April 8, 2008, April 11, 2008, and on other dates during the time after March 21, 2008, and before May 18, 2008, a series of articles were published in *The Hutchinson News* which documented several of these attacks on elderly women in the area.

37. From these articles and the information which had been provided to Defendants by ▓▓▓▓ ▓▓▓▓, Defendants knew or should have known that attacks on elderly women in the area were ongoing and that it was likely that ▓▓▓▓ or some other elderly women at Defendants' facility would be attacked again if Defendants failed to take reasonable steps to

ensure the safety of their residents.

38. However, following actual knowledge of an attack at their own facility and after being made aware of ongoing attacks on other elderly women at other facilities, Defendants negligently, in breach of their duty, did nothing to prevent further attacks from occurring at their facility.

39. Defendants negligently failed to investigate the initial attack, negligently failed to investigate to determine whether other elderly women in the area had also been attacked, negligently failed to provide additional security at the facility, negligently failed to provide additional lighting or monitoring or security cameras, negligently failed to report the attack to police and other authorities, negligently failed to notify other residents and staff members of the attack and need for heightened security, negligently failed to take reasonable steps to ensure that other attacks would not occur at Defendants' facility, and were negligent in other respects.

40. As a result of Defendants' negligence, Gifford again returned to Defendants' facility on or about May 18, 2008, where he raped and strangled ████████ until she died.

41. Following the murder of ████████, Defendant Pankratz instructed employees not to talk to law enforcement investigators concerning the attack and murder.

42. As a result of Defendants' negligence, on May 18, 2008, ████████ endured severe mental anguish, pain and suffering, which culminated in her death.

43. As a result of Defendants' negligence, on May 18, 2008, ████████ suffered a loss of her time.

44. The Estate of ████████ brings this action for her conscious pain, suffering, mental anguish, loss of time, and funeral and burial expenses, arising from the attack on or about May 18, 2008.

45.   Plaintiffs ▮▮▮▮▮▮▮▮▮▮▮▮▮▮▮▮▮▮▮▮▮▮ and ▮▮▮▮▮

bring this action for the May 18, 2008, wrongful death of their mother, and for all damages

allowed by the Kansas Wrongful Death Act.

WHEREFORE, Plaintiffs pray for judgment against each of the Defendants in an amount in excess

of $75,000.00, and for such other and further relief as the Court deems just and equitable.

Respectfully submitted,

_____

Matthew L. Bretz #15466
Attorney for Plaintiffs

REQUEST FOR JURY TRIAL

Plaintiffs hereby demand trial by jury of all issues herein.

_____

Matthew L. Bretz

APPENDIX 11
NURSING HOME PETITION—NEGLECT

This is another wrongful death case against a nursing home, but is based on neglect rather than on assault.

In a case involving neglect by the nursing home and its employees, one must state all of the claims being made in the lawsuit. However, the petition does not have to be quite as fact-intensive as a nursing home petition which is based on an assault by a non-employee such as shown in Appendix 10.

BRETZ & YOUNG
1227 N. MAIN STREET
P.O. Box 1782
Hutchinson, Kansas 67504-1782
Phone (620) 662-3435
Fax (620) 662-3445

IN THE DISTRICT COURT OF RENO COUNTY, KANSAS
(Pursuant to K.S.A. Chapter 60)

THE ESTATE OF ███████████ ,) by and through its duly appointed special) administrator, ████████████ ,) ██████ ,████ and) █████████ and, heirs at law of) ██████████ , deceased,)) Plaintiffs,)) vs.)) LIVING CENTER, INC.,)) Defendant.))	Case No.: 13 CV 341

PETITION

COME NOW the Plaintiffs, and for their causes of action against the Defendant, state and allege as follows:

1. Plaintiff the Estate of ████████████ has been duly opened in the Reno County District Court, and ██████████████ has been appointed Administrator of the Estate.

2. Plaintiff ████████████ is a resident of the State of Kansas and is an heir at law of ██████████ .

3. Plaintiff ██████████ is a resident of the State of Kansas and is an heir at law of ██████████ .

4.   Plaintiff ▮▮▮▮▮▮▮▮▮▮ is a resident of the State of Kansas and is an heir at law of ▮▮▮▮▮▮▮▮▮▮ .

5.   Defendant Living Center, Inc. is a Kansas for not for profit corporation. Living Center, Inc.'s registered agent for service of process is Kevin J. Miller, 1701 East 23rd Street, Hutchinson, Kansas 67502.

6.   Defendant Living Center, Inc., does business as Ray E. Dillon Living Center Inc.

7.   This Court has jurisdiction over the subject matter and over the parties named herein, and venue is proper in the Reno County District Court pursuant to K.S.A. 60-604(2).

8.   Defendant was negligent in their care of ▮▮▮▮▮▮▮▮▮▮ , causing her to suffer injuries and ultimately causing her death.

9.   On or about August 14, 2013, Defendant left ▮▮▮▮▮▮▮▮▮▮ unattended in the bathroom, despite the "fall risk" tag attached to her wrist.

10.   Defendants failed to respond to ▮▮▮▮▮▮▮▮▮▮ 's verbal calls for assistance to leave the bathroom.

11.   As a result of Defendants' failure to provide assistance ▮▮▮▮▮▮▮▮▮▮ fell off the toilet and fractured her hip.

12.   Defendants were negligent in one or more of the following, and other respects:

       a.   Negligently providing care and treatment;

       b.   Negligently failing to monitor; and

       c.   Negligently leaving ▮▮▮▮▮ unattended

13.   As a result of Defendant's negligence, ▮▮▮▮▮▮▮▮▮▮ endured severe mental anguish, pain and suffering.

14.   As a result of Defendant's negligence, ▮▮▮▮▮▮▮▮▮ died on August 20, 2013.

15.   The Estate of ▮▮▮▮▮▮▮▮▮ brings this action for the pain, suffering, mental anguish, physical distress and death suffered by ▮▮▮▮▮▮▮▮▮.

16.   The Estate of ▮▮▮▮▮▮▮▮▮ also brings this action for medical, nursing expenses and funeral expenses.

17.   ▮▮▮▮▮▮▮▮▮, ▮▮▮▮▮▮▮ and ▮▮▮▮▮▮▮▮ bring this action for the wrongful death of their mother and seek all damages available under the Kansas Wrongful Death Act.

WHEREFORE, Plaintiffs pray for judgment against Defendants in an amount in excess of $75,000.00, together with the costs of this action, interest, and for such other and further relief as the Court deems just and proper.

BRETZ & YOUNG

By: _____
       Matthew L. Bretz, SC#15466
       Attorney for Plaintiffs

REQUEST FOR JURY TRIAL

COME NOW the Plaintiffs, pursuant to applicable Kansas law, and respectfully makes demand for trial by a jury of twelve (12) persons of all issues herein above joined.

BRETZ & YOUNG

By: _____
       Matthew L. Bretz, SC#15466
       Attorney for Plaintiffs

APPENDIX 12

MEDICAL MALPRACTICE COMPLAINT— OVERDOSE

This case arises from a young mother's trip to the emergency room for heartburn, resulting in her being prescribed a deadly dose of a high-powered pain killer — a pain killer normally reserved for people in the end stages of terminal cancer who are in intractable pain.

Most states have additional requirements for filing medical malpractice claims, including special requirements for filing a petition or complaint. There are often other special requirements for medical malpractice claims such as special notice which must be given after an incident, shorter deadlines, screening panels, special notice which must be given upon filing a lawsuit, retention and designation of expert witnesses, and the like. If you are contemplating a medical malpractice action, be especially careful.

BRETZ & YOUNG
P.O. Box 1782
1227 North Main Street
Hutchinson, KS 67504-1782
Phone (620) 662-3435
Fax (620) 662-3445

**IN THE UNITED STATES DISTRICT COURT
FOR THE DISTRICT OF KANSAS**

THE ESTATE OF ███████████ ,)
by and through its Executor,)
███████ , and)
███████ .)
███ , and ███████ , heirs at)
law of ███████ deceased,)
)
vs.)   Case No.:
)
███████████ .,)
                    Defendant.)
_____)

COMPLAINT

COME NOW the Plaintiffs, by and through their attorney, Matthew L. Bretz, and for their

cause of action against the Defendant, ███████ , M.D., allege and state as follows:

1.   The Estate of ███████ has been duly opened in Reno County, Kansas, and

██████ , has been appointed as Executor of the Estate.

2.   Plaintiffs ███████████████ and ███████

███ , are individuals and citizens of the State of Kansas and are the heirs at law of ███

███ , deceased.

3.   ███████████ and ███████ are the surviving children of ███████

███ and bring this action together with and by and through their father and next friend, ███

███ , for the wrongful death of ███████ .

-1-

4. The Estate of ▨▨▨▨ brings this action for all claims properly made by the Estate for conscious pain and suffering, and medical and funeral expenses.

5. Defendant is an individual and a citizen of the State of Oklahoma.

6. There is complete diversity of citizenship and the matter in controversy exceeds, exclusive of interest and costs, the sum specified by 28 U.S.C. § 1332.

7. This Court has personal jurisdiction over the parties and subject matter jurisdiction pursuant to 28 U.S.C. § 1332.

8. On or about February 18, 2013, ▨▨▨▨ entered the Hutchinson Regional Medical Center emergency department in Hutchinson, Reno County, Kansas, with the complaint of chronic epigastric burning pain that had increased in intensity earlier that evening.

9. Her pain was similar to multiple previous episodes, though it was more severe than usual.

10. Her home medications at that time included Zoloft, Dexilant, Carafate and Nitroglycerin. She was not reported as having taken any recent narcotic pain medications.

11. ▨▨▨▨ was seen by Defendant ▨▨▨▨.

12. Dr. ▨▨ ordered multiple medications including Fentanyl transdermal patch 75mcg/hour which was administered at 10:45pm in the emergency room.

13. ▨▨▨▨ was discharged from the emergency room at 12:20am on February 19, 2013, with an instruction to see her primary care physician, Dr. David Richman, in two to three days.

14. On the morning of February 19, 2013, approximately 10 hours after leaving the emergency department ▨▨▨▨ was found by her husband to be unresponsive with agonal respirations. EMS arrived at 10:36am and noted that she was pulseless and was receiving CPR that had been started by her husband. The EMS technicians found the Fentanyl 75mcg/hour patch that had been ordered by Defendant on ▨▨▨▨ and immediately

removed it and started Narcan to counter the effects of the Fentanyl overdose which had been ordered by Defendant.

15.   was taken back to Hutchinson Regional Medical Center for further treatment and was diagnosed with anoxic encephalopathy.

16.   After   was taken back to Hutchinson Regional Medical Center on February 19, 2013, Defendant was notified of the Fentanyl overdose which he had ordered. Defendant then wrote a note in the medical chart at 10:27pm on February 19, 2013, falsely claiming that he had recommended admission to the hospital on the previous evening. There was no notation or documentation in the record on the evening of February 18 or at the time of discharge from the emergency room at 12:20am on February 19, 2013, that   left against medical advice.

17.   's condition never improved and she was declared brain dead on February 27, 2013.

18.   An autopsy determined that her death was due to Fentanyl toxicity.

19.   Defendant was negligent, clearly departing from the accepted standard of care, when he prescribed a 75 mcg Fentanyl patch for a narcotic naive patient such as   .

20.   As a result of the negligence of the Defendant   died leaving three young children and her husband.

21.   The Estate of   brings this action for medical bills, funeral bills, loss of consortium prior to her death, and all damages properly pursued by the Estate.

22.   's children and husband bring this action for the wrongful death of   , and make claim for mental anguish, suffering and bereavement, loss of society, companionship, comfort and protection, loss of marital care, attention, advice and counsel,

loss of filial care and attention, loss of parental care, training, guidance and education, loss of income, and reasonable funeral expenses.

23.   Plaintiffs have been damaged and will be damaged in the future in the form of medical bills, funeral bills, wrongful death.

WHEREFORE, Plaintiff prays for judgment against the above-named Defendant for an amount in excess of $75,000.00, plus costs, and for such other and further relief as the Court deems just and equitable.

Respectfully submitted,

    /s Matthew L. Bretz
    Matthew L. Bretz, SC #15466
    Attorney for Plaintiffs

REQUEST FOR JURY TRIAL and
DESIGNATION OF WICHITA, KANSAS, FOR TRIAL

COME NOW the Plaintiffs and respectfully make demand for trial by jury of all issues herein joined. Plaintiffs hereby designates Wichita, Kansas, as the place of trial for this matter.

    /s Matthew L. Bretz
    Matthew L. Bretz, SC #15466
    Attorney for Plaintiffs

-4-

<u>NOTICE OF SUIT</u>

Pursuant to K.S.A. 40-3409 the Board of Governors for the Health Care Stabilization Fund is hereby notified of the commencement of this action, said notice being sent via Registered Mail on August 16, 2013.

/s Matthew L. Bretz
Matthew L. Bretz, SC #15466
Attorney for Plaintiffs

APPENDIX 13

MEDICAL MALPRACTICE PETITION—DRUG ADDICT SURGEON

This is another medical malpractice claim, though this one is a bit different than most because it arises from problems with a surgeon who is an admitted drug addict.

Most people do not know that drug addicts are allowed to practice medicine, and are shocked to find out that there is no easy way to find out whether their doctor is a drug addict.

This petition is included to show how precise factual allegations can back a defendant into admitting things which he otherwise would be likely to deny.

BRETZ LAW OFFICES, LLC
1227 N. Main Street
P.O. Box 1782
Hutchinson, Kansas 67504-1782
(620) 662-3435
Fax (620) 662-3445

IN THE DISTRICT COURT OF SEDGWICK COUNTY KANSAS
(Pursuant to K.S.A. Chapter 60)

▬▬▬▬▬, Plaintiff,	)))	
vs.	)))	Case No.: 12 CV 3752
KRIS LEWONOWSKI, M.D., and VIA CHRISTI HOSPITALS WICHITA, INC., fka VIA CHRISTI REGIONAL MEDICAL CENTER, INC., Defendants.	)))))))	

FIRST AMENDED PETITION

COMES NOW the Plaintiff, ▬▬▬▬, by and through her attorney, Matthew L. Bretz, and for Plaintiff's causes of action against the Defendants state as follows:

1.   Plaintiff ▬▬▬▬ is an individual and resident of the State of Kansas, residing in Wichita, Sedgwick County, Kansas.

2.   Defendant Kris Lewonowski, M.D., is an individual and resident of the State of Kansas, and may be served with process at his residential address, ▬▬▬▬▬▬▬▬▬▬▬ ▬▬▬▬.

3.   Defendant Via Christi Hospitals Wichita, Inc., is a Kansas corporation formerly known as Via Christi Regional Medical Center, Inc., and may be served with process by serving its registered agent, Gary E. Knight, 8200 East Thorn, Wichita, KS 67226. Defendant Via Christi Hospitals Wichita, Inc., is hereinafter referred to alternatively as "Via Christi", the

-1-

"hospital", and "St. Francis".

4. This Court has subject matter jurisdiction over the controversy and personal jurisdiction over the parties.

5. Venue is proper in this district.

6. _____ was born on March 3, 1934, making her 76 to 77 years old at the time of the events giving rise to this action.

7. _____ had a left knee arthroplasty which was done in 1989. This was followed by a revision surgery in 1991 and a second revision in 1994.

8. _____ had a right total knee arthroplasty in 1996.

9. _____ was diagnosed with chronic synovitis in the knees for which she received injections given by Dr. Lewonowski.

10. On December 22, 2009, a progress note from Kansas Orthopaedic Center by Dr. Lewonowski verifies bilateral knee injections with the combination of lidocaine, Marcaine, and Solu-Medrol for chronic synovitis of the knees.

11. Bilateral knee injections were again repeated by Dr. Lewonowski on February 22, 2010, April 23, 2010, June 28, 2010 and August 30, 2010.

12. The chart note by Dr. Lewonowski on August 30, 2010, indicates, "She has known osteoarthritis of her bilateral knees." This of course is not a true statement given the fact that she has bilateral total knee arthroplasties making it impossible to have osteoarthritis of her bilateral knees.

13. In the first week of December 2010, _____ underwent additional bilateral knee injections by Dr. Lewonowski and then immediately developed increasing pain and difficulty with the left knee to the point that she was unable to weight bear.

14. Following the December 2010 injection by Dr. Lewonowski, _____ was seen at the Emergency Department at Via Christi Emergency and was found to be in need of a knee aspiration.

15. There is an operative report dated December 19, 2010, in which the surgeon of record is listed as

Kris Lewonowski, M.D., "available by phone" with first assistant, Lucas Casey Armstrong, M.D. and second assistant, Seth Harrer, M.D.

16. The postoperative diagnosis was "postoperative left periprosthetic knee infection" and she underwent an aspiration of the left knee.

17. At the conclusion of the body of the procedure report, it indicates, "Dr. Lewonowski was available by phone during this entire procedure." Even though Dr. Lewonowski was identified as the surgeon of record, he obviously was not present for this procedure.

18. On December 20, 2010, ▓▓▓▓ was seen in infectious disease consultation by Dr. Assi who found the impression to be "(1) Left total knee arthroplasty infection with alpha hemolytic streptococcus. (2) Multiple antibiotic allergies, (3) Diabetes mellitus type 2. (4) Dyslipidemia. (5) Clotting disorder on Coumadin."

19. In his plan, Dr. Lewonowski identified the continuation of vancomycin and follow-up on the knee aspirate cultures and agreed with the performance of a two-stage procedure with initial removal of knee joint and antibiotics spacer replacement with IV antibiotics. Dr. Lewonowski wrote: "She will need long-term IV antibiotics for approximately the next six weeks prior to the knee being able to be reimplanted."

20. On December 22, 2010, ▓▓▓▓ was taken back to surgery by Kris Lewonowski, M.D. with the diagnosis, "Septic revision left total knee arthroplasty" and the procedure performed, "Removal of infected left revision total knee arthroplasty with irrigation and debridement of skin, fat, fascia, muscle, tendon, and bone with implantation of antibiotic-impregnated articulated spacer and closure over drains."

21. In the indications, Dr. Lewonowski recorded that ▓▓▓▓ had a two-week history of left knee pain, "The patient had bilateral knee pain and underwent bilateral steroid injections into her bilateral total knees approximately two weeks ago. Subsequently, the right knee resolved and the pain dissipated, however, the left knee continued to get worse."

-3-

22.   In the body of the operative report, Dr. Lewonowski indicates, "It should be noted that the case was extended over 45 minutes to an hour due to late arrival of implants. Apparently, they were supposed to be here at 8 o'clock in the morning and the implants did not arrive until approximately 45 minutes to an hour after they were to be used. That was the reason for the delay in putting up the tourniquet. FedEx apparently made stops instead of coming directly to the hospital as they were instructed and we were not informed of this portion until the case was underway, however, there were no complications."

23.   was eventually discharged on December 27, 2010, with the discharge diagnosis, "Septic left revision of total knee arthroplasty" and she was transferred to a skilled nursing facility.

24.   was seen by Dr. Lewonowski on February 4, 2011,. Dr. Lewonowski's note indicates, "The patient has been on IV antibiotic for the last six weeks and they were discontinued yesterday and she is now on oral antibiotics."

25.   In his plan, Dr. Lewonowski indicated that   was to continue the oral antibiotics for the next six weeks. "I will need to see her in one week after her last antibiotic treatment and aspirate her knee. If the cultures are negative, then we will replace her total knee arthroplasty."

26.   On April 4, 2011,   was seen at Via Christi Regional Medical Center in which preoperative orders indicated that she was to be given vancomycin 1 gram IV preoperatively and she was scheduled to undergo revision of the left total knee arthroplasty.

27.   The admitting history and physical for the April 4, 2011, admission by Dr. Lewonowski indicates that the infection was "most likely she may have developed this secondary to steroid injections of the knees or possibly even from a colonoscopy, which was done in mid-November 2010."

28.   Dr. Lewonowski indicates, "On December 22, 2010, she underwent septic revision of the left total knee arthroplasty with implantation of antibiotic-impregnated articulating spacer and closure of her drains. Since that time, she has been on a six-week course of IV antibiotics and then a six-week course of oral antibiotics. At this time, the patient is stable and okay for explantation of the

antibiotic spacer and will undergo revision of the left total knee arthroplasty on April 4, 2011."

29.   In Dr. Lewonowski's plan he indicates, "She will be readmitted to Via Christi Hospital on North St. Francis in order to revise the left total knee arthroplasty status post infection."

30.   However, a procedure note April 4, 2011 indicates, "Unfortunately, the final aspiration for cultures was not performed to ensure that patient's infection has completely resolved. As a result, the patient's surgery must be cancelled today. We will do her aspiration at bedside in preop today. If culture results are negative, patient will be readmitted April 8, 2011 for explantation of antibiotic spacer and revision of total knee arthroplasty."

31.   In review of the order sheets from April 4, 2011, it is noted that at 1230 hours,   was given 1 gram of vancomycin IV preoperatively and the aspiration of the left knee was performed just one hour later at 1330 hours. Administration of the vancomycin one hour before the aspiration would result in a false negative for any test results.

32.   eventually was readmitted to Via Christi Hospital on April 8, 2011, by Dr. Lewonowski and taken to surgery on April 8, 2011, to undergo explantation and the second stage revision left total knee arthroplasty. Dr. Lewonowski arrived late for the scheduled surgery and, referencing all the needle marks on his hand, said "they couldn't get in the vein".

33.   However, an event took place in the operating room in which there is sparse documentation. There is a discharge note from April 8, 2011, dictated by physician assistant Amanda Dimitroff, PA that indicates that "The patient was taken to the operating room. During this time, it was determined by OR management, as well as Via Christi that they did not in fact feel comfortable with Dr. Lewonowski performing the surgery secondary to concern for an infected IV site at that time. Unfortunately, the surgery had to be cancelled. The patient was awakened without any surgical procedure being performed." When   awoke following anesthesia for the surgery which ultimately was aborted and learned that she again had not had the surgery, she was told Dr. Lewonowski was asked to submit to a drug screen because he was using bad language

and cursing in front of the office, that he blew up and refused, and that she was just left in surgery and ultimately the surgery was not performed at all.

34. A telephone call April 12, 2011, to Kansas Orthopaedic Center indicates that the patient was upset, "She said she was taken to the OR and administered anesthesia and then woken up and told the surgery wasn't done but OR staff wouldn't explain why. She said no one from the hospital spoke with her about the situation."

35. On April 14, 2012, ▓▓▓▓ was seen by Dr. Mahomed, M.D. in place of Dr. Lewonowski. In his consultation, April 14, 2011, he indicates, "On April 4, 2011, she was in St. Francis and was put to sleep but decided to do knee aspiration since it had not been done and they woke her. She stayed in St. Francis and then on April 8, 2011, she was put to sleep to have her revision done. At that point, there was some concern about Dr. Lewonowski's IV site, which had some complication and so the surgery was cancelled by the hospital administration. The patient is quite distraught that she awoke in the OR rather than in recovery room and that her doctor and nurses were not there and she was not given a good answer as to why her surgery could not go forth. Both she and her daughter and her son were quite upset and verging on hostility."

36. The Board of Healing Arts of the State of Kansas records reveal that there was an *ex parte* emergency order of suspension in regards to the license to practice medicine of Kris Lewonowski, M.D., on April 12, 2011.

37. The *ex parte* emergency order does not list any of the specific issues in regards to the suspension only to indicate "confidential." However, it found that Kris Lewonowski was in violation of the Kansas Healing Arts Act "**in that he committed conduct likely to deceive, defraud, or harm the public in violation of the Kansas Healing Arts Act**" and "**In that he has been sanctioned or disciplinary actions have been taken against the licensee by a peer review committee, health care facility, a governmental agency, or department or a professional association or society for acts or conducts similar to acts or conduct, which would constitute grounds for disciplinary**

action under the Kansas Healing Arts Act."

38.   The Board of Healing Arts records indicated that, "**The presiding officer found that the licensee is an imminent danger to the public health, safety or welfare**" but only identified as "confidential" the specific circumstances that took place.

39.   The records from the Healing Arts of the State of Kansas contain a consent order, April 13, 2012, that again identified Kris Lewonowski, M.D., "**On or about April 6, 2011, licensee was observed by an anesthesiologist to be agitated and had a bandage on his left wrist and hand.**" The remainder of the information and circumstances is identified as "confidential". The document furthermore indicates, "Licensee's license to practice medicine in surgery should be suspended for violating the Kansas Healing Arts Act, licensee's license to practice medicine in surgery has been suspended for the period of time between April 12, 2011 and April 13, 2012. No other specific information can be obtained from that document."

40.   On October 4, 2011, she was admitted to Wesley Medical Center by Dr. Paul Pappademos, M.D. and in the history of present illness, he notes, "She apparently had some difficulty with Dr. Lewonowski. He has since left the city and is not practicing. The patient was transferred to Dr. Pappademos for consideration for knee reimplantation." His plan was for a total knee arthroplasty revision and reconstruction of the left knee.

41.   Consultation by Dr. Assi, M.D. from infection disease October 4, 2011, found that ▓▓▓▓ was "postoperative left knee and status post reimplanted on the left total knee on October 4, 2011" and that he would "discontinue antibiotics after tonight's dose. There is no evidence of acute infection at this point."

42.   The discharge summary from the admission of October 4, 2011, indicated that at the time of discharge, there was no growth from cultures obtained intraoperatively.

43.   Defendant Lewonowski was negligent in his care and treatment of ▓▓▓▓ in the following, and other, manners:

A.   Falsely representing himself as the surgeon of record for the December 19, 2010, knee aspiration (and presumably billing for the same) when in fact he was not even present for the procedure.

B.   Failure to perform knee aspirations to verify the absence of infection prior to admitting ▮▮▮▮ for the second stage revision implantation surgery on April 4, 2011.

C.   Administering intravenous vancomycin on April 4, 2011, one hour prior to performing a knee aspiration to determine if the knee was free of infection.

D.   Attempting to perform knee revision surgery April 8, 2011, while in a compromised physical/mental state.

E.   Commencing the December 22, 2010, operation without all of the necessary equipment and supplies thereby exposing ▮▮▮▮ to increased risk of mortality and morbidity from surgery and anesthesia which was longer than necessary.

44.   Defendant Via Christi was negligent in allowing Defendant Lewonowski to enter the operating suite, place the patient under anesthesia, and attempt to perform knee replacement surgery when they knew or should have known that he was in a compromised physical or mental state.

45.   Unbeknownst to ▮▮▮▮ , Dr. Lewonowski is a known drug and alcohol addict.

46.   In 1985 Dr. Lewonowski was removed from the USC Orthopedic Residency Program for admitted drug and alcohol use.

47.   In 1985 Dr. Lewonowski entered a drug and alcohol rehabilitation program in Long Beach, California.

48. In 1993 Dr. Lewonowski was mandated to submit to urinalysis due to drug use. In an attempt to disguise sleeping medication use he substituted his urine sample with Pedialyte. This resulted in a positive screen for alcohol and Dr. Lewonowski stated that Pedialyte has an "alcohol base". It does not.

49. In 1993 Dr. Lewonowski entered another rehabilitation program in Pasadena, California.

50. In 1995 Dr. Lewonowski was licensed by the Kansas Board of Healing Arts to practice medicine in Kansas.

51. In 1997 or 1998 Dr. Lewonowski entered another rehabilitation program in Portland, Oregon.

52. In 2008 Dr. Lewonowski started writing prescriptions for narcotics to a person without any doctor/patient relationship and without any diagnosis. This person died in September, 2009.

53. Dr. Lewonowski has also admitted to addiction to pain medications following a lyposuction surgery.

54. On June 4, 2011, Dr. Lewonowski's license to practice medicine in California was suspended.

55. On October 31, 2011, Dr. Lewonowski's license to practice medicine in Arkansas expired.

56. Unfortunately, neither Dr. Lewonowski nor Defendant Via Christi informed ▇▇▇▇ that Dr. Lewonowski was a drug and alcohol addict and that she was going to be operated on by a drug and alcohol addict, or that her scheduled surgeries might not take place due to Dr. Lewonowski's drug and alcohol abuse and addiction, and malpractice.

57. Defendants were negligent in failing to inform ▇▇▇▇ that Dr. Lewonowski was a drug and alcohol addict, that due to his drug and alcohol addiction her surgery might be cancelled, and that she was at risk for injury due to his drug and alcohol addiction.

58.   Had Defendants properly informed ▨▨▨ about Dr. Lewonowski's drug and alcohol addiction, ▨▨▨ would not have consented to treatment by Dr. Lewonowski.

59.   As a result of the negligence of the Defendants, ▨▨▨ has incurred and will incur in the future medical and surgical expenses, pain, suffering and disability, great emotional distress including the fear of death, the risk of death and increased morbidity from repeated anesthesia, six unnecessary months without a knee, and in other respects.

WHEREFORE, Plaintiffs pray for judgment against each of the Defendants in an amount in excess of $75,000.00, for costs of this action, and for such other and further relief as the Court deems just and equitable.

Respectfully submitted,

By:_____
Matthew L. Bretz, #15466
Attorney for Plaintiff

REQUEST FOR JURY TRIAL

COME NOW the Plaintiffs and respectfully make demand for trial by a jury of twelve persons of all issues herein joined.

_____
Matthew L. Bretz, #15466
Attorney for Plaintiff

NOTICE OF SUIT

Pursuant to K.S.A. 40-3409 the Board of Governors for the Health Care Stabilization Fund is hereby notified of the commencement of this action, said notice being sent via Registered Mail on November 9, 2012.

_____
Matthew L. Bretz

APPENDIX 14

PREMESIS LIABILITY PETITION

This petition is from a premises liability claim. The client was shopping in a Dollar General store when she was hit by a truck whose driver was attempting to park in front of the store and ended up coming over the sidewalk and into the store.

We attach this petition as an example for lawyers to dig deep and investigate potential claims and potential insurance, rather than roll over and just take the easy and obvious claim.

In a case like this, the obvious claim would be against the driver of the truck which went over the curb and into the building. If the driver had an unlimited amount of insurance then only pursuing the motor vehicle liability claim might be enough. But when the motor vehicle liability insurance limits are not high enough to cover all of the damages, then the experienced zealous attorney looks elsewhere for any other potential claims.

In investigating this case we found that Dollar General designed their store and parking lot to allow parking up against the sidewalk apron in front of the store. There was a handicapped parking sign in front of the store which had been hit many times by vehicles being parked, and the sidewalk apron was only about 2 inches higher than the parking lot. Essentially, there was nothing to prevent a driver from going over the sidewalk into the building.

Through our investigation we were able to obtain architectural and construction drawings which showed that the sidewalk was supposed to have a 6 inch elevation rather than the 2 inch elevation which was constructed. A 6 inch elevation would have been more likely than a 2 inch elevation to stop a truck as it was being parked in front of the store.

BRETZ LAW OFFICES, LLC
1227 North Main Street
P.O. Box 1782
Hutchinson, KS 67504-1782
Phone (620) 662-3435
Fax (620) 662-3445

IN THE DISTRICT COURT OF RENO COUNTY, KANSAS
(Pursuant to K.S.A. Chapter 60)

, Plaintiff,	)))	
vs.	))	Case No. 2010 CV 0033
DG RETAIL, LLC, KEYSTONE PROPERTIES, INC., and CATHY HOWES,	)))))	
Defendants.	)))	

SECOND AMENDED PETITION

COMES NOW the Plaintiff,   , and for her cause of action against the Defendants and states and alleges as follows:

1. Plaintiff is a resident and citizen of the State of Kansas, residing in Hutchinson, Reno County, Kansas.

2. Defendant DG Retail, LLC, does business as "Dollar General" at 3030 North Lorraine Street in Hutchinson, Kansas, and may be served with process by serving its attorney, Pamela J. Welch, at Franke Schultz & Mullen, 8900 Ward Parkway, Kansas City, MO 64114.

3. Defendant Keystone Properties, Inc., is an Oklahoma corporation and may be served by serving its registered agent for service of process, Harry M. Bass, 112 W. Laurel, Independence, Kansas 67301.

-1-

4. Defendant Keystone Properties, Inc., owns and maintains the business premises and parking lot at the Dollar General store at 3030 North Lorraine in Hutchinson, Reno County, Kansas.

5. Defendant Cathy Howes is an individual and resident of the State of Kansas, and may personally be served with process at her place of business, 3030 North Lorraine in Hutchinson, Kansas 67502.

6. Defendant Cathy Howes is the manager of Dollar General in Hutchinson, Kansas, and is responsible for the operations of the Dollar General store, including, but not limited to, parking, policies and procedures, safety equipment, and customer safety.

7. This Court has jurisdiction over the subject matter and over the parties named herein, and venue is proper in the Reno County District Court pursuant to K.S.A. 60-603 and K.S.A. 60-604.

8. On April 5, 2009, Plaintiff was shopping inside the Dollar General store located at 3030 North Lorraine in Hutchinson, Kansas, when she was struck by a motor vehicle which came over a short parking curb and into the store, causing extensive injuries to Plaintiff.

9. Defendants Keystone Properties, Inc., Dollar General and its manager Cathy Howes were negligent in the following, and other, respects:

   a. Failing to provide a safe place to shop;

   b. Failing to ensure the safety of their customers;

   c. Failing to have a parking curb which was tall enough to stop a vehicle attempting to park against the curb;

   d. Allowing parking perpendicular to the store without an adequate parking curb;

   e. Allowing parking perpendicular to the store without any barricades to prevent vehicles from coming over the curb and into the store;

f.   Failing to conduct any safety studies to address the risk to customers from inadequate protection from vehicles parking perpendicular to the store;

g.   Failing to implement any safety measures designed to protect customers from the risk of injury created by allowing customers to park perpendicular to the store;

h.   In creating an unreasonably dangerous condition;

i.   In maintaining an unreasonably dangerous condition;

j.   In failing to provide adequate warning of the dangerous condition;

k.   In failing to inspect the business premises; and

l.   In other respects.

10.   As a direct and proximate result of the above-mentioned negligence by the Defendants, Plaintiff has suffered, and will continue to suffer in the future, pain, permanent injuries and disability, mental anguish, disfigurement, loss of enjoyment of life, hospital, medical, nursing home and incidental expenses.

WHEREFORE, Plaintiff prays for judgment against each of the Defendants in an amount in excess of $75,000.00, costs, and for such other and further relief as the Court deems just and proper.

BRETZ LAW OFFICES, LLC

By: _____
       Matthew L. Bretz, SC #15466
       Attorney for Plaintiff

REQUEST FOR JURY TRIAL

COMES NOW the Plaintiff, pursuant to applicable Kansas law, and respectfully makes demand for trial by a jury of twelve (12) persons of all issues herein above joined.

By: _____

Matthew L. Bretz, SC #15466
Attorney for Plaintiff

JOURNAL ENTRIES OF JUDGMENT

The two journal entries which are attached are included because they demonstrate how ethical and zealous attorneys can get a much better result than can a person without an attorney or a person with a TV lawyer/ambulance chaser.

The first journal entry of judgment also demonstrates how comparison of fault works when the actions of more than one person cause a wreck and the client's injuries.

IN THE DISTRICT COURT OF SEDGWICK COUNTY KANSAS
(Pursuant to K.S.A. Chapter 60)

Plaintiff,)	
	)
vs.)	Case No. 13 CV 1577
	)
CODY WICKHAM, and CHAD SHEPLER)	
Defendants.)	

JOURNAL ENTRY OF JUDGMENT

On April 1, 2013, this matter came on for trial by jury. Plaintiff appeared in person and with her attorney, Matthew L. Bretz. Defendant Cody Wickham appeared in person. Defendant Chad Shepler appeared in person and with his attorney, Bradley D. Serafine. There were no other appearances.

Whereupon, 21 potential jurors were seated for *voir dire* and were passed for cause by all parties. The parties then exercised their peremptory challenges and a jury of 12 was empaneled and sworn. The parties presented their respective cases by the testimony of witnesses and the introduction of documentary evidence and rested.

Whereupon, the jury was instructed on the law applicable to the case by the Court, and after the parties gave their closing arguments the jury retired to deliberate.

On April 2, 2013, the jury returned a special verdict finding for Plaintiff. The parties found Defendant Wickham to be 75% at fault and Defendant Shepler to be 25% at fault. The jury awarded Plaintiff $25,000.00 in medical expenses to date, $7,200.00 for economic loss to date, $40,000.00 for noneconomic loss to date, and $175,000.00 for future noneconomic loss, for a total damage award of $247,200.00. The verdict was by agreement of ten or more jurors.

The Court hereby enters judgment in Plaintiff's favor in the amount of $247,200.00.

-1-

Applying the jury's determination for apportionment of fault, the Court hereby enters judgment in Plaintiff's favor against Defendant Wickham in the amount of 75% of Plaintiff's total damages, for a judgment against Defendant Wickham in the amount of $185,400.00, plus interest at the statutory rate from April 2, 2014, plus statutory court costs. The Court further enters judgment in Plaintiff's favor against Defendant Shepler in the amount of 25% of Plaintiff's total damages, for a judgment against Defendant Shepler in the amount of $61,800.00, plus interest at the statutory rate from April 2, 2014, plus statutory court costs.

IT IS SO ORDERED.

Dated this ___ day of April, 2014, at Wichita, Kansas.

_____
Judge of the District Court

Approved:

By:_____
      Matthew L. Bretz, SC #15466
      Attorney for Plaintiff

By:_____
      Bradley D. Serafine, SC #24135
      Attorney for Defendant Chad Shepler

By:_____
      Cody Wickham

**IN THE DISTRICT COURT OF MONTGOMERY COUNTY, KANSAS
SITTING IN INDEPENDENCE**

_____,	)	
Plaintiff,	)	
	)	
vs.	)	Case No. 11 CV 331
	)	
DON ARMITAGE,	)	
Defendant.	)	
	)	

JOURNAL ENTRY OF JUDGMENT

NOW on this day of March 4, 2014, the above captioned matter comes on for jury trial before the Honorable Gary L. House. Plaintiff appears in person and through her attorney, Matthew L. Bretz of Bretz & Young. Defendant Appears in person and through his attorney, Jeffrey A. Chubb of Emert, Chubb & Gettler, LLC. There are no other appearances.

WHEREUPON, a jury of twelve jurors and one alternate was impaneled.

AND WHEREUPON, on March 4 and 5, 2014, the parties presented evidence to the jury and rested.

AND WHEREUPON, on March 6, 2014, the jury was instructed on applicable law, deliberated and entered the following general verdict:

1. On plaintiff's claim, the jury found for the plaintiff and awarded the following damages:

Medical Expenses:	$18,048.32
Non-economic loss to date:	$50,000.00
Future non-economic loss:	$131,951.68
TOTAL	$200,000.00

2. On defendant's counterclaim, the jury found for the defendant and awarded the following damages:

Property Damage: $703.52

WHEREUPON, the Court after hearing the verdict of the jury, and evidence and arguments of the parties, makes the following findings:

1. Defendant is given a credit in the sum of $18,923.79 against the judgement entered against him.

2. After deduction for the credit and the amount of the defendant's counterclaim, plaintiff is granted judgment against defendant in the sum of $180,372.69 plus statutory interest as allowed by law, plus statutory court costs.

IT IS THEREFOR ORDERED, ADJUDGED AND DECREED that the above findings are made the order of the Court.

_____
JUDGE

SUBMITTED BY:

_____
Jeffrey A. Chubb (#9925)
EMERT, CHUBB & GETTLER, LLC
304 North 6th - P.O. Box 747
Independence, KS 67301
(620) 331-1800
Attorneys for Defendant

APPROVED BY:

_____
Matthew L. Bretz (#15466)
BRETZ & YOUNG
P.O. Box 1782
Hutchinson, KS 67504-1782
(620) 662-3435
Attorney for Plaintiff

Page -2-

ABOUT THE AUTHOR

Matthew Bretz received a B.S. from Kansas State University, where he taught both classical and contemporary physics. He graduated from Pepperdine University School of Law where he received the Vincent Dalsimer Moot Court Award from U.S. Solicitor General Kenneth Starr. After graduation, he practiced with the Los Angeles firm of *Erin Brockovich*, *Delta Force II*, and *The Twilight Zone* fame, Engstrom Lipscomb & Lack, litigating aviation, toxic tort and catastrophic injury cases.

After returning to Kansas, Mr. Bretz was a litigation partner with Gilliland & Hayes, P.A., until starting Bretz Law Offices in 1997. Mr. Bretz handles all types of injury claims, including primarily automobile, commercial trucking, product liability, nursing home, and premises liability matters. He has been recognized by CNN and by local and state news media for trial and settlement results in numerous cases.

Mr. Bretz is licensed in Kansas and California, by the United States District Courts in Kansas, the Central District of California, the Northern District of Illinois, the Western District of Missouri, Colorado, the Eastern and Western District of Oklahoma, Nebraska, and by the Tenth Circuit Court of Appeals. He is a Member of the Board of Governors for the Kansas Trial Lawyers Association, and formerly was the Medical Legal Editor for the Journal of the Kansas Trial Lawyers Association.

Matt Bretz serves on the National Board of Directors for Mothers Against Drunk Drivers (MADD), the Training and Evaluation Center of Hutchinson (TECH), and he is a former board member for the American Red Cross, United Way, Interfaith Housing and Big Brothers.

Matt may be reached at matt@bretzinjurylaw.com.

In the last 30 years, Matt Bretz has litigated cases in more than 25 states, Washington, D.C., and from four foreign countries. He has received, among others, the following awards and accolades:

"AV PREEMINENT" rated by Martindale Hubbell™— the highest rating possible for professional ability and ethics

"10.0 SUPERB" rated by AVVO™

CLIENT DISTINCTION AWARD from Martindale Hubbell™— an award earned by fewer than 1% of all attorneys

Named to the **TOP 100 TRIAL ATTORNEYS** by the National Trial Lawyers Association™

10 BEST CLIENT SATISFACTION AWARD from American Institute of Personal Injury Attorneys™

Recognized as Kansas and Missouri **SUPER LAWYERS** by KC Magazine™

MULTI-MILLION DOLLAR ADVOCATE FORUM— one of only six Kansas attorneys to have earned this distinction at the time his book was first published

LAWYER OF THE YEAR for Wichita Personal Injury Litigation— Plaintiffs from Best Lawyers in America™

A PERSONAL NOTE FROM THE AUTHOR

The best way to get to know me and find out why I love being a trial lawyer is to understand where I come from. I grew up with a single mother and three sisters and spent a lot of time with my grandparents. An inquisitive kid, my mom and grandparents pushed and challenged me, helping me develop a passion for learning. With their support I got my first job at the age of 11, earned the rank of Eagle Scout by 13, and then graduated college and started teaching classical and quantum physics at Kansas State University by the age of 20.

One of the side jobs I did as a kid was yard work for a local retired lawyer. I didn't know what lawyers did, but I admired this man and wanted to be like him. Physics and teaching intrigued me, but I could not get the idea of being a lawyer out of my mind.

I think there are three primary things that have made me who I am as a trial lawyer. The first was an opportunity to get out of Kansas and attend Pepperdine University School of Law in California on a scholarship. I didn't realize the importance of it at the time, but I received an education from one of the top law schools in the country. For me – a small-town Kansas boy – this was an eye-opening and horizon-expanding experience.

The second career-defining opportunity was lucking into a job during law school with the Los Angeles firm of *Erin Brockovich*, *Delta Force II* and *The Twilight Zone* fame, Engstrom Lipscomb & Lack. At Pepperdine I learned "the law," but at EL&L I learned how to be a trial lawyer, litigating aviation and catastrophic injury cases from around the globe.

The third, and by far the most formative event in my life, occurred on Valentine's Day in 1992. On that day my 16-year-old sister, Marlee, and two of her friends were delivering baskets of flowers when their car was struck by a train, instantly killing all three of the girls in the car. Going through that devastation with my family at the time and in the years since has given me a personal understanding of the crushing pain suffered by those who have lost a loved one. Since then, I have devoted both my professional and personal life to helping those who have been seriously injured or who have lost a loved one, and to making the community a safer and better place to live.

My professional and personal lives bleed together. I am on the National Board of Directors for MADD with the singular goal of bringing an end to the mayhem caused by drunk and drugged drivers. I also volunteer time with the United Way, Red Cross, Interfaith Housing, ABATE, and the Training and Evaluation Center of Hutchinson.

Even after 30 years, I still enjoy teaching. As a trial lawyer I get to teach juries, insurance companies and sometimes defense experts. I've also been able to teach through the local community college, the Boy Scouts, and Sunday School. In recent years I have also started teaching trial lawyers from Seattle to Atlanta and every place in between at the Keenan Trial Institute.

I handle motor vehicle, medical malpractice, defective product and premises liability cases. I've been fortunate to receive accolades from CNN, Martindale-Hubbell, and AVVO, but the recognition most dear to me was a handwritten note from a client saying: *"You treat me like your only client, and I so appreciate that."*

My wife of 28 years, Amy, and I have two compassionate and driven daughters, Lauren and Hannah. Lauren received her Master's Degree in speech language pathology in 2020 and works as an SLP with the Blue Valley School District in Kansas City. Hannah graduated from Kansas State University in 2021 with a degree in philosophy, with plans to attend Brooklyn Law School in New York this fall.

BRETZ | INJURY LAW

3 Compound Drive | PO Box 1782 | Hutchinson, Kansas 67504-1782
620-662-3435 | toll-free 888-259-4406 | www.bretzinjurylaw.com

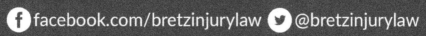 facebook.com/bretzinjurylaw @bretzinjurylaw

Printed in the USA
CPSIA information can be obtained
at www.ICGtesting.com
JSHW061631010823
45731JS00002B/9

9 780990 614302